NEW VISION New Zealand

Calling the Whole Church
to take the Whole Gospel
to the Whole Nation

Bruce Patrick, Editor

Norman Brookes
Brian Carrell
John Evans
Bob Hall
Brian Hathaway
John Hitchen
Peter Lineham
Ray Muller
Jill Richards
Max Scott
John Stenhouse
Lionel Stewart
Barry Tetley
Harold Turner
Alan Withy

Auckland, New Zealand 1993

Cover Design and Illustrations
Brian Pollard.

Typesetting and Page Makeup
Graham Jones of Petros Marketing Ltd, Auckland.

Filmwork and Plates
Cityscan Communications Ltd, Auckland.

Printing
Academy Interprint Ltd, Auckland.

Mission Statement of VISION New Zealand

"Calling the Whole Church to take the Whole Gospel to the Whole Nation."

VISION New Zealand has a two-fold focus
for this Decade of Evangelism:

We will study obstacles
posed by our secular society
to the advance of the kingdom of God,
and seek ways to overcome these.

We will encourage Christian leaders
to strengthen the quality
and multiply the number
of growing, caring, Christ-centred churches
until there are sufficient
to affect the spiritual and social climate
of New Zealand.

The task of evangelizing New Zealand
will be attainable
when there is at least one such congregation
sharing Christ within easy access
geographically, culturally, and linguistically
of every person,
ie. approximately one for every 500 people.

We will encourage every denomination
in their commitment to growth,
and every specialist ministry
to assist denominations and churches in mission.
Together we can do it!

Authors

Norman E. Brookes MA(Hons)
Superintendent of the Development Division, including the Making Disciples Task Group, of the Methodist Church of Aotearoa New Zealand.

Brian Carrell   MA, BD
Assistant Bishop, Anglican Diocese of Wellington; former General Secretary of New Zealand Church Missionary Society, and Vicar of All Saints, Palmerston North.

John O. Evans   MDiv, DMin
Minister of Greyfriars Presbyterian Church, Mt Eden; Chairman of the Evangelical Fellowship of New Zealand and of VISION New Zealand; Moderator-Designate of the General Assembly 1993, Presbyterian Church of Aotearoa New Zealand.

Bob Hall   BA(Hons), MA, PhD
Senior Lecturer in Sociology, University of Canterbury; National Coordinator, Centre for Mission Direction.

Brian Hathaway MSc(Hons), DipTchg
Member of Pastoral Team at Te Atatu Bible Chapel; Author of "Beyond Renewal, the Kingdom of God".

John M. Hitchen BA, BD(Hons), PhD
National Principal, Bible College of New Zealand; former Lecturer and Principal, Christian Leaders' Training College of Papua New Guinea.

Peter Lineham   MA, BD, PhD
Senior Lecturer in History, Massey University; Coordinator of Commissions for the Evangelical Fellowship of New Zealand; Immediate Past Chairperson of Scripture Union Council; Chairperson of Tertiary Students Christian Fellowship.

Raymond J. Muller   LTh, DMin
Parish Consultant responsible for Evangelism and Church Growth, Anglican Diocese of Wellington; Executive member of the Anglican

Commission for Evangelism; graduate, Fuller Theological Seminary; Editor, Kiwi Growth Report.

Bruce Patrick   **BSc, BD(Hons), DipEd, ALBC**
Until recently Home Mission Director for the Baptist Churches of Aotearoa New Zealand; Coordinator of VISION New Zealand; Candidate, DMin; Pastor, Auckland Baptist Tabernacle

Jill Richards
Parish minister with 20 years experience in community research and development; Parish Mission Consultant, Development Division of the Methodist Church.

Max Scott   **MSc(Hons), BD, DipTchg**
Vicar of St Margarets, Hillsborough; Archdeacon of Maungawhau; past Chairperson of the Evangelism Council of the Diocese of Auckland; Chairperson of Christian Lovelink New Zealand.

John Stenhouse   **BA(Hons), PhD**
Formerly with Youth With A Mission; Lecturer in History, University of Otago.

Lionel Stewart
Tumuaki (Superintendent) of Baptist Maori Ministries, Baptist Churches of New Zealand (Ko Nga Hahi Iriri o Aotearoa).

Barry Tetley   **LTh, MDiv(Hons)**
Former evangelist with Open Air Campaigners in Philippines and producer of Sowers Programme; presently Lecturer and Fieldwork Supervisor at the Bible College of New Zealand.

Harold Turner   **MA, DD, HonDD**
Presbyterian Minister, retired after 35 years teaching in overseas universities; initiator of Gospel and Cultures Trust.

Alan Withy   **RS, DipTP, ThC**
Planning Consultant, Surveyor, Research Analyst; Manager of VISION New Zealand.

Editorial Group
Norman Brookes, John Evans, John Fulford, Stuart Kirkpatrick, Ray Muller, Bruce Patrick (chairman), Margaret Reid-Martin, Jill Richards, Max Scott, Barry Tetley, Alan Withy (secretary).

Research Assistance
All-New Zealand church survey: Overseen by Alan Withy.
North Island: Major researcher: Johanna Cooke, with Syd Beale, Bruce Bradburn, Barry Buckley, Garey Clark, Dawn Cookson, Angela Cossey, John Fulford, Rona Grieve, Pam McCroskie, John McMullan, Lindsay Martin, Teresa Megerny, Brian Michell, Mark Munro, Peter Murch, Muriel Nacey, Kay Officer, Joyce Relph, Ann Rhodes, Jeff Smith, Selwyn Stevens, Raewyn Trail, Ian Whye, and many others.
South Island: Major researcher: Lynne Taylor, with Lorraine Adams, John Bigwood, Shirley Bond, Jean Cain, Unity Clark, Athlyn Coppard, Allan Coussell, Ian Dodge, Hugh Donald, Geoff Dunham, Shelley Hawke, Elizabeth James, Ian Kennedy, Allan Ladbrook, David Lee, Alan McCrostie, Brian Mitchell, Vivienne Nelson, Gordon Pearce, Doug Robb, Roly Scott, Val Smith, Shirley Taylor, Pam Wadsworth, Alistair and Jenny Yule, and many others.

Special research: Johanna Cooke, Bob Hall, Ray Muller, Bruce Patrick, Max Scott, Barry Tetley.
New Zealand Evangelism Survey: Major researcher: Ray Muller, with Murray Collingwood, Alistair Davis.
Special assistance with Maori factors: Muru Walters, Frank Harrison, Lionel Stewart, Bob Joyce.

Computer Programming, Graph Generation, and Interpretation
Murray Collingwood, Graham Jones.

Prayer
Intercessors for New Zealand, Fiona Fountain, Gwen Chapman and a host of others.

Data Entry
Jocelyn Black, Keri Chisholm, Jane Collingwood, Ludwig Felderhof, Gayanne Frater, Alison Heckler, Dennis Long, Peter Moyer, Mary Pincott, Rilma Sands, Bruce and LeeAnne Tetley, Dale Withy, Denise Woodside, and others.

Word Processing
Pat Keats, Creina Penfold, Janet Regan and Judy Stainton.

Proof Reading
Ruth Burnham, John Fulford, Marilyn McSaveny, Christine Tetley, Barry Tetley.

Contents

Foreword

by Brian Davis

This is a book for those who are concerned to see the gospel vision at the centre of our nation's life. *NEW VISION New Zealand* brings together new information, including the fruits of recent research, to stimulate thinking and motivate the churches for evangelistic action.

NEW VISION provides a wealth of material on the methodology and theology of evangelism. Many of our churches are committed to making the last ten years of this century a Decade of Evangelism, and to working together to achieve our goals. *NEW VISION* is a joint exercise, supporting and resourcing the Decade.

NEW VISION recognizes the importance of understanding the particular Aotearoa New Zealand context in which our churches are called to proclaim the gospel. We have our own unique geography and history. The writers address this from a variety of Christian traditions.

Whether we describe our nation as essentially Christian or as post-Christian, secular or even pagan, statisticians point to declining membership figures in mainstream New Zealand churches. It is clear that Christian vision and Christian values compete with many alternate beliefs in an increasingly secularized society. Anglicans, who have been the largest religious group, are expected in the next (1996) census to be headed off by those who claim to have no religious affiliation.

At the same time, world-wide, there is growing evidence that the key notions of humanistic secularism, the assumptions that have shaped the life of our society, are now being seriously questioned or abandoned by leading scientists and philosophers. There is also increasing awareness of spiritual need. Secularism has not meant the end of religious or moral consciousness. People still have spiritual hunger and ask deep questions about life's meaning, purpose and value. People still look for something worth living and dying for. The boredom and emptiness, the alienation and deadness, of much modern life is all too obvious.

It could be that the churches now have a better opportunity for proclaiming the truth of the gospel than for many years. But there is much ignorance and naivety about what the Church is and what gospel truth is all about. Increasingly in our gospel outreach we are going to be meeting people who have no understanding whatsoever of the Christian message and tradition. This must affect the way we do evangelism, the way we welcome enquirers, and the way we nurture and incorporate new believers within our congregations.

We in the churches need to know clearly what our mission is. We have to understand the context in which we are called to proclaim Jesus Christ as Lord. And we must tell the story of God's salvation in a way that relates to the perceived needs of secularized people. *NEW VISION New Zealand* addresses these issues. The fresh research and insights it provides are born out of the challenge of being a Christian in these islands of the South Pacific.

We are deeply grateful to Bruce Patrick and all contributors for what they have provided. I warmly commend the book to the churches and church people, confident that it will help us all respond more fully to the challenge to take the whole gospel to the whole nation.

Brian N. Davis
Primate and Archbishop/Te Pihopa Matamua
The Anglican Church in Aotearoa, New Zealand and Polynesia
Bishop of Wellington

Introduction :
New Vision

by Bruce Patrick

The Church in New Zealand is searching for a new vision. What was presumed to be a churched culture is now seen as a mission field.[1] Nominal Christianity is a dead option. Christians in this new New Zealand of the 1990s are adjusting to a social climate of apathy and antipathy. We also face each day the reality "that evangelism means calling people to believe something which is radically different from what is normally accepted as public truth, and that it calls for a conversion not only of the heart and will but of the mind."[2]

Our increasingly secular society is also searching. "It is clever at devising means, but not so clever at understanding ultimate ends," says Anglican Archbishop Brian Davis. "We have tended to lose sight of any clear boundaries to human conduct, and ridicule those who seek to preserve standards. Worship of God and reverence for life is being seriously eroded. As a consequence there has been an alarming increase of crime and violence, the victims often being women and children."[3]

In their concern the leaders of many of our denominations have declared the 1990s to be a Decade of Evangelism. But what might this mean? In a recent book, theologian William J. Abraham states in his opening sentence, "One of the undeniable features of modern theology is the scant attention it has given to the topic of evangelism. It is virtually impossible to find a critical, in-depth study of the subject by a major theologian." He goes on, "I consider it nothing short of a disaster..." He writes of the rift between evangelism and theology. He says there are only three categories of substantial contemporary studies on evangelism: "the wealth of material on church growth", the volumes produced from "various world-wide conferences on evangelism", and "here and there a really solid work". He says, "Christianity has been part of the fabric of the West for so long that it has been assumed that Christians do not really need to evangelize... There has been therefore a deep sense of ease about the survival of Christianity in the West. Where evangelism has been taken seriously by the mainline traditions it has been relegated to a position of minor importance. Overall it has failed to fire the imaginations of the leaders of the central ecclesiastical institutions; most of these have been committed primarily to the maintenance of the institutions..."[4]

Many of our Christian leaders are now looking for what some have found: the key to the recovery of apostolic confidence, and thus the means of growing the kingdom of God in the alien soil of our new culture. As Christian leaders we are called to look ahead in order to lead our organizations. Visionaries, every now and then we lift our heads out of the papers on our desks and ponder how the Lord is going to accomplish the task of making disciples of the people groups of our nation.[5]

Exactly 200 years ago this month (as I write in October 1992) an unknown pastor named William Carey dared to challenge the prevailing mentality of his circle. In his day too, Christian leaders wondered how God would bring about the conversion of the nations. The religious fraternity of which he was a part expected a sovereign God somehow to save the people groups of the world. In God's time, in God's way. They were not convinced he would need or desire their involvement.

Carey had become an avid student of scientific and geographic journals. In the tiny village of Moulton, England, he devoured the reports of explorers such as Captain James Cook. He recorded demographic information and charted population sizes on an emerging world map. His concern for unevangelized peoples grew. His heart broke for the vast needs of peoples in the South Sea Islands, including Maori of Aotearoa, the islands named New Zealand in 1642 by Dutch explorer Abel Tasman, charted and explored by Cook in 1769. His growing passion and missionary vision caused him to clash with senior colleagues. One of them rebuked him: "Young man, sit down. When God pleases to convert the heathen, he will do it without your aid or mine!" Carey sat down. But he would not be silenced. "He saw that his first task must be to pass on to others the information that had stirred his own heart; he must transmit to them his vision."[7]

In 1792 this cobbler and pastor, aged 31, published a small volume of 87 pages. Its ornate title and subtitle confronted the prevailing theological determinism and ecclesiastical comfort of his day. Its contents led to a revolution in world mission.

AN ENQUIRY into the OBLIGATIONS OF CHRISTIANS TO USE MEANS for the CONVERSION OF THE HEATHENS,
in which the Religious State of the Different Nations of the World,
the Success of Former Undertakings,
and the Practicability of Further Undertakings,
are Considered.

One modern biographer describes the Enquiry in superlative terms: "This remarkable pamphlet was one of the greatest achievements of Carey's career, and an important landmark of modern missions. It was in every way unique... Carey's pamphlet was a reasoned statement of Christian obligation, of world needs, of existing opportunities, and practical proposals... Even today we read with amazement the product of his indefatigable industry and heart passion."[8]

The modern mission movement was launched through the information William Carey gathered, information that had stirred his own heart and shaped his thinking. Through the power of information God had given him a vision, and he passed it on. In its world-wide survey the Enquiry lists "New Zealand (footnote: two islands): Length 960 Miles, Breadth 180 Miles, Number of Inhabitants 1,120,000; Religion, pagans; 1 or 2 Ministers are there."[9] No armchair theorist, it was Carey's initial intention to become a missionary to the South Seas islands. He was provoked by Cook who had dismissed the Church's motivation for mission in this part of the world with these words: "It is very unlikely that any measure of this kind should ever be seriously thought of, as it can neither serve the purpose of (fame or fortune); and without such inducements I may pronounce that it will never be undertaken."[10] Carey might have come to New Zealand, but he went to India and served there for 41 years.[11]

Two decades after Carey arrived in India, on Christmas day, Sunday 25 December 1814, Samuel Marsden first preached the gospel on New Zealand soil. His text was Luke 2:10, "And the angel said unto them: Fear not, for behold, I bring you good tidings of great joy!" (AV).

Much can be said about the progress of the gospel and the establishment of the Church since 1814. Hundreds of thousands of committed believers, Maori, Pakeha,[12] and others have sacrificed to serve Christ in each generation. Multi-millions of dollars have been generously given away for compassionate ministries and for ministry facilities. In all contemporary endeavours we stand on the shoulders of our Christian predecessors. Where our history's high water mark is for the kingdom of God, may not be clear.[13] What is clear is that in the 1990s the tide is on the ebb. We have a generation of New Zealanders most of whom have never heard or understood the good tidings of great joy. In 1988 Ralph Neighbour studied our largest urban population. He entitled his report: *A City that Rejects its Religious Institutions: Auckland, Resistant, and Neglected.*[14] The word 'neglected' is there to goad the Church. The situation has worsened since this report was published. In only five years another 78,000 people have moved into greater Auckland.[15] For too long, too many have focused only on their own local church, their own ministry, their own denomination. We have lost sight of the big picture. We must see the whole nation as our mission field, we must see the whole Church as the mission force, and we must discover what God wants us to do. We must accept responsibility before God for our nation. We need a new vision for a new day of mission.

NEW VISION for New Zealand

In accepting the gospel of the kingdom as Jesus lived and proclaimed it, we as his disciples have been burdened by it. We are also New Zealanders, whatever our tribe racially, socially, or spiritually, and in our hearts we long to see our nation in touch with the love of Christ.

This publication, *NEW VISION New Zealand,* follows in the tradition of Carey's *Enquiry.* It comes out of a passionate commitment to see Christ's kingdom grow in New Zealand. It is essentially an enquiry into our obligations as Christians to use appropriate means to take the gospel to the people of our nation. In a number of chapters these means will be considered in detail. In other chapters, various writers describe factors relevant to the religious state of the different people groups of the nation (for Carey, *The Religious State of the Different Nations of the World*). Other writers examine the state of the Church and the churches[16] (for Carey, *The Success of Former Undertakings*). Finally, *The Practicability of Further Undertakings are Considered.* What must we do?

VISION New Zealand

VISION New Zealand has been common property from the day it was presented to a broadly representative meeting of leaders, women and men who came together from around New Zealand on 27 September 1990. On that day we were aware there were no other plans to be compared with the plan we had gathered to consider, a plan that would lead us toward the answer to the question: How will all the people of our nation hear the gospel? How will New Zealand be evangelized? We were also aware of the challenge to broaden the base for New Zealand's already prodigious contribution to the work of world mission, especially in the physically needier places on the planet. From that day, VISION New Zealand has been dedicated to the growth of the kingdom of God "by all possible means".[17] The koru symbol in the VISION logo is a Maori motif representing continual growth.

There was little time spent that day describing the state of New Zealand, or wringing our hands over the condition of the Church. In fact we took encouragement from some genuine signs of hope. God is stirring up his people, giving visions and dreams, and new gifts. Denominations and churches are setting goals in evangelism and church planting for the 1990s and some are growing rapidly, against the overall trends. God is calling people to pray. Intercessors are praying around the clock for New Zealand. But we acknowledged that our country has never known a Christian revival, nor a bold, united, sustained thrust for mission by Christians in their various organizations. Many Christians and leaders want to be part of such a move. Whole denominations have variously designated the 1990s a Decade of Evangelism, Mission, Harvest, Release, etc. It is clear that many believe this is the time, this is the hour, that it can happen in the 1990s.

A few weeks after this preliminary meeting, the publisher of a Christian newspaper asked the crucial question. He returned from a training seminar on evangelism held in a provincial centre and wrote, "The cry of those who wanted to be more effective in telling the community about the love of Jesus and seeing them responding in believing faith is still ringing in my ears. Lord, how can we reach our community and our nation more effectively?"[18]

The Potter's Hands

How could an effective mission thrust come together, and what primary strategies would it employ? My thinking has been shaped by a multi-denominational background, experience as the senior pastor for nine years of a growing church where we discovered there were many reachable people, and seven years as the home mission director for the Baptist churches in New Zealand. This denominational ministry has encompassed evangelism and church strengthening, with the focus on church planting. But my preoccupation throughout this period has been the basic question, how can New Zealand be evangelized? Concurrently I have been chairman of the Dawn Strategy Committee for New Zealand since it started in 1987.[19] With some enthusiasm we have noticed the denominations that are growing in New Zealand are those that since 1987 have applied Dawn principles. We have been learning from their experience how this may best be done in New Zealand's unique spiritual and cultural context.

I was greatly stimulated by the experience of attending the Lausanne II Congress on World Evangelization in Manila in mid 1989. Before my departure for Manila, editor Suzanne Sands had requested an article for the Bible College of New Zealand magazine, *The Reaper*, on how Lausanne II could impact New Zealand.[20] That assignment kept me alert, listening and praying for ten days during the most representative gathering of national Christian leaders ever assembled to consider the challenge of world evangelization. This vision began to clarify. The Dawn process was given some prominence at Manila; I believed more than ever that it was the process we needed. I now saw that the Lausanne Congress itself provided the model of a major event such as was needed in New Zealand. Such a congress had the potential to bring the whole Church in our nation together to consider the ultimate New

Testament challenge, the evangelization of New Zealand in our generation. In this way the international momentum of the Dawn and the Lausanne Movements would have wider impact in New Zealand. A third international movement sprang out of Lausanne II, led by the retiring Executive Director of the Lausanne Committee, Thomas Wang, and Luis Bush. This was the AD2000 and Beyond Movement. Promoting a clearer and more intentional approach to the task, AD2000 emphasizes the acceptance of God-given goals by which denominations and other mission agencies can measure progress.

It is one thing to understand principles which have their roots in Scripture, to read of antecedents in history, to observe global movements that are currently impacting whole Churches in various nations for the gospel, and to note the positive effects of the adaptation and application of such principles in one's own nation. It is another to navigate endemic factors of Kiwi culture, initiate a thoroughly democratic process, ensure adequate representation, demonstrate genuine openness to modification, build positive faith and hope, validate integrity, build widespread mutual trust despite the acknowledgement of overseas influences, and at the end of the process gain majority ownership of the vision. Only God can accomplish that. It must be recorded that prayer and waiting on God has been central as the Potter has worked at shaping a new vessel for a new day.

To Evangelize Our Nation

The simple conviction underlying VISION New Zealand is that God has given the whole body of Christ in this country all the resources needed to evangelize the whole nation. No one denomination or organization can accomplish the task alone, but together and with God it is possible. Two vital questions immediately surface: first, what is meant by evangelize? Second, how might that be accomplished on a national scale?

A definition of evangelization was proposed in 1978 by Anglican theologian John Stott as chairperson of the Lausanne Movement's Theology Working Group. This was adopted by the Lausanne Committee as its working definition:

> The nature of evangelization is the communication of the good news.
>
> The purpose of evangelization is to give individuals a valid opportunity to accept Jesus Christ.
>
> The goal of evangelization is the persuading of men and women to accept Jesus Christ as Lord and Saviour, and serve him in the fellowship of his Church.

In the secular West few individuals are won to Christ by a single event. Evangelism is a process. Certainly no nation is evangelized by an event but rather by a comprehensive process over time. We must think in 20 or 40 year terms, and pray and plan and work accordingly. What tested process is there that best facilitates the evangelization of a nation? We are talking missiology here. How does the body of Christ in a nation begin to increase its impact on that nation?

Obviously we must think in terms of many ministries, the multi-faceted, flexible initiatives of our creative God. He has given spiritual gifts and talents to every believer, and all are needed. We have to talk about reaching all the people groups: Maori, European, Pacific Islander, Laotian, Indian, Chinese, Bengali, etc. We have to talk about preaching good news to the poor: the unemployed, the disabled or differently abled, the drug dependent, the alcoholic, the abandoned, the abused, the prisoner, the disadvantaged, the children, the sick, the terminally ill. We have to understand basic missiological and church growth principles. George Hunter summarizes numerous church growth principles in just six. He says churches grow as they:

1 Identify receptive people to reach
2 Reach into social networks to contact people
3 Multiply recruiting groups (cells, congregations, churches) and ports of entry
4 Minister to the needs of people
5 Indigenize ministries to fit the culture of their community
6 Plan to achieve the future they intend.[21]

Every pastor knows that church growth is complex. Every pastor knows that healthy growth must occur in at least four dimensions: in members' maturity, in deepening relationships, in costly community service, and in evangelism and numbers.[22] Growth is dependent on numerous factors, not least the sovereign power of the Holy Spirit of God!

Multiplication

Older denominations have a twin growth challenge: to strengthen and to plant. And in some places, to replant. The Decade of Evangelism brings the microscope to bear on all existing denominational paraphernalia: overall vision, orientation to a biblical mission theology, adoption of growth goals, mobilization of genuinely spiritually-gifted leaders at every level, fruitful and pragmatic leadership, missionary training objectives and methods, lean national and regional structures, renewal and revival of all existing local churches, and the liberation of God's people into lifestyle evangelism and marketplace ministry. Other chapters including chapter 19 take up some of these points.

Having said all of the above, it is now widely acknowledged that the most important and central strategy for the growth of the Church in nations is Hunter's third principle: multiply recruiting groups (cells, congregations, churches) and ports of entry. This is as true for virgin territory as it is for the once churched, now post-Christian West. Every existing church must be revived and strengthened, and effective new congregations planted. This is the basis of the strategy that grows the national Church. Prior to the Lausanne II Congress in 1989, to earth vague and wishful dreams and schemes for world evangelization, Jim Montgomery wrote a book: *DAWN 2000: 7 Million Churches to Go!* From a global perspective, that was his estimate of the number of churches needed. In his view, "When the Church of every country has an intentional plan for saturating its land with cells of believers, one for every 400 to 600 in rural villages, and one for every 1,000 to 1,500 in its cities distributed among all the cultural, ethnolinguistic, and societal groupings in the land, we will be in high gear for completing the Great Commission in our time."[23]

There are several points that need to be understood. First, it is not assumed that when this has been accomplished the Great Commission will have been achieved and a nation fully evangelized. But this is the crucial strategic objective. It is a practical and measurable goal that can be attained. Second, with a witnessing congregation in every small community of people, Christ is incarnate relationally and long-term in their culture and context. Third, every person then has a genuine opportunity to see, hear and understand the gospel, and be nurtured as a disciple should he or she become a believer.

New Zealander Jeff Fountain, now YWAM[24] Director for Europe, made an important discovery at Lausanne II in Manila. He realized that for years YWAM's evangelistic strategies have been non-relational. They have largely used street drama, street witnessing, door to door visiting, tracts, films, one-off campaigns, often hit and run evangelism. But effective evangelism today is relational. At Manila he saw that most people come to Christ through a relationship with a Christian family member or a trusted friend. Churches with community ministries build relational bridges into their communities, bridges for the gospel. There are wider personal networks, nurtured through the workplace, the telephone and the car. Lifestyle evangelism is effective because it builds on a caring relational process over time.

This is why the loving local church has always been the heart of God's primary evangelistic strategy. Jeff Fountain's conclusion: post-Christian Europe needs many thousands of new Christ-centred Spirit-filled churches. There is no other process that can evangelize the dark neighbourhoods of Europe. It has been noted that in the New Testament, patterns of evangelism centred on winning individuals and families to Christ and forming them into churches. "It is not enough to do evangelism or to plant a single congregation. We have not done our job unless a movement of fully indigenous, mission-minded, multiplying churches is planted in a people group and nation... Such a church planting vision is one of the most essential concepts for world evangelization."[25] YWAM is now committed to raising up church planting movements across Europe. This is evangelism in the 1990s, the exciting cutting edge of mission!

God is a Strategist

Theological statements abound, but until 1992 I had never heard a speaker say "God is a strategist." Immediately I thought of God's strategies involved in the exodus from Egypt, the conquest of Canaan, and the Acts of the Apostles. At every significant turning point in the recorded history of the people of God, men and women listened as the Lord gave directions. I have come to believe God is speaking today, directing whole Churches to adopt and adapt national strategies to evangelize their nations. In the 1990s similar strategies are being applied in dozens of nations worldwide.[26] Without yielding to the basic urge to re-invent the wheel, VISION New Zealand is inviting Christian leaders in our nation to share responsibility for its evangelization. Together we are adapting four simple and tested steps to our unique context:

First, research is undertaken to dispel the fog of vague impressions and ignorance, and to reveal the facts. The Bible says, "What a shame, yes, how stupid, to decide before knowing the facts."[27] Jesus said, "Open your eyes and look at the fields."[28] William

Carey studied *The Religious State of the Different Nations*, the Harvest Field. He looked at the fields. Carey also studied *The Success of Former Undertakings*, the Harvest Force. Is the church growing, and if so where, and how? What is God blessing? Facts often immediately suggest responses.

On the basis of the facts, God's revealed word in Scripture, and urgent prayer, a prophetic message emerges. What is God saying to the Church in our nation? Carey concluded his *Enquiry* with a consideration of *The Practicability of Further Undertakings*. One role of the prophet is to communicate vision. Can we describe what can happen, what ought to happen, what God wants to happen? Without such a vision, "the people perish". But given a clear vision of what God wants to accomplish, people's hearts are fired. The purpose and goal of research is a visionary message through which God may guide the Church into the most fruitful steps to be taken to make disciples of all the people groups in the nation.

Second, leaders are brought together to consider the facts and the vision, and to make their response. In nations where such a conference or congress has been held, it has been a history-making event, a catalyst that convinces the body of Christ to adopt a tested strategy for the discipling of the people groups in the nation. These are top leaders, women and men of influence whose leadership qualifies them to mobilize virtually the whole body of Christ in their nation. Carey's revolutionary approach produced a revolution in world mission. Here in New Zealand there were immediate responses to the initial Dawn conference in 1987 where Wolfgang Fernandez presented the first Dawn Report.[29] These responses have led to dramatic growth.

Third, goals for growth are prayerfully set by every church, denomination and organization that identifies with the objective of the evangelization of the nation. How their goals are set, what goals, and how their attainment is measured, is the prerogative of every agency. These goals become a focus for the mobilization of the mission force as leaders make plans to reach their goals using their own resources. Numerous denominations in New Zealand have already set growth goals, as reported in chapter 8. Some have grown so rapidly they have had to increase their goals after only a few years. This theme will be developed in the final chapter of this book. Where such congresses have been held these goals are normally totalled to give a cumulative and exciting picture of the overall growth rates being targeted.

Fourth, progress is monitored through ongoing research. Further conferences are held periodically to report on progress, and to enable leaders to discuss and reassess strategies. They are able to work most effectively, putting resources where they will have greatest long-term effect for the growth and the conservation of the body of Christ.

In this volume the writers wrestle with broad issues, issues that must be considered if the whole Church in New Zealand is to take the whole gospel to the whole nation. Some new possibilities and challenges (for New Zealand) are presented. Perhaps the major challenge is for each part of the body of Christ, as it sets goals for growth, to recognize and assist all others as working partners in the greatest enterprise on earth. "There are two choices ahead... We can build our (personal) empire... and go to glory knowing we did all that any individual could. Or we can believe that God is building his Church, and work through our part of the vision in partnership with all those to whom God has given another part. In this way our voices will be united and our resources shared. What is more, by adopting mutual encouragement and support, we obey the Lord Jesus and have the power to challenge our nation to listen to him."[30] Let us "Expect great things from God; attempt great things for God" (William Carey).

FOOTNOTES

[1] Kennon L. Callahan, *Effective Church Leadership*, (San Francisco: Harper and Row, 1990): "The day of the professional minister is over. The day of the missionary pastor has come. The day of the churched culture is over. The day of the mission field has come" (pages 3 and 13).

[2] Lesslie Newbigin, *Truth to Tell, the Gospel as Public Truth*, (Grand Rapids: Eerdmans, 1991), page 2.

[3] Reported in *Challenge Weekly*, (Auckland, 21 May 1992).

[4] William J. Abraham, *The Logic of Evangelism*, (Grand Rapids: Eerdmans, 1989), pages 1 - 4.

[5] In the Great Commission in Matthew 28:18-20, we are commanded to make disciples of "panta ta ethne" (New Testament Greek), "all the ethnic groups".

[6] The words of John Collett Ryland, as quoted in Deaville F. Walker, *William Carey, Missionary Pioneer and Statesman*, (Chicago: Moody Press, 1980), page 54.

[7] Ibid., page 55.

[8] Ibid., pages 67 - 68.

[9] William Carey, *An Enquiry*, originally published in Leicester, England, (a recent edition, Dallas: Criswell Publications, 1988), page 38.

[10] S. Pearce Carey, *William Carey*, (London; Hodder and Stoughton, 7th edition, 1926), page 39.

[11] It is of interest to note, "Carey structured his ministry in India on five foundational points: the dissemination of the Gospel by every feasible means; Bible distribution in the language of the people to enhance awareness of the Gospel; establishment of churches at the earliest moment possible; in depth study of the background and thought of the non-Christian recipient peoples; and provision for early indigenous leadership training." (Ibid., Keith E. Eitel, Introduction: Echoes from the Past, page xv.)

[12] Maori are the indigenous people of New Zealand. Pakeha is the Maori word for a New Zealander of European origin.

[13] See Chapter 2.

[14] Ralph Neighbour, *Auckland, Resistant and Neglected*, (Auckland: Touch Ministries, 1988).

[15] An initial release from the Department of Statistics following the 1991 census showed the following net increases (the five highest in New Zealand): Manukau City 19,187; Auckland City 14,497; Waitakere City 14,019; Rodney District 9,925; and North Shore City 7,181.

[16] This book will observe the common convention: Church with a capital C = the whole body of Christ in New Zealand, and sometimes a national Church (eg. the Methodist Church); church with a small c = a local church.

[17] 1 Corinthians 9:22.

[18] John Massam in *Challenge Weekly*, Auckland, 25 October 1990.

[19] Dawn is an acronym for "Discipling A Whole Nation", essentially a strategy devised by James Montgomery and field-tested in the Philippines, Guatemala, and other countries. The Dawn strategy was introduced to New Zealand by layman

Con Belmont, editor of *Church Growth Ministries Magazine*. New Zealand became the first Western nation to begin to implement the Dawn strategy.

[20] Bruce Patrick, "Influencing the Growth of the Church in New Zealand", *The Reaper*, (Auckland: Institute Press, October/November 1989), pages 13 - 14.

[21] Slightly adapted from George Hunter, *To Spread the Power*, (Nashville: Abingdon, 1987), page 36.

[22] Orlando Costas, *The Church and its Mission*, (Tyndale, 1974), commenting on Acts 2:42-47.

[23] James Montgomery, *DAWN 2000: 7 Million Churches To Go*, (Pasadena, CA: William Carey Library, 1989), page 77.

[24] YWAM is an international mission agency, Youth With A Mission.

[25] Floyd McClung jnr, Executive Vice President of YWAM, in *Dawn Report*, (Pasadena: Dawn Ministries, Issue no. 14, April 1992) page 8.

[26] Numerous European countries are now applying these principles. Two examples: in England 'Challenge 2000' is working for 20,000 new churches and congregations by AD 2000; in Denmark goals have been set for 2000 new churches and congregations by AD 2000.

[27] Proverbs 18:13 (LB).

[28] John 4:35.

[29] Bob Hall and Wolfgang Fernandez, *Initial Findings of a Research Analysis on the People and the Church of New Zealand*, (Wellington: Dawn Strategy Committee, 30 September 1987). Wolfgang Fernandez is a member of the small international Dawn Ministries team.

[30] Brian Hathaway recorded this pertinent statement from Clive Calver, the General Director of the Evangelical Alliance of Great Britain, here slightly adapted, in the Evangelical Fellowship Newsletter *Workout*, (Auckland, September 1990), page 4.

2

The History of the Christian Movement in New Zealand

by John Stenhouse

The aim of this chapter is to examine where Christianity in New Zealand came from and what happened to it once it arrived. I discuss the main factors which hindered and facilitated the progress of the gospel. To do all this in a few pages entails considerable compression. Inevitably there will be omissions which will annoy readers. Some may also feel that the tone of the chapter is too negative, for I discuss hindrances to the gospel at some length. Voltaire once called history the devil's Bible, a dark record of the follies, errors and crimes of humankind. Some may see too much gloom and too little celebration of the triumphs of the gospel here. However, if we do not learn from the mistakes of the past we are liable to repeat them.

Christianity was brought to Aotearoa New Zealand at the beginning of the 19th century, when religious revival in Britain was in full swing. Thanks to John Wesley's tireless preaching and extraordinary talent for leadership and organization, tens of thousands of Britons, including many ordinary working people, had been converted to vital Christianity Methodist-style from the mid-18th century. Led by Charles Simeon, the evangelical revival was awakening the Church of England from its lazy 18th century slumber. As well as transforming individual lives by preaching the gospel, evangelicals were determined to redeem the nation. With great energy and success they led the way to abolish practices which they believed a Christian conscience should not tolerate. William Wilberforce led the campaign to abolish slavery, for example, and fellow evangelical and politician Lord Shaftesbury had factory legislation passed to ensure that women and children would not be abused as cheap labour. Believing that the gospel concerned the whole of life they united evangelism and social concern and had a huge impact on the Victorian Britain of our forebears.

Missionaries brought Christianity to New Zealand at the beginning of what came to be a great century of foreign missions. The Anglican Church Missionary Society under the leadership of Samuel Marsden was the first to attempt to convert Maori. By the 1830s, after a slow start, vast numbers of Maori began flocking to CMS and Wesleyan Missionary Society stations and, after 1838, to French Catholic missions.[1] Yet many became disillusioned with Pakeha Christianity, especially after the wars of the 1860s. Tragically, they had reason so to do. The wars began when the Governor Thomas Gore Browne seized the Waitara block in Taranaki over the protests of its rightful Te Ati Awa owners (most of whom were Anglican Christians). Government troops fired on those who peacefully resisted Waitara's occupation. Later when the war spread to the Waikato a number of missionaries, including Bishop Selwyn, acted as chaplains to government troops. This seemed like a stab in the back to many Christian Maori. Then the Pakeha parliament, after passing the appropriate legislation, began to confiscate huge areas of Maori land. Little wonder Maori became disillusioned with the Pakeha and his religion. They realised too late that when it came to land and power many Pakeha did not take the Christian ethic seriously.[2]

Some evangelical Christians, suspicious of the social concerns of the mainstream churches which they associate with bankrupt theological liberalism, might see the preceding discussion as irrelevant, a diversion into social and political issues. It is not. Too many 'Christian' Pakeha placed stumbling blocks in the way of newly converted Maori. Religious hypocrisy did not help the gospel take root then, and it never will.

Yet while we must acknowledge wrongdoing where it existed, we must beware the current fashion for reinterpreting the whole of New Zealand history in light of Pakeha skullduggery. If Maori-Pakeha relations have been relatively good in comparison with race relations elsewhere in the world, then evangelical Christianity has had a great deal to do with it. Professor Sir Keith Sinclair, who could never be accused of having a religious axe to grind, has argued exactly this. The fact that Maori rights and welfare were respected and protected as much as they were in New Zealand, enshrined in the Treaty of Waitangi and in subsequent legislation, shows how important Christian attitudes were in setting positive standards for Pakeha attitudes and behaviour from the beginning of settlement.[3] It was precisely because early 19th century evangelicals believed in *both* revivalism and social reform, because they evangelized *and* acted politically, that our race relations got off to such a comparatively good start.

During the 1840s a growing number of British settlers trickled in to the new colony. Many brought a Bible in their baggage and Christian faith in their hearts. Was the colonial era an age of exemplary faith and practice in which everyone went to church, worshipped God and loved their neighbour? Sometimes evangelical Christians, appalled by the secularism of the late 20th century, are tempted to call the nation back to such a golden age which they presume to have existed early in our history.

It never did. There were some who hoped it would. John Robert Godley, the leader of the Canterbury settlement for example, wanted to create a society composed exclusively of respectable churchgoing Anglicans; and the leaders of Otago were intent on peopling the province with devout evangelical Presbyterians like themselves.[4] Visions of church-based societies shaped the character of Canterbury and Otago, and in positive ways. In its early years for example, Otago was remarkably free of serious crime. Throughout the colony Christian faith played a real and important role in shaping beliefs and behaviour.

Yet most did not go to church. By 1874 only 23.5% of the European population were regular churchgoers, and although this figure grew later in the century, it never rose above 30%. Church attendance was markedly lower in New Zealand than in Britain throughout the 19th century, and probably even lower than in New South Wales which had begun as a penal colony.[5] Most settlers came here to get on in life, not to worship God.

There were signs too, from the beginning, that committed Christians who stood up to be counted on matters of principle were liable to encounter hostility. Robert FitzRoy for example, was an evangelical Anglican who became our second Governor in 1843. Like most humanitarians he tried to ensure that the disasters which had befallen the North American Indian and Australian Aborigine as a result of European colonization should not occur in New Zealand. The first to describe the Treaty of Waitangi as our Magna Carta, FitzRoy did everything he could to protect Maori rights and welfare. Just how unpopular this policy was is evidenced by the fact that when he was recalled to England in 1845 settlers at Nelson burnt FitzRoy in effigy.

One of FitzRoy's fiercest opponents was the lawyer and politician Alfred Domett. He deplored the "pernicious influence" of Christian humanitarians like FitzRoy. Unlike most missionaries, he rubbished the Treaty of Waitangi: "the rights of the aborigines to land, of the capabilities of which they cannot avail themselves, are not to be considered of any great value or entitled to much respect."[6] Early in 1863 he suggested that funds voted by the British government for the civilization of Maori should more properly be spent on their conquest. As Premier he recommended that all the lands of the

Waikato and Taranaki tribes that were suitable for European settlement should be confiscated for that purpose.[7]

Like most Pakeha, Domett believed in a god, but his was not the God of the Christians. According to a close friend, he never set foot inside a Christian church.[8] His god was Power, and in ethics he insisted that might was right. As he put it in 1844, "The land [of New Zealand] is, first, God's, who made it, next, theirs to whom he has given skill to use it best and strength to hold it fastest... might is the test of right after all."[9] These arguments were popular with the New Zealand Company and many of the settlers. Beneath the thin veneer of civilization, Domett was a power-hungry, Christian-despising pagan, and found this no barrier to popularity and political success. The professed religion of the vast majority of British immigrants was Christianity; their actual religion, as Domett illustrates, could be quite different. Most Protestants in this period (and according to the census they numbered almost 90% of the Pakeha population) believed that New Zealand was a Christian country and that, while Maori needed to be converted, their fellow Pakeha did not. It was a dangerous assumption. Sheltering beneath the 'Christian New Zealand' idea lurked all kinds of sub-Christian and anti-Christian beliefs and behaviours, as this brief biography of Domett suggests. The gospel had a foothold, but New Zealand was scarcely the kingdom of God.

Although some like Domett had murky motives for distancing themselves from Christianity, it must be said that the behaviour of professing Christians turned non-churchgoers off too. Sectarian conflict, generally of a Protestant-versus-Catholic variety, tainted the gospel by association. Sectarianism was part of the cultural baggage settlers imported from Britain, where for centuries Protestants had tended to identify Catholicism with religious error and political disloyalty, and Catholics had tended to see Protestants as heretics and oppressors. Ireland, where conflict was ever smouldering, kept such antagonisms alive. Sometimes they burst into flame here. In Christchurch on Boxing Day 1879 for example, a parade of Protestants flaunting Orange scarves and banners was attacked outside the Borough hotel by a group of Irish Catholics armed with pick handles. Five Orangemen were hospitalized, and by nightfall a huge crowd estimated at well over 3,000 surrounded the pub and pelted it with stones. The First World War aroused even more intense hostilities, stirred up this time by a rabidly anti-Catholic Auckland Baptist minister named Howard Elliot.[10] None of these activities commended the gospel to non-believers. Instead they reinforced the belief that religion was divisive, anti-social and should not be taken too seriously. As the 20th century wore on, sectarian alliances changed. In the second half of the century conservative Protestants and Catholics often found themselves united over issues like abortion and Homosexual Law Reform against liberals, both secular and religious. In these debates both sides displayed much of the misunderstanding, bitterness and intolerance which characterized earlier sectarianism.

This is only part of the story however. Colonial Christians wanted their churches to grow, and revivals sometimes occurred, particularly during the depression years of the 1880s. Smaller sects and denominations which were more oriented to evangelism grew faster than the larger churches. The Brethren, for example, gifted with outstanding preachers like Gordon Forlong, grew three times as fast as the total population between 1881 and 1886 (though they still numbered only just over 3000 adherents).[11] In 1883 the Salvation Army arrived and their combination of music, marches and mayhem soon gained them a following of almost 2% of the population.[12] Among the major Protestant denominations, the Methodists grew rapidly in the last third of the century.[13] The Catholics too, had their touring missioners. But New Zealand never experienced widespread dramatic revival on the scale of the Second Great Awakening in Britain and the United States. By contrast to the mercurial Methodists and Baptists blazing a gospel trail across large parts of the U.S., in New Zealand affable Anglicans and pious Presbyterians predominated, both numerically and socially. Their desire for respectability, tolerance of nominal religion and repugnance toward revivalism became widely shared. Even the small-scale revivals which did occur here were more restrained and dignified than in the U.S.

The power of the early 19th century religious revival,[14] which sought to Christianize both individuals and society, and held evangelism and social reform in fruitful tension, was gradually dissipated. The main denominations, Anglicans, Presbyterians and (by the 20th century) Methodists, began increasingly to neglect evangelism for social issues. The smaller evangelical groups, Baptists, Brethren, Salvation Army etc., went the other way, concentrated on "plucking brands from the burning", and tended to leave the wider society, the 'wicked world', to its fiery fate.[15] Protestantism was gradually separated into comfortable liberal Churchianity on the one hand, and combative evangelical groups on the other.

One of the other problems the gospel faced around the turn of the century was moralism. There was a growing tendency for mainstream society to value Christianity not for its own sake but for secular reasons. Two were regarded as especially important. First, Christianity was useful because it produced moral, law-abiding individuals. Second, a society composed of such citizens would be cohesive, strong and competitive. The emphasis was increasingly on morality and nation building rather than on Christianity. Just how private and peripheral Christian belief was becoming may be illustrated by the fact that New Zealand elected not just one but two freethinkers, Robert Stout and John Ballance, as Premier (ie. Prime Minister) during the last two decades of the century. The fact that both of these men made no secret of rejecting Christianity did not apparently trouble their electors. They were morally upright leaders and that, it would seem, was all that mattered.

The major Protestant denominations had themselves contributed substantially to the moralistic atmosphere of the late 19th and early

20th century. The great social crusades of the period, against alcohol and gambling, and for Bible-in-Schools and Sabbath observance etc., consumed enormous amounts of Christian energy. But, apart from trying to reach the next generation of churchgoers' children in Sunday School and Bible Class, evangelism of non-churchgoers was increasingly neglected for the social gospel. And identifying Christianity with morally correct behaviour, avoiding alcohol, going to church, not swearing etc., as many tended to do, was dangerous. It turned a gospel of unmerited grace into a religion of law and condemnation. The lesson for modern Christians is a crucial one.

In the 20th century the major Protestant denominations (Anglicans, Presbyterians and Methodists) experienced a slow but steady decline. By 1918 more New Zealanders attended the new picture theatres than went to church. Since Church and State had been separate from the beginning and nobody was legally obliged to go to church here, the churches had to compete with a growing range of attractive alternative activities on Sundays. Presbyterians fought a rearguard action against Sabbath desecration, but the tide was against them. In the 20th century a growing number of sporting and leisure pursuits replaced churchgoing as preferred Sunday activities. When services were dry and boring it was little wonder that many preferred to go tramping or watch television than go to church.

The 1950s, a decade of church growth, were an exception to this general trend. Presbyterians began a New Life Movement and the Methodists a Campaign for Christ and His Kingdom. New churches were built in the growing suburbs. Billy Graham arrived for a crusade in 1959 at the invitation of the National Council of Churches. He reached over half a million New Zealanders, almost ten and a half thousand of whom made first time decisions for Christ. This was the closest New Zealand had ever come to a general spiritual revival.

But there were deeper problems which this brief period of success masked. The churches were still declining in relation to the population as a whole. Growing numbers of young people were going to Sunday school and Bible class. This trend peaked in the late 1950s, but then began to decline. The baby-boomers' children were going to be largely lost to the churches. Few students in university courses today have the biblical knowledge their parents' generation gained in Sunday school or Bible class.

From the mid 1960s decline in the major Protestant denominations was more rapid. Presbyterian church membership was almost cut in half between 1966 and 1989. Whereas nominal Anglicans were well over a third of the population in 1956, by 1991 they were only just over a fifth.[16] Those who continued to attend the mainline Protestant churches (Anglican, Presbyterian and Methodist) were older people and the majority were women. These churches, led by educated middle-class male ministers, tended to be liberal and secular in their orientation. Their social conscience was active, their theology uncertain, their God unwell if alive at all. Theological opinion was divided on this last point, as the Geering controversy in the late 1960s illustrated. One indication of how much society was changing was the relative lack of success of Billy Graham's second crusade in 1969. Mainstream culture was now much less receptive to a conservative evangelical message.[17]

The picture was not all doom and gloom however. Beginning in the 1960s the charismatic movement breathed new life and hope into the mainstream churches, both Protestant and Catholic. Charismatic and pentecostal churches grew particularly fast in the 1970s and 1980s, their vibrant worship and close fellowship attracting many, particularly young people. Pentecostal churches had been in New Zealand for almost half a century before this without making much impact; pentecostalism may be a key but cannot be the key to church growth. The Baptist denomination, which was conservative and evangelical and included a number of charismatic congregations, grew in the 1980s from 1.6% of the population in 1981 to 2.1% in 1991. Despite deep differences, these growing churches possessed certain common features relevant to their success: deep conviction of the supernatural reality of God; an outward orientation emphasizing conversion of non-members; most emphasized the importance of close personal relationships in both evangelism and church fellowship; and most insisted that becoming a member must make a clear difference to beliefs and behaviour, sustaining the kind of moral and intellectual tension between church and world which the liberal churches did not.

Yet a number of academics have argued that the churches' decline is inevitable and will continue. New Zealand's future is not religious, they argue, it is secular. Lloyd Geering is the most well-known of those who argue that the process of secularization, the withering away of the Church, is not only irreversible but desirable. The Webster and Perry Values Survey affirms this prognosis.[18] There is some empirical evidence which makes this interpretation plausible. As well as dying mainstream churches, the 1991 census revealed that almost 30% of the population refused to declare even nominal Christian adherence.

How believable are these prophets of Christian doom? The simple answer is: not very. First, the defection of the faithful is no new thing in the history of Christianity. The disciples fell away from Jesus in his hour of trial. Subsequent church history has been characterized by long periods of gradual decline followed by short bright bursts of renewal and revitalization. Second, as the Bible reminds us again and again, numbers are not everything. A lone Elijah faced 450 prophets of Baal, but God was not with the big battalions (1 Kings 18:20-40). Christianity began as a tiny, obscure Jewish sect in a far-flung outpost of the mighty Roman Empire. Ignored by the great, despised by intellectuals, within two centuries it was dominating the known world. American sociologists of religion writing on religious prospects in the late 20th century world argue that massive religious renewal might well be triggered by only a single effective religious movement.[19]

It would certainly be unduly pessimistic to see the 30% of non-Christian New Zealanders as impervious to the gospel. U.S. research suggests that almost 60% of Americans brought up in non-religious homes become committed religious believers of one sort or another as adults.[20] Dynamic churches could easily have a similar impact here on the unchurched.

What lessons does this historical survey have for us? What sort of renewal movement might be effective here? First, it must be one which, unlike weak and worldly liberal churches, provides strong positive answers to the ultimate questions most people ask: Is there a God? Why am I here? Is death the end? It must believe and preach the Christian gospel, fearlessly emphasizing the supernatural reality of God, the resurrection of Christ and God's unconditional offer of forgiveness and salvation. Second, it must avoid the sectarian spirit toward opponents which in the past has put people off Christianity: the anger, bitterness and loveless self-righteousness which are the besetting sins of religious people. Displaying the fruit of the Spirit, love, joy, peace, patience, gentleness and humility, in all our dealings is the way to commend the gospel; if we have them, Paul tells us, we cannot be faulted (Galatians 5:22). Third, it must concern itself with the whole of life, with politics as well as evangelism, social justice as well as individual salvation, with the life of the mind as well as the passions of the heart, for Christ is Lord of all. Fourth, it must insist that Christianity makes a difference not only to the way we think but also to the way we live. In a world of frequent divorce, stable loving Christian marriages will speak volumes. So too, in an increasingly aggressive, self-oriented culture, will the quiet kindness of Christians. Fifth, it will be outgoing, evangelistic and other-oriented, rather than self-absorbed. Outdated, offensive methods of evangelism undoubtedly need to be changed. Singing on street corners, handing out tracts, street preaching, even mass evangelistic rallies, have probably had their day. Careful study of recent attempts at revival by evangelists Leighton Ford and Luis Palau, for example, has shown them to be essentially 'in house' affairs: convinced Christians speaking to convinced Christians, failing to reach the unchurched.[21] Sensitive, committed friendship evangelism, where the friendship is genuine and not ulterior, is the way to go.

In the 1990s New Zealanders are less optimistic, more fearful, more lonely than ever. Rising crime, divorce, poverty and unemployment statistics indicate that the secular, materialistic foundations on which modern New Zealand has been built are cracking. Mammon has proven a false, heartless god. In this dark situation, Christians who incarnate the opposite truth will shine like beacons. "God is love, and he who abides in love abides in God, and God abides in him" (1 John 4:16).

FURTHER READING

Colless, Brian and Peter Donovan (eds), *Religion in New Zealand Society*, second edition (Palmerston North: Dunmore Press, 1985).

Davidson, Allan, *Christianity in Aotearoa: A History of Church and Society in New Zealand*, (Wellington: Education for Ministry, 1991), a very useful general survey.

Davidson, Allan and Peter J. Lineham, *Transplanted Christianity: Documents Illustrating Aspects of New Zealand Church History*, second edition (Palmerston North: Dunmore Press, 1989), a book of original documents and commentary.

Donovan, Peter (ed), *Religions of New Zealanders*, (Palmerston North: Dunmore Press, 1990)

Lineham, Peter J. and Anthony R. Grigg, *Religious History of New Zealand: A Bibliography*, third edition, (Palmerston North: Department of History, Massey University, 1989), the indispensable bibliography for further reading on any topic discussed above.

Jackson, H.R., *Churches and People in Australia and New Zealand 1860-1930*, (Wellington: Allen and Unwin, 1987), a study of major themes including revivalism, sectarianism and doctrine.

Pratt, Douglas (ed.), *Rescue the Perishing: Comparative Perspectives on Evangelism and Revivalism. Waikato Studies in Religion Volume 1*, (Auckland: College Communications, 1989), on evangelism and revivals in New Zealand and elsewhere.

FOOTNOTES

[1] For more on the missionaries, and a useful select bibliography on this topic, see Allan Davidson, *Christianity in Aotearoa: A History of Church and Society in New Zealand,* (Wellington: Education for Ministry, 1991), chapters 2-3.

[2] For a fuller discussion see Davidson, *Christianity in Aotearoa*, chapter 5.

[3] Keith Sinclair, *Why are Race Relations in New Zealand Better Than in South Africa, South Australia or South Dakota?*, New Zealand Journal of History, 5:2 (1971), pages 121-127. There were, of course, plenty of Pakeha who were openly hostile to the evangelical humanitarian position that Maori were human beings and ought to be treated as such. Historians like James Belich are right to stress that the Maori side of the race relations equation was vital too. It was not only Pakeha humanitarianism, but also their own strong right arm, which earned respect for Maori.

[4] A couple of other much smaller religious settlements were established at Albertland and Waipu in the north of the North Island, but their impact on the wider society was limited. For a fuller treatment see Davidson, *Christianity in Aotearoa*, chapter 6, and Jeanine Graham, *Settler Society* in W.H. Oliver with B.R. Williams, *The Oxford History of New Zealand*, (Wellington: Oxford University Press, 1991), 112-140, on pages 126-129.

[5] For a more thorough analysis of church attendance statistics see H.R. Jackson, *Churchgoing in 19th Century New Zealand*, New Zealand Journal of History, 17:1 (1983), pages 43-59.

[6] E.A. Horsman (ed.), *The Diary of Alfred Domett, 1872-1885* (London: Oxford University Press, 1953), pages 16, 31.

[7] For a brief biography of Domett see *The Dictionary of New Zealand Biography* volume 1, 1769-1869, (Wellington: Allen and Unwin and Department of Internal Affairs, 1990), page 111.

[8] C.W. Richmond to Emily E. Richmond, 18 September 1857, quoted in Guy H. Scholefield (ed.) *The Richmond-Atkinson Papers*, volume 1, (Wellington: Government Printer, 1960), page 308.

[9] Horsman, *The Diary of Alfred Domett*, page 18.

[10] For a fuller discussion of sectarianism see Davidson, *Christianity in Aotearoa*, chapter 9.

[11] Peter Lineham, *There We Found Brethren: A History of the Assemblies of the Brethren in New Zealand*, (Palmerston North: Gospel Publishing House Society, 1977), pages 59-62.

[12] Cyril R. Bradwell, *Fight the Good Fight: The Story of the Salvation Army in New Zealand 1883-1983*, (Wellington: Reed, 1982).

[13] For a useful analysis of the growth and decline of Methodism see Peter J. Lineham, *New Zealanders and the Methodist Evangel: An Interpretation of the Policies and Performance of the Methodist Church of New Zealand*, (Wesley Historical Society Proceedings, no. 42, 1983).

[14] This revival, an evangelical Protestant phenomenon, is described more fully in the second paragraph of this chapter.

[15] For a fuller account of 19th century revivalism see H.R. Jackson, *Churches and People in Australia and New Zealand 1860-1930*, (Wellington: Allen and Unwin, 1987), chapter 3 and Peter J. Lineham, "When The Roll is Called Up Yonder, Who'll be There? An Analysis of 19th Century Transatlantic Revivalism in New Zealand and Canada," in Douglas Pratt (ed.), *Rescue the Perishing: Comparative Perspectives on Evangelism and Revivalism*, Waikato Studies in Religion Volume 1, (Auckland: College Communications, 1989), pages 1-22.

[16] These and the following figures are taken from *New Zealand Census of Population and Dwellings*, 1971, 1986, 1991.

[17] Bryan Gilling, "Mass Evangelism in Mid 20th Century New Zealand", in Pratt, *Rescue the Perishing*, pages 43-56.

[18] See for example Lloyd Geering, "New Zealand Enters the Secular Age", in Christopher Nichol and James Veitch, *Religion in New Zealand*, (Wellington: Tertiary Christian Studies Programme of the Combined Chaplaincies and The Religious Studies Department Victoria University, 1980), pages 238-263; Alan C. Webster and Paul E. Perry, *The Religious Factor in New Zealand Society*, (Palmerston North: Alpha Publications, 1989).

[19] Rodney Stark and William Sims Bainbridge, *The Future of Religion: Secularization, Revival and Cult Formation*, (Berkeley and Los Angeles: University of California Press, 1985).

[20] Ibid., pages 48-49.

[21] Bryan Gilling, "Convinced Christians Convincing Convinced Christians? A Study of Attenders at a Luis Palau Crusade Meeting", in Pratt, *Rescue the Perishing*, pages 77-96.

New Culture, New Challenge

by Brian Carrell

The mid-1960s were years of great expectations for the civilized world. The decade had begun with putting a man into orbit around the earth, and concluded with putting a man and a machine on the moon. They were the years which introduced to New Zealand cheap international travel, domestic television, and a host of dazzling technological innovations. This was also the period when the music of the Beatles, the free-wheeling lifestyle of *Easy Rider*, the effervescent optimism of flower power, and the liberal theology represented by *Honest to God* captured the spirit of the Western world. But this would eventually prove also to be the decade in which the form of Christianity identified with European nations for over 1300 years, and with their former colonies such as New Zealand for more than a century, began to go into dramatic decline. This decade would in fact witness the demise of Christendom, arguably a more obvious end in this country than in any other Western nation.

Looking back on that span of ten years, it is not too surprising that this happened. For some time before this the acids of modernity[1] had been eating into the fabric of traditional religion in the West. The recipe for this had been concocted three hundred years previously when, in the aftermath of the Renaissance and Reformation, the Enlightenment had subtly shifted the centre of European spirituality from heaven to earth, from God to nature, from revelation to reason, from hope in the future to life in the present, from an aspiration to become divine to a preoccupation with being more human, from worship of the transcendent to obsession with the transient.

While it was the Enlightenment which provided the intellectual revolution, questioning the reality and relevance of God as the centre of the universe, another cataclysm, the French Revolution of 1789, introduced a succession of seismic shocks in the body politic of the Western world. This shifted the centre of human aspiration from seeking the glory of God to the pursuit of human happiness through struggles for freedom and equality and for a variety of human rights. Add to these a third radical social change in Europe during the 18th century, the industrial and agrarian revolutions, and all the necessary ingredients were incubating in preparation for the great paradigm change in the role of religion in Western society which eventually has taken place over the past thirty years.

The catalyst which precipitated this final death-blow to Christendom as the Western world had known it, was the impact of modernity. Two world wars within one generation shook to the core the confidence of Western man and woman in the faith of their forebears as it had been handed down to them. But it was the rapid and spectacular advances of science and technology in the immediate post World War II period which powerfully suggested the unspoken message that there were saviours other than the Lord of the Church, deliverers other than the God of the Bible, explanations for the mysteries of life and the universe other than the theology of the Christian faith to which modern man or woman could turn.

The impact of modernity on a society whose eyes had already been distracted to fix on planet earth, personal rights and human happiness was devastating so far as traditional religion was concerned. And the devastation steadily increases, particularly in a country such as New Zealand which has little vestigial evidence of its Christian roots or collective memory of its spiritual foundations. This total process we call "secularization". It has produced for us who live in New Zealand at the end of the 20th century, a new culture; and for us who are concerned Christians in this country, a new challenge. Evidence of the impact of secularization on our society can be seen in a number of ways.

The Impact of Secularization

Church attendance and adherence have been significantly altered. All of the traditional 'mainline' churches have suffered a decline in both active membership and nominal affiliation because they have been primarily shaped to serve Christians in a superseded world, and they represent a Christendom which no longer exists. Paradoxically, along with this steady decline in mainstream Christianity since the 1960s has occurred a significant emergence or regrowth of both new, independent and usually charismatic churches, and of older Baptist or pentecostal churches. These appealed to many as more appropriate alternatives to traditional churches in this new kind of world New Zealanders sensed around them.

Yet remarkable as these developments have been, such churches on the growing edge of Christianity in this country still only represent a small percentage of the total population. There are also indications that much of this new growth has been by transfer from other older churches rather than by fresh inroads into secular society. Traditional forms of faith and worship are no longer deemed by some to serve the spirit of this age with its insistence on entertainment as the medium of communication, and instant returns as the expectation of a consumer society.

A marked shift in religious profession has occurred. In the anonymity of the regular census returns, no citizen need feel under obligation to conform to social expectations or even family precedents. Honesty in answers is generally assumed. These returns show that although as recently as the 1976 census only

3.2% of the population indicated they professed "No Religion", fifteen years later in the 1991 census returns this percentage had risen to 19.6%. Combine with this latter figure those who in 1991 "Object to State" (7.4%) and together these represent 27% of the population - more than one in every four New Zealanders. Significantly (and for the first time ever in the history of this country) this group together are now more numerous than the next largest single block of church adherents, Anglicans, who dropped from 29.3% of the population in 1976 to 21.4% in 1991.

Another effect is an observable loss of a sense of the sacred. Buildings formerly regarded as sacred are today no longer treated with the respect once taken for granted. Most churches now need to be locked during the day if unattended, as well as overnight. Arson, burglary, desecration and vandalism of places of worship are widespread. Sacred days and sacred seasons are fast losing their significance. Sundays have been opened to commerce, public sporting events, and now gambling opportunities. Sundays and holy days are considered to be days for Christians to do their thing, rather than for the nation to pause and remember God, such has been the flood-tide of secularization.

Moral behaviour patterns and ethical standards have been affected. Once God is minimalized and religious observances ostracized, the traditional values of a society lose their imperative and the moral direction of a people becomes confused. This also has become increasingly apparent in our nation, especially over the last decade. There is a reluctance to acknowledge any moral authority outside a supposed social consensus. Yet this consensus is often engineered by a vociferous minority who have a cause to capture, or by media merchants who have a product to sell and tailor their material to match their market. When this market is represented by people who have lost touch with their Christian roots and forgotten their culture's foundational values, it is a case of reinforcing an ethical outlook now largely shaped by convenience and self-gratification.

What works, goes; what the public buys, sells. There is no obligation to anyone outside oneself.

Although the much-lauded and long-awaited secularist's promise of a new liberation of the spirit, which would flow on as inevitably as day emerges from night, has not yet arrived, still the doughty defenders and advocates of secularism speak of the economic, or educational, or political miracle which is about to achieve this, without benefit of God. They seem to disregard the negative effects of secularization on our nation: the horrific increase in homicides and crimes of violence; the prevalence of white-collar crime and misappropriation of trust funds on a scale hitherto unknown; the growing sense of insecurity of either persons or property; the rampant individualism which saps corporate voluntary activities and community enterprises; the low esteem in which politics and politicians are held today; continuing offences of a sexual nature in a society supposedly freed from the restrictions and inhibitions of Victorian puritanism.

New gods have arisen to capture the devotion and commitment of the ordinary Kiwi. By a strange quirk of fancy, secular New Zealanders have not given up on all semblance of religion or worship. In many cases they have simply created substitute idols and pseudo-gods. Hope for the future is expressed through Lotto investments by a staggering proportion of people; character building of children is largely entrusted, often in blind faith, to a secular education system; a yearning for the New Heaven is transmuted into creating a renewed planet earth.

The western origins of secularization, and its particular relevance to those of European descent whose faith and values have been nurtured in "Christendom", means that the impact of this process in New Zealand has been largely felt by the Pakeha. Maori and Polynesian cultures and values, though informed and even in part transformed by the gospel brought to them by Europeans, have never lost their innate spirituality. Yet even they are not immune to the cold winds of secularization, and certainly not untouched by the subtle ravages of modernity. This has produced an all-pervasive new universal culture which, with the help of Coca-Cola, jeans, McDonald's and satellite television, eventually will consume all nations, peoples and cultures. So this 'new culture, new challenge', while principally a concern of the Pakeha, must also be of concern to Maori and Polynesian. The inroads of this secular spirit are already being felt in these cultures. On maraes around New Zealand a phrase increasingly quoted today is: "Kua ngaro te tapu". Addressing the issue of "wairuatanga"[2], this draws attention to a growing sense of loss of the numinous and the sacred even in Maoridom.

Such then is the changed climate in which the Christian Church operates in the West today. It is an environment which calls for a new and appropriate response, in the way that the gospel in the 1st century Mediterranean region had to vary its response in its encounter with Judaism in Palestine, compared with its engagement with Greek or Roman Gentile society in Europe.

What any church in New Zealand must take into account if it is merely to survive well into the 21st century, much less make inroads into our increasingly pagan communities through effective evangelism, are the characteristics of this new culture we confront today:

Characteristics of the New Culture

We no longer enjoy the plausibility structure of Christendom. What was formerly for the most part a user-friendly environment for the gospel and the Church is now distinctly cool and detached. Today Christians can carry into society no assumptions that their message will be welcomed, their story understood. The dominant contemporary attitude to religion, whether Christianity of the traditional denominations or of the newer independent churches, is one of disdain or just disinterest.

We are now a people whose expectations have been conditioned by a full generation of television viewing. The subtleties of how constant exposure to television changes the perceptions and critical perspectives of viewers has been well-explored in Neil Postman's *Amusing Ourselves To Death*.[3] Television has conditioned us to be motivated through entertainment, to lay more weight on appearance than on substance, and to have our news and information presented to us in attractive short segments. For good or ill, the Church in its worship and Christians in their communication of the Gospel have to compete in this kind of climate today. Some churches (and many Christians) are not geared to cope with this becuse of their being locked into Christendom models of denominationalism and discipleship.

We face a new set of public values, often at variance with the exclusive claims of the gospel. We live in a society which lays great store by toleration, relativism and pluralism. No longer can any faith claim to be true in an absolute sense. There is some truth in every religion. All must be allowed. No-one must be given preference or privilege. Whether in education, the administration of justice, or political decision-making, religion and the values it represents must have no public role. The consequence of all this is a Church which becomes increasingly marginalized, a faith which becomes increasingly privatized, and a morality which becomes increasingly relativized.

Implications for Evangelism

All this has major implications for how we communicate the gospel in a secularized society. A new culture issues a challenge to provide a different kind of evangelism. Such evangelism is likely to take into account these seven features:

Pre-evangelism becomes much more important. We have to begin further back. One way will be by challenging the key secular assumptions underpinning contemporary society. Often these are at variance with the gospel, though sometimes sadly confused by Christians with gospel values. These are likely to include such staple features of Western liberal democracies as consumerism, individualism, the artificial separation of facts from values (scientism), and freedom as the ultimate human value.

Our communication needs to be more authentic and visual. The message which will get through in a secular setting is one seen visibly to be lived out in distinctive communities of faith. We need much more to show as well as tell our gospel. This means the solitary Christian in her daily round of neighbourhood activities; the contribution of a group of Christians in an office, school, factory, to the atmosphere of their work-place; the way a local church engages itself in the joys and pains of its surrounding community.

A priority must first be de-secularizing the Church.
Somewhere along the line, the Church herself has unconsciously imbibed something of the secular spirit. Her message and ministry at times sound as though for Christians also the sole gospel goal is human happiness. While in her architecture the cross still holds centre-stage, in deference to the spirit of the age the Church often mutes the offence of a crucified Saviour, and trades the sin of 'rebelliousness' for lesser and socially more admissible misdemeanours of 'inappropriate behaviour'. 'Sins' are acceptable; 'sin' is not. And while vigorously decrying the excesses of capitalism and market forces, we endorse meekly a supermarket mentality over issues of church mobility. ("By all means worship where you feel comfortable; choice and change is everyone's right.") What look like secular values have seeped into the heartland of faith itself.

This seepage of secularism has infiltrated the whole Christian spectrum, from liberal to fundamentalist, in one form or another.

For example, evangelical emphasis on the salvation of the individual and personal sanctification may unwittingly owe as much to the Enlightenment as to the Gospel and serve to reinforce secular pressures towards privatized faith.[4]

The emphasis in evangelism needs to shift from event to process, from making decisions to making disciples. In an age such as Christendom when most people lived close to professed faith, a call to make a decisive response and take that final step of commitment was appropriate. But in a society where most people are ignorant of Christ, oblivious to the cross, and a long way from God, discipleship becomes much more a journey towards faith and a growing into Christ.

A new measure of mutuality across the whole Christian Church front is required. When Christianity is more or less accepted as the faith of the nation, a society can afford the luxury of competing denominations. But when the grey cloud of secularism descends upon a people, Christians have to stand together (or at least respect with integrity the differences between them) and affirm one another publicly and sincerely as brothers and sisters in Christ. Rash criticism, cheap jibes, or uninformed condemnation of other churches only wounds the body of Christ in the eyes of the watching world, and negates our gospel.

Faith needs resolutely to move out of the private closet and into the public arena. Christians in the West, in contrast with those in Africa or South America, have too easily allowed themselves to be duped by the secular spirit of the age into regarding religious faith as a purely private virtue which has no appropriate place in public life. We have to change this, as a public expression of our evangelism. We need to be bold and insistent that the death and resurrection of Jesus Christ are of vital relevance to every aspect of our political, social and economic life, civic or national. As Lesslie Newbigin has reminded us, this is "public truth". We will not allow Christ to be kept in the wardrobe.

More effort needs to be put into 'forming' Christians.
We have a new task of helping Christians discover what it means to be disciples in the face of modernity. We can no longer take for granted that all people in a country such as ours live close to the Christian ethic, and are at least unconsciously aware of the gospel distinctions between right and wrong, good and evil. Just as the New Testament epistles were written to help new believers know how to live in an alien culture, so today in a fresh way we need to equip disciples of Christ for translating their faith into life in a secular society as it enters the 21st century.

FOOTNOTES

[1] Modernity sums up all those convergent forces which have created our modern world: urbanization, scientific advances, technology, industrialization, and hyper-rationalism (eg. in theology and Biblical criticism). See Andrew Walker, *Enemy Territory*, (Hodder and Stoughton, 1987).

[2] Maori spirituality.

[3] Neil Postman, *Amusing Ourselves To Death*, (Methuen,1987).

[4] See Os Guinness, *The Gravedigger File*, (Hodder and Stoughton, 1983) pages 73-109, and Lesslie Newbigin, *Truth To Tell*, (Eerdmans 1991) pages 68-85, for a wider discussion of this example.

The Three Levels of Mission in New Zealand

by Harold Turner

Christian missions have been part of New Zealand's history in the modern period, initially as missions to the Maori people. After these missions became Maori churches, cross-cultural concern was redirected into foreign missions. New Zealand personnel eventually served in every continent of the world. For a small country we have a notable record. Besides denominational mission agencies, the list of independent missionary societies or local representatives of overseas societies runs into many scores.

Holistic Overseas Missions

In most of this overseas work there has been a holistic approach in the sense that the gospel was addressed to all three levels of human existence: the individual personal, the public social, and the deeper cultural. Such a comprehensive approach was demanded by the nature of the local situation. Missionaries had to start at the first level, with sole converts or small groups. They also had to address the second level: social systems and the structures of marriage, the place of women, the treatment of disease, pay-back revenge, and many other areas demanding reform in the direction of God's kingdom.

Beyond these two levels missionaries had to address the basic culture itself. Language is the first expression of the basic culture.

The local language was learned, given written form, and used for translating the Scriptures. This study was extended by the use of anthropology to help reach the very roots of a people's life. Missionaries were pioneers in the development of the modern sciences of linguistics and anthropology. They then brought the gospel to bear on the roots of the culture. They were engaged in what I am calling "deep mission".

Learning From Our Missionaries

The holistic approach we have learned abroad in other societies and cultures offers a radical critique of what we have been doing in New Zealand. Here the evangelism of the 'evangelical' and the more recent 'charismatic' constituencies has been focused on level 1, the individual, as its chief emphasis. Christian bookstores concentrate on this and on the nurture of the personal religious life. The more 'liberal' constituency, especially in the mainline churches, is much more involved in the reform of social systems and structures, level 2 of our existence, especially through its focus on issues such as rights, ecology, peace, feminism, etc. For some two decades evangelicals have shown increasing concern for social transformation. Brian Hathaway's *Beyond Renewal, The Kingdom of God* provides striking evidence of this.[1] Nevertheless there continues to be a degree of polarization between the individual and the social emphases within our Christian community, polarization that has been less evident on overseas mission fields.

While our missionaries overseas study world-views and the basic assumptions of tribal and other cultures, level 3, in order to bring a biblical critique to bear at this level, concern in New Zealand to bring the gospel to bear on the very roots of our culture has been almost totally absent. There are various reasons for this.

Surface Culture as Social Custom

First, we operate with a surface view of culture, the popular view that limits culture to our various traditions: foods, clothing, housing, entertainment and parties, music, art styles, greetings, births, marriages and funerals, anniversaries, etc. I call this surface or expressive culture. It is equivalent to social customs rather than to any deeper basic worldview. 'Cultural presentations' consist of music, drama, dance, costumes, foods, ways of greeting, all of which are interesting to others and contribute to the self-identity of groups. These presentations may reflect the original root culture only little or not at all. To that extent they restrict the basic meaning of culture to social customs. So we come to believe, to quote from an Auckland mayor's publicity, that "all challenges of a cultural nature can be resolved by fostering understanding, communication and working together with a love for all in our community." This is superficial blah, but Christians fall for it like everyone else.

To illustrate further, consider the very distinctive 'cultures' of the English, the Welsh, the Scots and the Irish within the one society and nation of the United Kingdom. Here in New Zealand these surface culture variations of Britain survive and are consciously nurtured. To these have been added surface cultures of Dalmatia, the Netherlands, Greece and many others. These peoples are however all Europeans. Beneath level 2 variations of social custom they are Europeans who share a common deeper-level, level 3, European tradition and worldview. The two levels are quite different.

From the Maori viewpoint they are all 'Pakeha.' Pakeha is primarily a cultural term rather than a racial one. New Zealanders will become even more conscious of our common surface culture when we see the impact of the current immigration of quite different Asian cultures, and understand what lies below the surface cultural variations of Taiwanese, Japanese, Indians and others. An Asian worldview has fundamental oppositions to the European worldview. This is a new and urgent question to which governments seem to be irresponsibly indifferent. How can these worldviews combine if there is a basic incompatibility between them? We just do not know what we are doing at these foundational levels of human life.

Flexible Relations
Between Surface and Deep Culture

The same word 'culture' can refer to social customs, ie. 'surface culture' (level 2, the social level of our lives), or to the basic axioms and convictions by which people live, ie. our 'deep' or 'foundational culture' (level 3, the deeper level). Like the foundations of a building the third level is often hidden. At some points there may be the closest inter-connection between these two levels. It is remarkable how at other points they may be separated.

A classic example of this is found in the Scriptures. Israel emerged from a background of tribal cultures and religions where rituals and festivals were linked with the fertility of crops and herds, with lambing and harvest festivals, and with pagan fertility rites. Remarkably, outward forms, the visible social customs, were retained and given new meaning that derived from the new biblical worldview. The feasts of Weeks, of Tabernacles and of Passover commemorated the specific acts of God within their history rather than the timeless fertility powers of nature. Israel's surface culture now carried a new meaning.

A similar process occurred in the early Jewish church. In Acts chapter 15 we read of the history-making decision not to impose on Gentile converts in other cultures even such a basic Jewish cultural requirement as circumcision. The requirement was removed, as it were, from level 3 to a position within the more surface culture of level 2, a fairly radical change for Jewish Christians. The same process occurred again when rabbits and eggs of pagan Europe's ancient fertility rites were given new historical meanings within the Christian context of Easter.

There is no necessary connection between the surface culture of social customs and the deep cultural forces that ultimately control our lives. For instance, we will not necessarily deal with the basics of Maori culture at the level of marae protocol, nor with the roots of Japanese culture by learning how to visit a Japanese home for a meal, important though these and all similar customs are. In identifying the ambiguities of this word 'culture', we relocate these more surface aspects of cultures to the area of the social. This places them among the concerns of the Christian social reformer who seeks a Christian life-style in these matters. There is much to be done here. What is a Christian wedding or funeral, a Christian style in furnishings or dress? Some styles are plainly un-Christian, and evangelism must certainly take account of this level of our existence. So I am not depreciating the importance of change or reform at this level. But we do not reach understanding of the culture of any people when we seek it only at the surface level of social custom, by learning only to be polite to one another, or attending one another's festivals.

The Analogy of Marxism

In illustration consider the history of Marxism. If Marx had been content to operate at our level 1, he might have left no more than a coterie of like-minded radical thinkers or at best a kind of Marxist Church. Such groups were founded in the 19th century in the name of humanism or secularism.

Or Marx might have been merely a radical social reformer, operating at our level 2, a social activist concerned with child labour, boy chimney sweeps, sweated seamstresses, or conditions in prisons or factories. He would have joined the band of similar and honoured social reformers who effected some improvement in these areas. But he would not have changed the face of the world in the next 80 years.

The immense global and practical influence of this one man, Karl Marx, depended on his theories which offered a worldview, an interpretation of history and of the meaning of human life. They offered the basic assumptions or axioms of a comprehensive philosophy of existence. They claimed to be true. They invoked the adjective "scientific" to support their claim. Marxism would win in the end because it was true! Correct theory, ie. Marxist orthodoxy, was paramount, and the worst enemy would come from within as deviationism or heresy. What Marxism offered was foundational truth which lay at our level 3. On these axioms all else was to be built. Therein lay its strength.

This provides vivid examples of several important principles. First, note the difference between focusing primarily on level 3, rather than on levels 1 or 2. If we focus on levels 1 or 2, the results will be only on those levels. We must also work at level 3. We sorely need to absorb this fact when we talk about evangelism.

Second, note the supreme importance at level 3 not of pragmatic results or of power but of truth. Marxism had practical results and power in plenty, but it was wrong. Its basic view of reality was simply untrue. No achievements in China or elsewhere can mask the final consequences of a worldview that does not correspond with the way things are created. What is remarkable is how quickly reality rebelled and exposed the falsity.

And third, the gospel could reach Marxism and critique it only at the fundamental level, level 3. It was not much use picking a moral quarrel with the life-style of individual Marxists, who often put half-hearted Christians to shame. Nor was it very effective to critique Marxist economic and political systems which had usually replaced something worse, often with remarkable achievements. Only the truth of the biblical worldview, and its version of the real structure and goal of human nature and the real forces in history, could be placed over against Marxist axioms. In the end history and reality could wait no longer. With the collapse of Marxism, it is at this third level that the real reconstruction of Eastern Europe must now be sought.

Deep Culture, Deep Mission

Now at last we come to consider the proper content of level 3 itself. Here we meet a major difficulty, that of bringing to consciousness for critical examination the underlying, axiomatic, unconsciously-assumed convictions that I have called deep or foundational culture. We may get the feel of this unfamiliar realm if we look at the wide variety of terms used to describe its contents: words like axioms, assumptions, paradigms, viewpoint, mind-set, fiduciary stance, belief-system, worldview, cultural roots. I shall use the general term worldview for the contents of this level. This is the level in need of deep mission which will critique its truth or error, its relation to the biblical worldview, and so its relation to reality itself.

Who among us could describe clearly the underlying assumptions of our lives? In the previous chapter Brian Carrell sets out some of the characteristics of modern Western culture that Christians share with those outside the Christian faith, characteristics that make us all so alike as New Zealanders. And who can tell us how far this secular humanist worldview has become the effective working basis in much of our church and personal life? As Brian Carrell puts it, "a priority must be de-secularizing the Church itself." Or, in other terms, de-indigenizing the Christian faith within New Zealand before we can think of genuine indigenization. The basic reason why the gospel has so little impact in this country is that it has lost its distinctives by assimilation to the prevailing culture within which we all live. There is no 'us' and 'them'. We are all 'them'.

Let me offer the simplest of examples. The regular Salvation Army advertisement for its holiday facilities at Russell includes the offer of a "luxury motel". When the Salvation Army goes up-market and gets into the business of selling luxury, we have to ask whether the gospel or our current consumer-oriented Western culture is in control. For a Christian in a poor world the criterion of luxury is a good guide as to what not to buy or do. If the Army should plead that its motel is really quite modest (as well it may be), then it has been caught up in current advertizing exaggeration to the point of untruth! I apologize to the Army for taking this example when more serious and complex illustrations can be found in any of our churches. But the very simplicity and unwitting nature of this example shows how easily we operate with the unconscious assumptions and attitudes of our culture.

Changing hearts and minds at the level of belief systems, to remove distortions and sheer errors: that is the new mission frontier for the gospel of Christ. This gospel brings its own special understanding of the way things really are. At this third level that is the question at every point.

Deep mission at this level is essential if we are to undergird the direct changes in the social order at level 2, and provide the cultural context for more holistic persons at level 1. Indeed, if Christianity is to do more than counsel individuals at the private level, or avoid becoming an increasingly weak and parasitic ally of liberal humanist forces operating mainly at level 2, it must cross this new mission frontier to level 3 and engage with all serious-minded people in a profound re-examination of the very bases of Western culture. This will demand hard thinking, the most relevant form of practical action for Christians in New Zealand today.

FOOTNOTE

[1] Brian Hathaway, *Beyond Renewal, The Kingdom of God*, (Milton Keynes, UK: Word, 1990).

Trends in The Nation

by Norman Brookes

Predicting the future on the basis of the past, or even of the present, is a risky business at best. The unexpected can always intervene. Who could have predicted in 1990 that within the space of eighteen months New Zealand would experience three mass murder events. Who can predict even now what effects those events will have on the future development of the New Zealand psyche? Nevertheless in considering the question, "How shall we proclaim the gospel in this context as we approach the year 2000?" an attempt needs to be made to understand the trends in our society. A hit and miss approach to evangelism is not good enough. Christians are called to use their minds as well as their hearts.

Trends, where discernible, can inform and influence our strategies for mission and evangelism. We are called to proclaim a multi-faceted gospel. Knowledge of social trends may even clarify which aspects of the gospel might speak most clearly to New Zealanders in this decade and in our context. In this chapter we will look at three key areas where trends are discernible. These are population and demographic trends, values and issues trends, and religious affiliation and belief trends. Each of these will help us sharpen our understanding of New Zealand society and therefore our ability to proclaim the gospel in that society.

Population and Demographic Trends

The 1991 census figures currently being released show that the New Zealand population now stands at 3,434,950, an increase of 3.5% over the 1986 figure.[1] Females outnumber males by 47,640. The most significant data to emerge from the census to date are the changing age profile and the ethnic mix.

The 3.5% growth rate in the population is not evenly spread over the country as a whole. The only area in which it is exactly reflected is the rural sector. The major cities have significant variations. Auckland shows the most dramatic growth with a 7.8% increase in the population of its urban area since the 1986 census. Hamilton is second with a 6.1% increase in its population. Christchurch shows a 2.4% growth in population, below the national average. Dunedin with a 1.7% increase, and Wellington with a zero increase, are well below the average. These figures highlight the trend that has been evident for several decades. It is the northern part of the North Island that is expanding. This expansion is partly the result of immigration but is also due to a northward drift of population from other parts of the country. In terms of evangelism strategy therefore, the northern part of the North Island presents, and will continue to present for the foreseeable future, the major challenge to the churches. There is an expanding mission field right on our doorstep.

The 1991 census shows that we are an aging population. This is seen in the 8.1% increase in those over the age of 60 when compared with the 1986 figure. It is also reflected in the 10.2% increase in the 45 to 59 age group. The next group, the 25 to 44 age group, includes most of the so-called baby-boomers and shows an 8.9% increase. The only other group to show a significant increase is the 0 to 4 age range which records a rise of 11.5%. On the other hand the 5 to 14 age group shows a decrease of 7.2%, and the 14 to 24 group a 4.4% decrease. If our churches were to reflect this pattern they should now have more elderly people (which many have), more people in the 25 to 44 age group (which most do not have), and there should also be an upturn in the presence of infants and little children. Of course the correlations are not as simple as that. In general terms however that is what one might reasonably expect if the churches were to reflect the population trends with respect to age groupings in our society.

In terms of ethnicity the major change since the 1986 census is seen in the influx of Asian people. The number of people of Chinese[2] origin resident in New Zealand increased by 88% during that period. Even more significant is the 112% increase in the number of people of Indian origin. In other words the Indian population of New Zealand has more than doubled in the space of five years. The total percentage of these two ethnic groups in the population as a whole is still low at 2%.[3] These trends present a growing challenge to the churches in terms of mission and evangelism. Fortunately many of these immigrants are themselves Christian. This is seen in the emergence of Chinese and Korean congregations in Auckland, and the presence of Sri Lankans and other Asian people in the life of many largely Pakeha congregations throughout the country. Such people undoubtedly are a key to the spread of the gospel within their ethnic communities. It is important that they are supported by the wider Christian community.

Another factor worth noting is the increase in the number of New Zealand residents who were born overseas. During the intercensal period (1986-91) these rose from 15% to 16%, a numerical increase of over 33,000 people, the equivalent of a city almost the size of Wanganui. The effect of this is to add to the diversification of society as a whole including a greater plurality of values and belief systems. New Zealand is no longer the relatively homogeneous, predominantly British country it once was. The increase in the Maori birth rate, and the Maori renaissance, has made that notion untenable. So too has the large influx of people from Samoa, Tonga, Raratonga, and other Pacific islands. The number of Samoan people in New Zealand now stands at 68,000 whereas five years ago it was 50,199, an increase of 35%. The number of Tongan people is now 18,157 which is almost a 100% increase on the figure of 9,225 returned at the previous census. While a high percentage of Samoan and Tongan people are Christian their presence nonetheless adds to the diversity of New Zealand society. Their Christianity is strongly community oriented, unlike much of Western Christianity which is often highly individualistic. As such it brings its own distinctive challenge to the Pakeha churches.

Values and Issues Trends

There is clear evidence in the New Testament that what we now call "contextual theology" was in fact alive and well. Each of the gospel writers, for instance, drew on the rich pool of information available about Jesus their Lord in a unique way. They did this in order to address the particular needs of the readers they had in mind. Paul did the same in his letters. Luke, in the Acts of the Apostles, also provides examples of this process. One example from Acts is Paul's address to the people of Athens from Mars Hill.

Two concerns lay behind the contextualizing approach taken by the New Testament writers in their proclamation of the gospel. The first was a deep conviction that the good news of the gospel was to be explained and communicated to the whole world. The second was the belief that for people to hear the good news it had to be related to their own particular context, and should touch base with the day to day realities of life. Today in Aotearoa New Zealand, many Christians are grappling with the same issues. Most endorse the conviction that the gospel is to be communicated to all people. At the same time an increasing number affirm the need to take our particular context seriously as we communicate the news that God has entrusted to us.

Aotearoa New Zealand is neither Palestine of the 1st century nor Britain of the 19th century. This means New Zealand Christians cannot simply assume that the language used in the New Testament era, or in Britain last century, will automatically communicate to New Zealanders today. The problem however is not just confined to language. The question of issues needs also to be addressed. The issues that were critical for the people of Jerusalem almost twenty centuries ago, or for the people of England in the industrial revolution, are not necessarily the critical issues of a country situated in the South Pacific at the end of the 20th century. What this means is that in proclaiming the gospel, both the language we use and the issues we choose to address must be readily understood by our hearers. The issues also need to be real to our hearers if we are to communicate effectively.

Updating the language is not too difficult. There are many excellent contemporary translations and paraphrases of the Bible to help us. Only those who want to treat the Bible as a fossil from the reign of the first Queen Elizabeth would choose to ignore this. The second matter, that of relating the gospel to contemporary issues is more difficult. That the gospel will provide us with insights for dealing with current contextual issues is of course true. The issues themselves however may be quite different from those addressed in the New Testament. Environmental issues for example are much more critical for us than they were in the 1st century. Ozone holes and CFC's[4] were unknown to the biblical writers, but the call to Christians to be responsible caring stewards of resources is certainly implicit in the Bible. For people to hear these things changing the language is not enough. We who seek to be communicators of the gospel must take seriously the context in which we live and the issues that emerge from that context.

Essential background : the 1980s. Much of what we are presently experiencing in New Zealand of the 1990s owes its origin to the previous decade. Therefore it is important to glimpse some of the key facets of the 1980s if we are to speak of trends in terms of values and issues. The following discoveries of the 1980s are important in seeking to identify the issues that continue to shape us as New Zealanders.

The year 1981 will long be remembered in New Zealand history. It was the year of the last Springbok tour. It erupted in a winter of discontent as the nation almost tore itself apart over whether the Springboks should or should not be in this country. The issues centred around racism and sport. Some believed that the evils of apartheid in South Africa were such that we as a nation must reject any involvement with that country. Others took the line that sport and politics should not be mixed. Be that as it may, the real legacy of the tour was an increasing awareness that it was not only South Africa that had a race problem. New Zealand too had a race problem. There were clear signs of racism in the relationship between the dominant white culture of New Zealand and the indigenous Maori people. Racism was no longer something out there, in distant South Africa. There were serious questions to be addressed in our context. Legislation to enhance the powers of the Waitangi Tribunal was one response to this new perception. So too was a spate of books, both from historians like Michael King[5] and novelists like Witi Ihimaera[6], creating a new awareness of our history as a nation. They also cast new light on injustices perpetrated against Maori people. These issues will not go away. The Maori cry is for justice. Christians, who as a matter of history were involved through missionary endeavour from the start, can play a significant part in this issue. As we do, the integrity of the Church and the gospel itself may be reclaimed in the eyes of Maori people. The evangelist cannot ignore these things.

A second discovery of the 1980s was that New Zealand could become nuclear free without disappearing from the face of the planet. This happened not long after the Labour Government took office in 1984. Although this was a political decision, it was clear, as many surveys have shown, that the government was responding to a rising groundswell of opposition to the visits to our ports of nuclear capable warships. The legislation itself went beyond this and outlawed nuclear power as well as nuclear weapons. This in turn led to the break-up of the ANZUS alliance. In a sense New Zealand became "the mouse that roared" in the South Pacific. That was achieved not without engendering a certain sense of pride for many. The discovery was made that we could stand alone in terms of our foreign policy. While not universally accepted, this still has strong support. The 1989 Study of New Zealand Values survey shows for example that only 39% of the population favour staying in ANZUS and letting in ships with a nuclear capacity[7]. A gospel that has a focus on peacemaking is a gospel that is both true to its biblical roots and relevant to the New Zealand scene.

The third discovery of the 1980s was that unbridled greed reaps its own reward. This was discovered by many in the October 1987 share market crash. 1984 to 1987 was the heyday of the Roger Douglas era. In part the government of the day was trying to open up New Zealand to the real world and to encourage us to become more efficient producers. This goal, while commendable, had two drastic and contradictory consequences. On the one hand unemployment started to soar. On the other, those with money took to the money market with a vengeance, playing with stocks and shares. Whole corporate edifices were built on the expanding money market scene. In October 1987 the day of reckoning dawned: many people were severely hurt, and many corporate edifices were shown to be built on shifting sands. Undoubtedly these events have contibuted to a growing cynicism with respect to politicians and government. In the 1989 survey mentioned above, 65% of New Zealanders saw "big business (as having) too much power"[8]. Certainly most people in New Zealand view alliances between the government and big business with deep suspicion.

A fourth discovery of the 1980s was that at certain times of the year a significant and growing ozone hole appears over the Antarctic. This, coupled with the scientific knowledge that this is caused in part by the use of CFCs in refrigerators, air-conditioning units, and as propellants in aerosol cans, has led to a growing concern about pollutants. Concern is also reflected in the move to use more lead-free petrol, and in the debate about the wise use of our present electricity generating capacity, and what might be required for the future. Increasing concern over the pollution of the Manukau and other harbours around the country, over the dumping of waste, and the adequate treatment of sewage, are also critical issues in the environmental scene. The 1989 survey indicates that 82% of the population sees the "recovery of environmental protection (as an) urgent problem".[9] It seems clear that we as a nation want to hold to our 'clean green image'. That, for Christians, points to the importance of our having a well thought out doctrine of creation. As evangelists we can note that the words from Genesis, "God saw all that he had made, and it was very good," are relevant words in our context.[10]

The final discovery came in 1990. The nation discovered that the Treaty of Waitangi is not simply an historic document but is a living covenant. How widespread that discovery is for Pakeha people is not clear. It appears to be very clear however for the vast majority of Maori. At the beginning of the 1980s many people were saying, "The Treaty is a fraud". Today we no longer hear that phrase. The emphasis now is on "Honour the Treaty". For the churches in our land this is particularly important. Three of the major churches were present when the Treaty was signed in 1840 and brought pressure to bear on key Maori chiefs to sign the Treaty believing it would protect Maori people from the worst excesses of the European settlers. The Treaty was to ensure that Maori retained their mana, and their treasures of language, forests and fisheries. The fact that their lands were subsequently taken, and that some missionaries betrayed Maori trust, has meant a significant loss of integrity on the part of the churches in the eyes of many Maori. It is a disturbing commentary on our present situation that in the 1989 survey only 16% of the population "favour special land and fishing rights (for) Maori, to make up for past injustice."[11] Does this mean that in the interests of communicating the gospel we should ignore past injustices for fear of losing the ear of the Pakeha majority? Or does this mean that on this issue a prophetic stance is called for? Perhaps the good news both for us who seek to communicate the gospel, and for Maori people, is that only 28% of New Zealanders believe that the "Treaty should be abolished."[12]

Other issues, gathering momentum during the 1980's, were: women's rights, such as equal employment and equal pay, along with questions of sexual harassment in the workforce; the widening gap between the rich and the poor due largely to a massive increase in unemployment, indicating the final demise of the egalitarian society if indeed it ever existed; and increasing interest in changes to the political system. Each of these is worthy of a chapter in its own right. Certainly the Christian communicator who seeks to speak clearly to our society cannot ignore these or other issues.

Trends in The 1990s. The most significant change to take place in the 1990s to date lies in the massive erosion of the welfare state. The safety net, the underlying security experienced by generations of New Zealanders, is now riddled with holes. The social contract which provided free healthcare, free schooling, almost free university education, as well as national superannuation and accident compensation, in some aspects of which we were world leaders, has been virtually rewritten. Of course New Zealanders paid for these things through taxation; they were never really free. They were however seen to be the responsibility of the state, and they did ensure that the elderly, the unemployed, the disabled, and others were given due care. New Zealanders can no longer take these things for granted. In proclaiming the gospel we now need to recognize that people are not just sinners. They are often the sinned against. Certainly that is how many unemployed, many poor people, see themselves. For middle-class Pakeha Christians to blame such people for a situation which is beyond their control can be the ultimate injustice. The gospel calls us to a different stance: to proclaim good news to the poor.

People and The Trends. The 1980s, and particularly the era of the first Labour Government, were something of a roller coaster ride for the country. Some were exhilarated by it, mostly the yuppies and the anti-nuclear lobby. Others found the accelerated pace of change not only confusing but also frightening. Still others were deeply hurt by the changes as factories were closed and businesses, some generations old, went to the wall. For some, Maori in particular, there were mixed messages. On the one hand the Waitangi Tribunal was strengthened and given a much more significant mandate in terms of time scale, while on the other, more and more Maori found themselves unemployed and economically marginalized. Currently we are still in the midst of the most severe recession since the 1930s, and we are in this recession in spite of almost eight years of belt tightening and restructuring which, we were told by successive governments, would bring about new growth, more jobs, and a better life for all. What this breeds for many is an increasing cynicism and sense of powerlessness. This is focused on the politicians and the institutions of the state. It can have negative spin-off for other sectors of society. Cynicism and powerlessness are in turn symptoms of a deeper malaise, in particular a lack of hope. Christians are called to be bearers of hope. Hope both for the present and for the future stands close to the heart of the Christian gospel. Our message, as evangelists, must be a message of hope.

The Churches and the Trends. The vast majority of people in the churches are immune from many of the factors described above because the churches, by and large, are made up of middle-class people. A recent survey in the Methodist Church showed that over 50% saw themselves as professionals while only 2% saw themselves as unskilled labourers,[13] an interesting finding in a Church with strong working-class origins, and an early focus on ministry alongside the poor. However this immunity on the part of most active Christians from the effects of poverty, and hence from the loss of hope and cynicism that goes with it, need not lead to an insensitivity to the issues and attitudes that are reality for an increasing proportion of our population. If it does, then Christians will have lost the ability to communicate with the very section of society which the history of revivals, of growth in the life of the Church, shows is the very area from which such growth often comes. This is what happened during John Wesley's ministry in an England on the verge of the Industrial Revolution. It happened again for William Booth in the late 19th century in the slums of London. It is happening in places in South America today. It is the poor that are often the most receptive to the gospel. Yet the churches put by far the largest part of their energies and their resources into ministering to the middle-class, often a low response area. An ability to break out of the straitjacket of the middle class may well be the key to the evangelization of New Zealand.

Affiliation and Belief Trends

In terms of census figures the three largest mainline churches, the Anglican, Presbyterian and Roman Catholic, account between them for 52% of the population of New Zealand.[14] The Methodists at 4%, and the Baptists at 2%, are the next largest in census terms. Ratana at 1.4% of the population is the largest of the indigenous Maori churches. Mormons account for a similar proportion of the population to Ratana. The only other religious group specified is "other religion" at 10.2%. This is a catch-all grouping which includes the smaller Christian Churches, members of eastern religions like Hinduism and Buddhism, along with Jews, Moslems and others.

These figures do not mean much in terms of Christian faith and commitment. The Methodist census figure of 138,273 for example is almost eight times the Methodist church membership figure which is about 17,500. Other Churches report the census figures to be equally unreliable in terms of their active membership. Where the church census figures seem to carry some weight is in the fact that they are trending downwards in a way that has some parallels to the decline in actual church membership figures. It is clear on both counts that the churches collectively, not just the mainline churches, account for a declining proportion of the New Zealand population as a whole. What needs to be further debated is the question: why?

The reverse side of this is seen in the increase in the percentage of the population who either indicate "no religion", or "object to state", or who are "not specified". The combined figure for these three categories in the 1991 census is 28.6%, up 2.5% from the 1986 census.[15] Males outnumber females in these categories by a significant majority. The reverse is true in terms of those who identify with the churches. The survey of active Methodists mentioned above indicated that females outnumber males in that Church by 2:1.[16] Other churches report similar findings. The "no religion" and related categories have grown to the extent that these now outnumber the combined census figures for the Anglican, Methodist and Baptist Churches. It is another clear indication that New Zealand is a growing mission field.

Over 75% of New Zealanders claim to believe in God, though the content of that belief is not necessarily what active Christians might mean by God.[17] A significant percentage also claim to believe in sin, life after death, the soul, and the devil.[18] For many these beliefs may be residual, owing much to attendance at Sunday School during one's childhood. They may also be distorted, misunderstood, a reason for the rejection of the gospel. On the other hand residual beliefs, coupled with good memories of childhood experiences of the faith, can be a basis on which, in God's good time, faith in Jesus Christ as Lord may be rekindled.

Conclusion

A major challenge now lies before us as Christians, and as evangelists, called to share the good news of the gospel in Aotearoa New Zealand at the end of the 20th century. This challenge calls us to note population trends and to identify areas of growth and potential for mission. It calls us to seek to understand our nation at depth noting the critical issues in its life, and to be prepared to speak for Christ into that context. It calls us to note, to learn, to wrestle with what is happening to the churches until answers emerge that are not facile or trite, but which point forward in hope because they spring from the God to whom the future belongs.

FOOTNOTES
[1] Figures given by the Department of Statistics, Auckland Office.
[2] Chinese and Indian may include those born outside China and India.
[3] Department of Statistics, Auckland Office.
[4] Aerosol pollutants.
[5] eg. *Being Pakeha.*
[6] eg. *The Matriarch.*
[7] H. Gold and A. Webster, *New Zealand Values Today*, 1989, Table 6.1c.
[8] Ibid., Table 3.
[9] Ibid., Table 7.3.
[10] Genesis 1:31.
[11] *New Zealand Values Today*, Table 5.1.
[12] Ibid., Table 5.2.
[13] *Towards a Profile of Methodism in the 1990s*, page 7.
[14] Department of Statistics.
[15] Ibid.
[16] *Towards a Profile of Methodism in the 1990s*, page 3.
[17] Webster and Perry, *The Religious Factor in New Zealand Society*, page 32. Note: this combines the two categories, "There is a personal God" and "There is some sort of spirit or life force".
[18] *New Zealand Values Today*, Table 8.9.

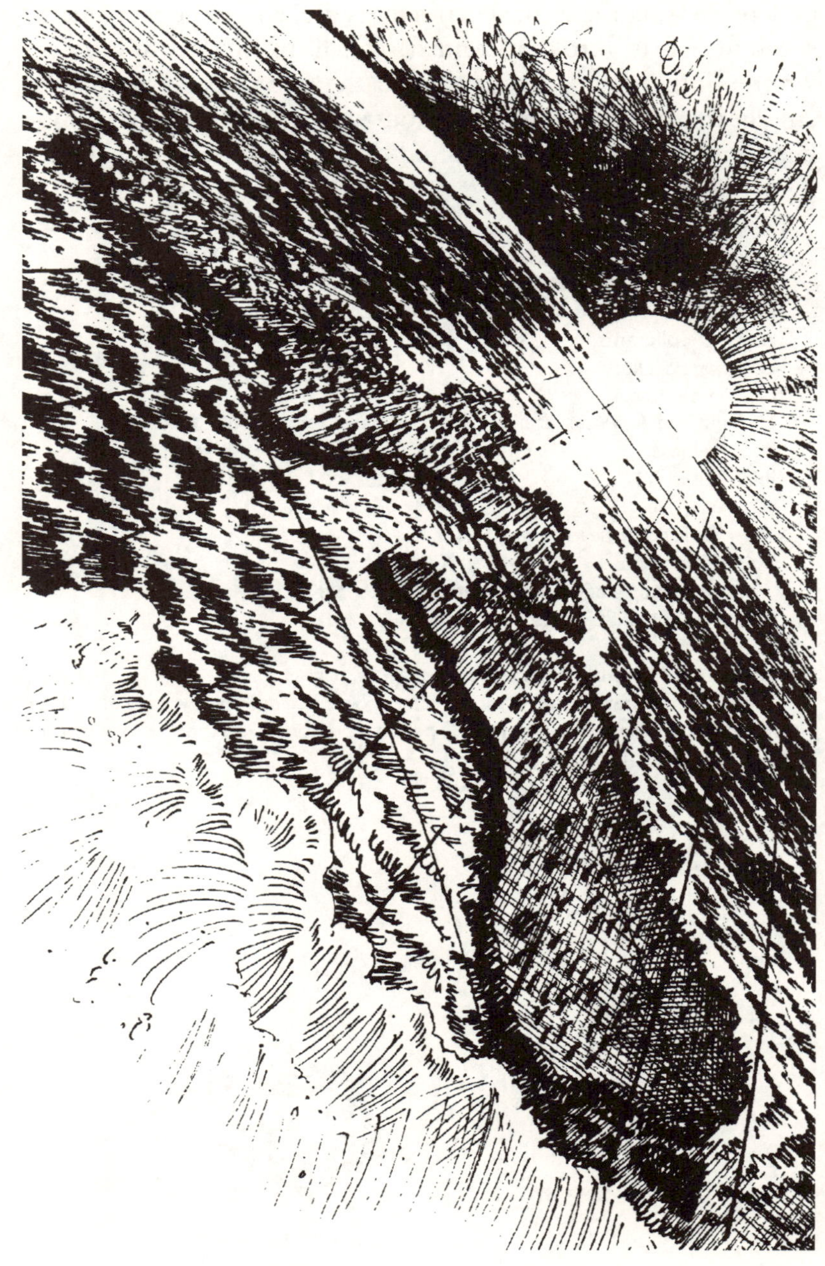

The People of New Zealand

by Bob Hall

Francis Schaeffer once observed that one of the key tasks facing the Church was to communicate unchanging truth into a changing world. Two implications can be drawn from this. First, we need to be convinced about the unchanging nature and universal relevance of the gospel (we require theological certainty). Second, we need to understand the changes that are taking place within society and be sensitive to the challenges and opportunities that these present for evangelism, church planting and church growth (we require a theologically informed social science). Given the degree and extent of change that has taken place within New Zealand society in recent years, Schaeffer's comment and the implications drawn from it are as relevant in 1993 as they were when first made. The purpose of this present chapter is therefore to explore the second of these implications by presenting a brief profile of contemporary New Zealand society.[1]

Population Structure

At the 1991 census New Zealand's total population stood at 3,434,950 (with 972 males for every 1,000 females). 75% of the population were living in the North Island (27% in the Auckland local government region alone) and 85% in urban areas in both the North and South Islands (68% in the 17 main urban areas). 48% of the country's population was located in the northern part of the North Island, Auckland's labour force being larger than the entire labour force of the South Island. Northward drift and increasing urbanization have been features of New Zealand's population growth for the last 100 years.

TABLE 1:   **NEW ZEALAND TOTAL POPULATION (1936-1991)**

Census	North Island	Propn	South Island	Propn	NZ Total	Maori	Propn
1936	1,018,038	64.7%	555,774	35.3%	1,573,812	82,326	5.2%
1945	1,146,292	6.7%	556,006	3.3%	17,023,298	98,744	5.8%
1951	1,313,869	67.7%	625,603	32.3%	1,939,472	115,676	6.0%
1956	1,497,366	8.9%	676,698	31.1%	2,174,062	137,151	6.3%
1961	1,684,785	69.8%	730,199	30.2%	2,414,984	167,086	6.9%
1966	1,893,326	70.7%	783,593	29.3%	2,676,919	201,159	7.5%
1971	2,051,363	71.7%	811,268	28.3%	2,862,631	227,414	7.9%
1976	2,268,393	72.5%	860,990	27.5%	3,129,383	270,035	8.6%
1981	2,322,989	73.1%	852,748	26.9%	3,175,737	279,252	8.8%
1986	2,441,615	73.8%	865,469	26.2%	3,307,084	295,659	8.9%
1991	2,553,413	74.3%	881,537	25.7%	3,434,950	321,396	9.4%

Source: Census 1991 Final Population and Dwellings

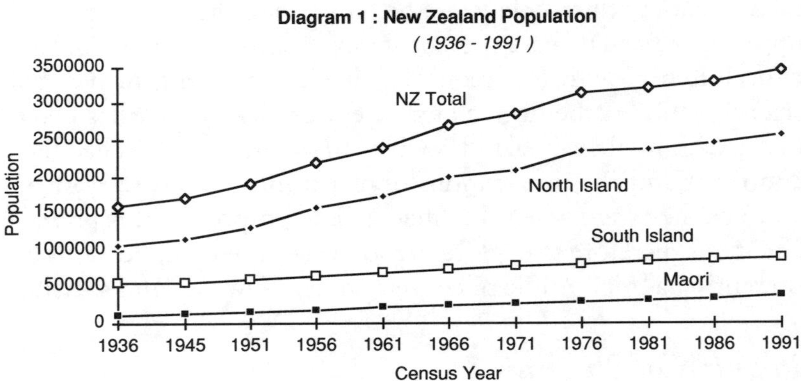

The New Zealand population is still predominantly European (74%) and Maori (13%) but ethnic diversity is growing with the incorporation of Polynesians (3.6%) and Asians (2%) into the society. Although the Maori population is growing at a slower rate than in the past its proportion of the overall population is still expected to reach 30% by AD 2020.

TABLE 2: **POPULATION OF REGIONAL COUNCILS (1981-1991)**

Regional Areas	1981 Census	1986 Census	1991 Census	1991 Propn	Increase Percent 1981-86	1986-91
Northland	114,409	127,656	131,620	3.8%	11.6%	3.0%
Auckland	821,816	881,011	953,980	27.8%	7.2%	8.2%
Waikato	313,515	325,220	338,959	9.9%	3.8%	4.1%
Bay of Plenty	178,495	194,622	208,163	6.1%	9.0%	6.9%
Gisborne	46,115	45,953	44,387	1.3%	-0.4%	-3.6%
Hawke's Bay	138,037	140,844	139,479	4.1%	2.1%	-1.2%
Taranaki	103,740	107,499	107,222	3.1%	3.6%	-0.4%
Manawatu-Wanganui	219,172	223,021	226,616	6.6%	1.7%	1.5%
Wellington	387,454	395,610	402,892	11.7%	2.1%	1.6%
North Island	2,322,989	2,441,615	2,550,370	74.2%	5.1%	4.5%
Nelson-Marlborough	102,466	106,775	113,487	3.3%	4.2%	5.9%
West Coast	35,553	36,375	35,380	1.0%	2.3%	-2.2%
Canterbury	424,742	433,017	442,392	12.9%	1.4%	1.9%
Otago	180,520	183,005	186,067	5.4%	-2.9%	1.2%
Southland	108,706	105,512	103,442	3.0%	4.1%	-2.1%
South Island	852,748	865,469	878,994	25.6%	1.5%	1.6%
Total	3,175,737	3,307,084	3,434,950	100.0%	4.1%	3.7%

Source:Census 1991 - Final Population and Dwellings

During the decade from 1981 to 1991 New Zealand's population grew by 8.2% or approximately 26,000 people a year. This was the smallest percentage increase recorded for any ten year period since the first national census in 1858. The population is expected to reach 4.4 million by AD 2031 but during that time it is expected there will be a marked slowdown in the rate of population growth (0.6% compared with a rate of 1% over the last two decades). Among the developed western countries only Australia (1.4%), Canada (1.1%) and the United States (1%) had population growth rates higher than New Zealand (0.8%) during 1981 - 1991. The low growth in the New Zealand population has been the product of a number of factors, principally low fertility rates, population ageing and net migration losses.

Fertility Rates

Two main characteristics of the New Zealand fertility rate can be identified: smaller families, and later motherhood. The New Zealand birth rate has fallen since last century when, for a whole

TABLE 3:   **TOTAL POPULATION OF URBAN AND RURAL AREAS (1981-1991)**

Main Urban Areas	1981 Census	1986 Census	1991 Census	1991 Percent	Increase 1981-86	Percent 1986-91
Whangarei	40,511	44,318	44,183	1.3%	9.4%	-0.3%
Auckland	770,331	821,647	885,571	25.8%	6.7%	7.8%
North Auckland Zone	*149,320*	*162,612*	*175,945*	*5.1%*	*8.9%*	*8.2%*
Western Auckland Zone	*116,979*	*125,899*	*140,251*	*4.1%*	*7.6%*	*11.4%*
Central Auckland Zone	*285,448*	*295,431*	*308,486*	*9.0%*	*3.5%*	*4.4%*
Southern Auckland Zone	*218,584*	*237,705*	*260,889*	*7.6%*	*8.7%*	*9.8%*
Hamilton	133,566	140,106	148,625	4.3%	4.9%	6.1%
Hamilton Zone	*111,189*	*115,741*	*123,295*	*3.6%*	*4.1%*	*6.5%*
Cambridge Zone	*10,194*	*11,873*	*12,454*	*0.4%*	*16.5%*	*4.9%*
Te Awamutu Zone	*12,183*	*12,492*	*12,876*	*0.4%*	*2.5%*	*3.1%*
Tauranga	55,983	63,254	70,803	2.1%	13.0%	11.9%
Rotorua	48,350	51,991	53,702	1.6%	7.5%	3.3%
Gisborne	32,062	32,238	31,484	0.9%	0.5%	-2.3%
Napier-Hastings	107,482	110,785	110,216	3.2%	3.1%	-0.5%
Napier Zone	*52,285*	*53,276*	*52,468*	*1.5%*	*1.9%*	*-1.5%*
Hastings Zone	*55,197*	*57,509*	*57,748*	*1.7%*	*4.2%*	*0.4%*
New Plymouth	44,065	47,384	48,519	1.4%	7.5%	2.4%
Wanganui	39,595	40,758	41,213	1.2%	2.9%	1.1%
Palmerston North	66,691	67,405	70,951	2.1%	1.1%	5.3%
Wellington	320,968	325,711	325,682	9.5%	1.5%	0.0%
Upper Hutt Zone	*36,525*	*36,046*	*35,565*	*1.0%*	*-1.3%*	*-1.3%*
Lower Hutt Zone	*94,701*	*94,837*	*93,974*	*2.7%*	*0.1%*	*-0.9%*
Porirua Zone	*42,363*	*45,567*	*46,493*	*1.4%*	*7.6%*	*2.0%*
Wellington Zone	*147,379*	*149,261*	*149,650*	*4.4%*	*1.3%*	*-0.3%*
Nelson	43,121	44,593	47,391	1.4%	3.4%	6.3%
Christchurch	290,680	300,052	307,179	8.9%	3.2%	2.4%
Dunedin	108,029	107,639	109,503	3.2%	-0.4%	1.7%
Invercargill	53,640	52,558	51,984	1.5%	-2.0%	-1.1%
Total Main Urban	2,155,074	2,250,439	2,347,006	68.3%	4.4%	4.3%
Secondary Urban Areas						
Pukekohe	13,343	13,931	15,009	0.4%	4.4%	7.7%
Tokoroa	19,342	18,193	16,636	0.5%	-5.9%	-8.6%
Taupo	15,388	17,602	18,369	0.5%	14.4%	4.4%
Whakatane	15,159	15,959	16,805	0.5%	5.3%	5.3%
Hawera	11,344	11,375	11,152	0.3%	0.3%	-2.0%
Feilding	12,203	12,802	13,370	0.4%	4.9%	4.4%
Levin	18,070	18,962	18,963	0.6%	4.9%	0.0%
Kapiti	20,083	23,203	27,380	0.8%	15.5%	18.0%
Masterton	20,193	19,930	20,007	0.6%	-1.3%	0.4%
Blenheim	22,104	22,681	23,637	0.7%	2.6%	4.2%
Greymouth	11,611	11,261	10,604	0.3%	-3.0%	-5.8%
Ashburton	15,328	15,229	15,172	0.4%	-0.6%	-0.4%
Timaru	29,285	28,676	27,637	0.8%	-2.1%	-3.6%
Oamaru	14,664	14,247	13,821	0.4%	-2.8%	-3.0%
Gore	12,065	11,249	10,998	0.3%	-6.8%	-2.2%
Total Secondary Urban	250,182	255,300	2,593,560	75.5%	2.0%	1.7%
Total M & S Urban	2,405,256	2,505,739	2,606,566	75.9%	4.2%	4.0%
Minor Urban Areas	287,986	301,021	309,816	9.0%	4.5%	2.9%
Rural Areas	479,023	497,730	515,227	15.0%	3.9%	3.5%
TOTAL	3,175,737	3,307,084	3,434,950	100.0%	4.1%	3.9%

Source:Census 1991 - Final Population and Dwellings

variety of reasons, women began having fewer babies. During the Depression of the 1930s the fertility rate was as low as 2.3 children per woman. The trend towards smaller families was temporarily interrupted by the baby-boom years of 1946 - 1975 (when the figure rose to a peak of 4.3 children in 1961) but since then the decline has continued. Like many other developed countries, New Zealand's fertility rate in recent years has been either below replacement level (2.1) or just on it. In 1983 the fertility rate was 1.9; now it is 2.2. Pakeha women average 2.1 children and Maori 2.3. The fall in Maori fertility has been even more spectacular than Pakeha fertility. In 1962 Maori women were averaging 6 babies each. The impact of the availability of legal abortions on the birth rate must not be ignored. In 1990 there were 11,173 legal abortions performed, as compared with 10,200 in 1989.

The other trend affecting the birth rate is the decision made by many women, especially Pakeha, to delay motherhood until their late 20s and 30s. For some women this has been a decision born of economic necessity. For others it has represented a new awareness of and willingness to take up career opportunities. Both factors have resulted from the impact of the feminist movement. These and other factors have served to reshape the New Zealand family.

Family Size and Structure

Surprising as it may seem, the stereotypical nuclear family of mum, dad and the children is no longer the predominant type of household in New Zealand. Just over one half of all families (54%) and one third of all households (34%) currently look like the stereotype, and the number is diminishing. Households with a breadwinner father and housewife mother are even more rare. Currently only one in eight households conform to this pattern. In contemporary New Zealand the most rapidly growing type of household is one person living alone. In 1971 this accounted for one in eight households (13%). Now the ratio is nearly one in five

(22%). Half of all households now consist of only one or two people.

TABLE 4:	HOUSEHOLD COMPOSITION (1971-1991)			
	1971	1981	1986	1991
One Person	13.2%	17.3%	18.6%	22.2%
Couple Only	20.0%	21.1%	23.2%	23.0%
Couple plus children	45.4%	39.2%	37.6%	28.8%
One Parent plus children	4.7%	6.5%	7.9%	9.3%
One family plus others	9.6%	8.0%	5.3%	7.7%
Two or more families	1.5%	1.7%	1.5%	0.6%
Non-family	5.5%	6.3%	6.0%	7.2%

Source: New Zealand Census 1971, 1981, 1986 and 1991

For cultural reasons extended family households will continue to be more common amongst Maori and Pacific Islanders. But increasingly many others will live in larger households through economic necessity. Separate homes for the elderly and independent flatting for young adults are becoming less of a possibility for many.

The proportion of one parent families in New Zealand doubled between 1971 (4.7%) and 1991 (9.3%). It is estimated that more than a third of New Zealand children will spend some of their childhood with a solo parent. Few however will pass their whole childhood this way since solo parenthood is often a temporary phase. Of concern however is the fact that the one parent family, usually headed by a woman, often lives on a low income (receiving only 41% of the income of two-parent families), with the disadvantages in housing and living standards that go with this.

Marriage is still popular although the never marrieds rose by 11% between the 1986 and 1991 census. Nevertheless, nearly everyone 35 or older in New Zealand has been married. The proportion of separated or divorced adults has increased from 2 in 100 in 1956, to 5 in 100, 35 years later. It seems to be a fact of modern life in New Zealand therefore that more marriages, both legal and de facto, are becoming unstable. Recent trends however, such as smaller families, later childbearing, and divorces occurring earlier in marriage have meant that marriage dissolutions are less likely to involve children than those granted a decade ago (66% in 1980 compared with 53% in 1990).

What of the family's future? In the years ahead we shall probably see an even smaller proportion of nuclear family households. The proportion of one parent families is likely to increase. There is also likely to be an increase in the number of reconstituted families as people remarry. Depending on economic circumstances, one-person households comprising mainly older women should also become even more common. The latter reflects changes in the age structure of the population.

Age Structure

New Zealand's age profile is characteristic of a mature population. The average age was 31.3 in 1991 and is expected to rise to 39.7 by AD 2031. Compared with most developed Western countries, New Zealand has always had a young population. Two factors have largely accounted for this: the large-scale immigration of mainly young adults, and a high birth rate for most of this century. This pattern is changing. By AD 2031 half the population is expected to be older than 40 years of age. This ageing of the population is a result of low birth rates, increasing life expectancy, and movement of the baby-boom generation up the age scale.

At the 1991 census the population aged 60 years and over comprised 15.4% of the total population compared with 14.8% in 1981. One in six New Zealanders are now 60 or older, and the proportion of older people will increase in the years ahead. The Nelson/Marlborough region has the highest ratio of elderly to total population. The number of 60-pluses increased by 8.1% between 1986 and 1991, while the total population grew by only 3.5%. In 30 years' time the baby-boomers born in the 1950s and 1960s will reach this age and, depending on what happens to the birth rate, will comprise about a quarter of the population.

According to the New Zealand Planning Council, the baby-boom generation is moving through New Zealand society like the bulge of a boa constrictor. Preceding it was a small Depression-age generation, now in their 50s. After it comes the 1970s age group, the generation that was too small to fill the primary schools opened for a swelling population in the 1950s and the 1960s. The baby-boom generation will not begin celebrating its 60th birthday until about AD 2010. This is when the 'greying' of New Zealand will begin for real. It is inevitable that the baby-boom elderly will dramatically change our ideas of what it means to be old. As generations age they carry with them values and preferences formed through differing historical events and social eras. In the next few decades we will therefore be seeing grandmothers who once wore hippie beads and flowers and grandfathers who once were yuppies.

Occupational Structure

Of the total 1991 population of 3.4 million, 2.6 million were of working age (ie. aged 15 and over) and 1.4 million were in paid employment (78% of them full-time). The labour force participation rate for men (73%) was higher than that for women (54%). The majority of full-time workers were men (64%), while part-time workers were mainly women (74%). Females made up 43% of the workforce and an increasing proportion of these were married. In 1976 one fifth of mothers with pre-schoolers were in full or part-time paid work. Now it is estimated that more than half of mothers with dependent children have some paid work. More than half the employed women are still concentrated in traditional female occupations (clerks, service, sales workers, nurses and teachers) while men are not as concentrated in any particular occupational group. Allowing for difficulties of definition, some 10% of the labour force would be classified as currently unemployed

(59% of these are men). This presents a problem of major magnitude.

Migration

In 1991 New Zealand had a net gain of 11,616 people as a result of migration. Over the last two decades however, net migration contributed only 2% to New Zealand's total population growth, as compared with Australia where net migration contributed 36% to total growth. Nevertheless the last two decades have witnessed major and unprecedented changes in New Zealand's external migration levels and patterns. The preponderance of immigrants coming from the British Isles has decreased and migration to and from Australia has become the largest in terms of volume. In the 1990-91 June year 287,500 New Zealanders were living in Australia, 1,400 fewer than a year earlier. Significantly, immigration from the South Pacific countries, although small in size, is continuing.

Immigrants are also now coming from Asian countries. For example in the year to 30 June 1991, 5,322 Hong Kong citizens were granted permanent resident status in New Zealand. This was twice the previous year's figure and was the first time Hong Kong had topped the list of the number of immigrants from one particular country. Since 1975 about 7,000 Indo-Chinese refugees have been resettled in New Zealand, accounting for over 90% of the total refugee intake during this period. Small numbers of Chilean, Russian Jew, East European and Assyrian refugees have also arrived at various times. Migrants from all sources are adding to ethnic diversity within New Zealand society.

Implications for the Church

Change has been a definite and pervasive feature of life in New Zealand society over the past decade. Economically, politically, socially and ideologically the secular context within which the Church is called to function has changed dramatically. A brief overview of some of these changes has been provided. Hopefully enough has been covered to give an indication of the changes that have been occurring in the areas of regional growth, family formation, age structure, labour force participation and cultural diversity. Further aspects of change have been covered in other chapters. How do we respond to all of this?

To ignore the realities of differential regional growth would be absurd. The northward drift and increasing urbanization need responses in the allocation of resources, development of strategic plans, and the setting of ministry priorities. But in the process we must not lose sight of provincial New Zealand where the impact of change may have been felt more severely. Cosmopolitan urbanites may be better equipped to take change in their stride, but for the rest, stress, disorientation, and at times despair have become all too common.

For increasing numbers of people however, it is not only the wider world that is changing. So too are their personal circumstances, and often as a direct result of those external changes. Redundancy and unemployment, ill health and a drop in living standards, separation and divorce, all of these and more are touching the lives of people. We need to address issues of unfulfilled economic expectations, broken family relationships, and personal stress, but we need to do so with understanding and compassion rather than with ignorance and condemnation. We must be informed enough to view social problems in structural rather than purely personal terms. We must be cosmopolitan enough not to be threatened by emerging post-modern forms of family relationship. We must be sensitive enough to identify with people at their point of need. Above all we must be honest enough to admit that we do not have simple solutions to life's problems, and bold enough to join the search. All of this will go some way towards improving our levels of compassion, our insightfulness into the contemporary human condition, and our standing in the eyes of a world that has become increasingly sceptical of our abilities and relevance in all of these areas.

Differential regional growth, increased urbanization, the drift north, changing family structures, an ageing population, the multi-faceted impact of economic and political change, unemployment, increased labour force participation of women, increased ethnic and cultural diversity, changing values: this is the changing world within which Francis Schaeffer would have us proclaim the unchanging truth of the Gospel. The challenge lies before us.

FOOTNOTES

[1] In preparing this chapter I have drawn heavily on a number of technical sources. These include publications of the Department of Statistics as well as of the New Zealand Planning Council. Those who want a concise but informative overview of these issues are advised to refer to two publications: Judith Davey and Jane Westaway, *Where to Now? New Zealand in the 1990s*, (New Zealand Planning Council, 1990); and *Facts New Zealand* (Department of Statistics, 1992). Reading these two documents in conjunction with the *1992 New Zealand Yearbook* and summary volumes from the 1991 census will provide information enough to satisfy most people.

The Condition of The Church

by Peter Lineham

Many New Zealand churches are in a positive mood. New Zealand has one of the strongest charismatic movements in the Western world, and numerous active movements and organizations. Many feel themselves to be growing: they claim a high level of interest in mission, they are contemporary in music and worship, they are lively, they are concerned and very involved in the community. This is a glowing picture but only a partial representation of the situation. If Christians are to take up the challenge of the evangelization of New Zealand there must be a more sober assessment of the Christian scene. In fact the churches face certain deep-set problems which will not be simply solved. If the churches embark upon a campaign to spread the gospel in this society but fail to address these factors, they could find their efforts less fruitful than in the past.

It is not the intention of this chapter to suggest that the mood should change to one of gloom. The Church has the deposit of an eternal gospel, the powers of the world and of the evil one cannot overthrow it, and God will ensure a witness to the truth until Jesus Christ returns. Our purpose is rather to lay groundwork for issues that other contributors to this book will address.

What are the trends? Adherence to Christianity in New Zealand has declined significantly in the past few years. In this chapter the 1991 census results for religious adherence (or affiliation) have been compared with a set of parallel statistics constructed from the 1971 figures. A range of other statistics are used to interpret these figures. The statistics for 1991 used extensively in this chapter have not yet been fully published, in particular for the smaller denominations. The comparison of 1991 with 1971 will help us understand the balance of problems and encouragements, challenges, threats and advances.

Patterns of Religious Change

Religious affiliation has changed very significantly. These changes show up in Chart 1 (gross statistics, not reflecting change in the New Zealand population) and Chart 2. Looking at these and the

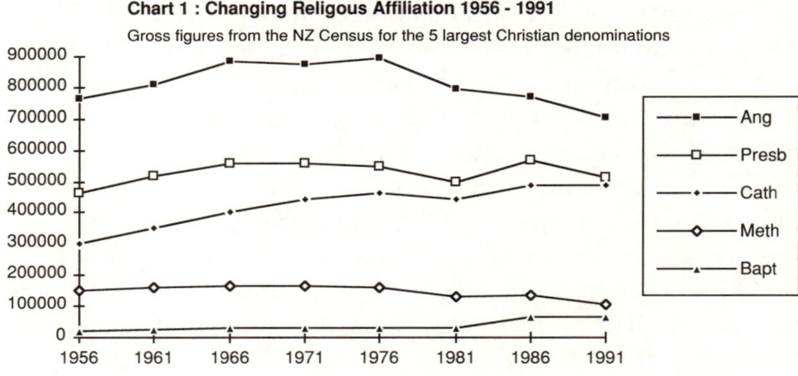

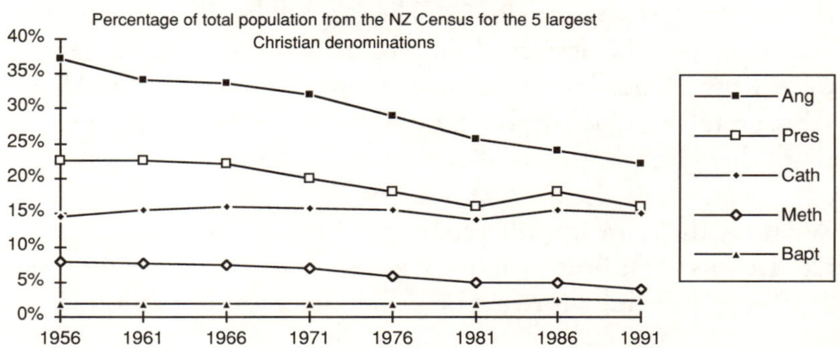

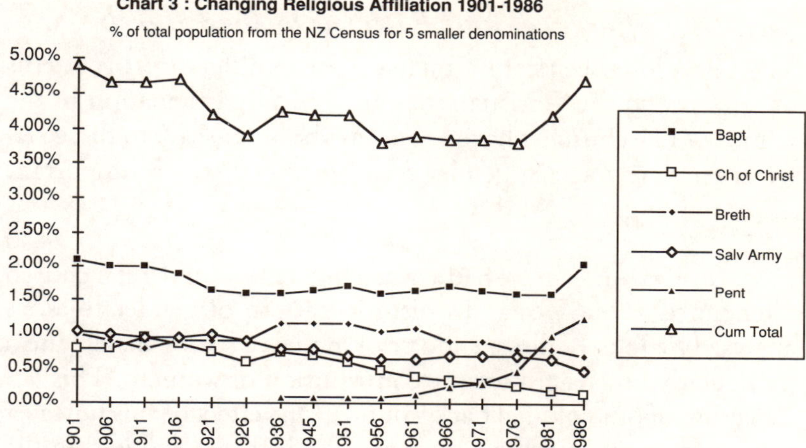

figures for the smaller groups up to 1986 (Chart 3) we may detect significant trends. Some denominations are in decline, while Catholic, Baptist, and particularly the pentecostal denominations, seem to be stable or rising.

The most striking growth is undoubtedly in the "religious nons",[1] various categories who make no claim to a religious persuasion, or in fact go further and describe their religion as none. Notice the growth in these figures since 1956, in Chart 4.

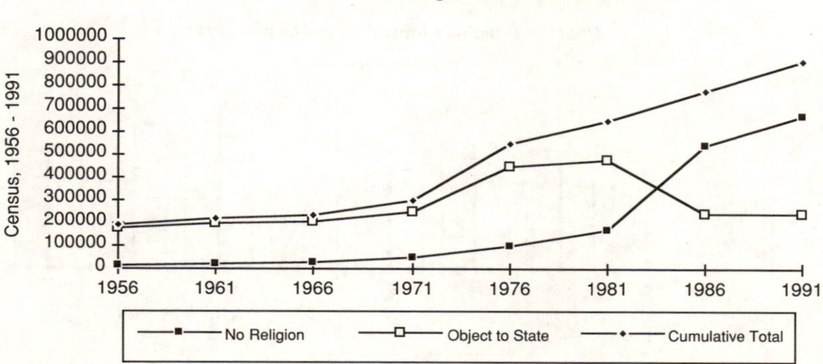

Gender Differences and Patterns of the Church

There have long been significant male/female differences in patterns of response to the Christian message and of participation in the Church. The churches have not always been sensitive to these. As we enter a new age in gender relationships there are important issues to ponder.

Historically women have had a much higher level of regular church attendance. New Zealand's historic pattern of gender roles, as analysed by Jock Phillips, endorses a model of strong males, and a particularly low regard for the contribution of women. This is a reflection of our colonial background. One effect of this however was a very active women's movement, which worked within the concept of 'a woman's role within the family' to influence many aspects of life. On this basis women received the vote in 1893. New Zealand was one of the first states to take this step, although historians have argued that the domestic pattern strengthened in the early years of the 20th century.

Patterns of nominal church adherence may be traced through the statistics of the five-yearly census. While these do not indicate actual church involvement, they have significance. The 1971 religious affiliation and gender graph (Chart 5) shows that particularly in smaller churches where the census reflects

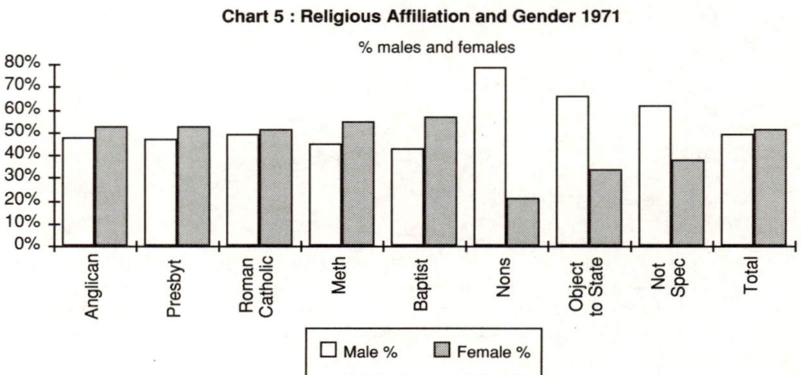

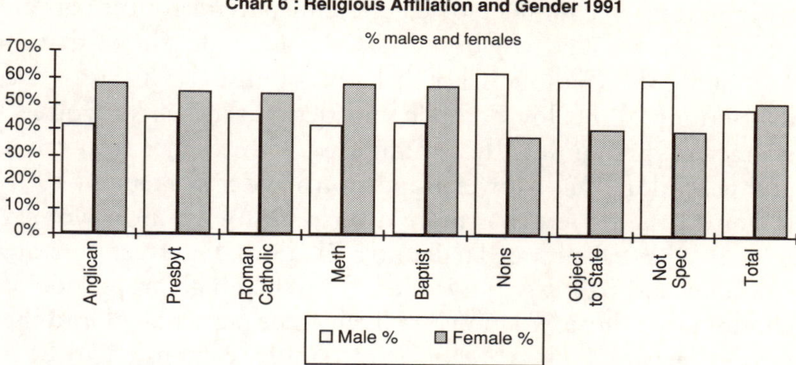

involvement more adequately, (eg. Baptist) there were lower ratios of men to women than one might expect. In contrast the ratio of those with no religion is strikingly over-balanced towards males.

The 1991 census provisional returns (graph 6) show striking evidence of further change: there are many more males in the religious nons categories. Overall 533,133 males (32% of the male population) are in these categories, compared with 433,182 women (25% of the female population). So levels of nominal unbelief or non-declaration of religion are nearly 20% higher among men than among women.

There are significant differences in gender ratios of adherence to different religious persuasions. Most successful at holding men adherents are the Catholic Church (45 : 55 ratio of men to women) and Other Religious Groups, which includes many evangelicals and charismatics (46 : 54). Presbyterians achieve 45 : 55, Baptists 43 : 57, Anglicans and Methodists 42 : 58. It is not easy to explain these ratios, but they deserve careful consideration. (Note however that there are 3% less men than women in our society, an imbalance largely produced by the longevity of women compared to men. This affects, for example, the gender ratios of the Anglican Church, whose supporters tend to be an aging group). The role of women in society has changed dramatically in the last 20 years. As women's opportunities and responsibilities have increased, have their patterns of church involvement tended to mirror the pattern of men? Chart 7 of religious affiliation of females shows that in 1971 only the Catholic Church had an unusual pattern of age distribution. Probably Catholic statistics reflect their supporters' character as predominantly working class, with a higher proportion of small children and a lower proportion of older women. By 1991 (Chart 8) the pattern was more diverse. More younger women tended to have abandoned religious affiliation. The exceptions are Catholics and Baptists. It is evident from their high proportion of children that those variations are likely to be perpetuated into the next generation. The percentage of Baptist women (Chart 8) is very stable through the age range, ie. it follows the proportion in the general population.

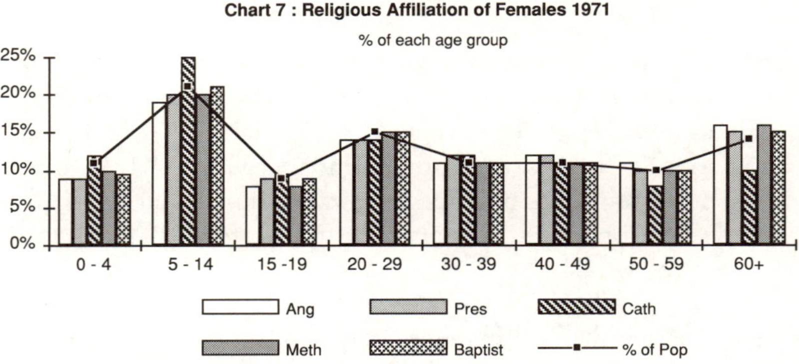

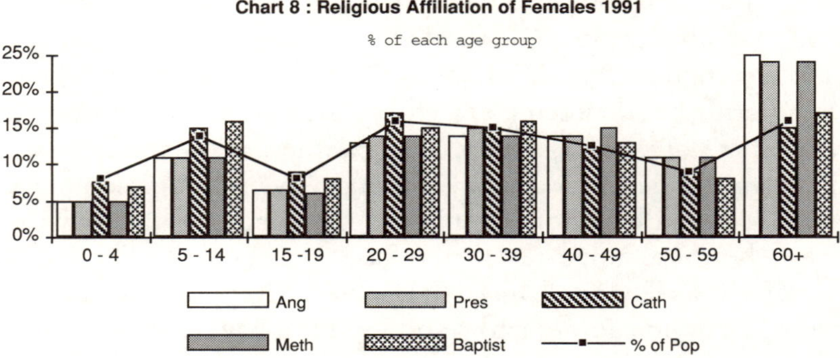

Chart 9 : Religious Affiliation of Males 1971

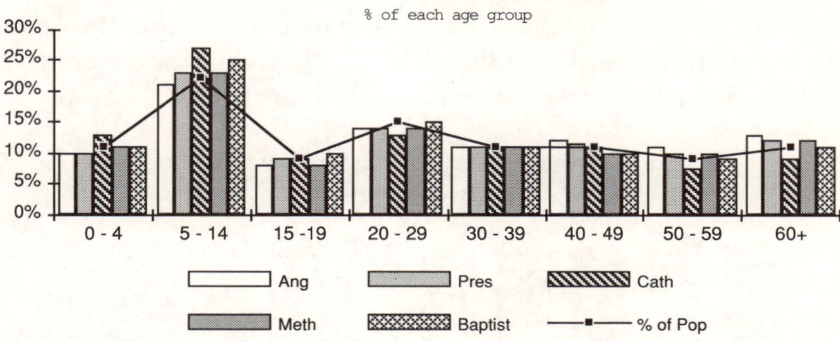

Chart 10 : Religious Affiliation of Males 1991

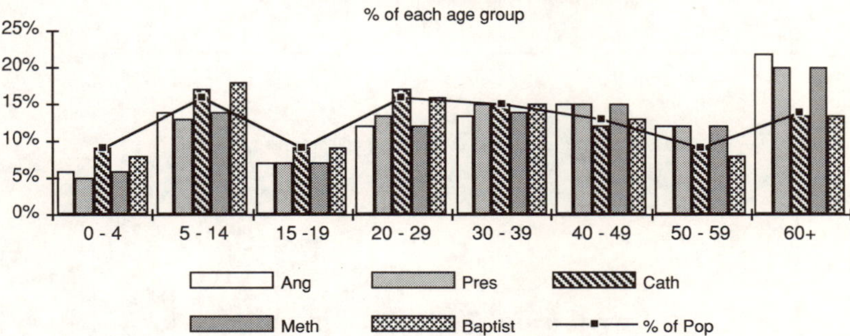

Age Patterns and the Church

There are significant variations in the patterns of affiliation and participation in different age groups. These important factors must be examined carefully by churches seeking to advance. (See Charts 7 and 8 on religious affiliation of females, and Charts 9 and 10, of males.)

Examining the proportions at different ages it is clear that more older males than younger males are affiliated to the larger and older declining traditional denominations. This higher proportion reflects denominational strengths a few years back.

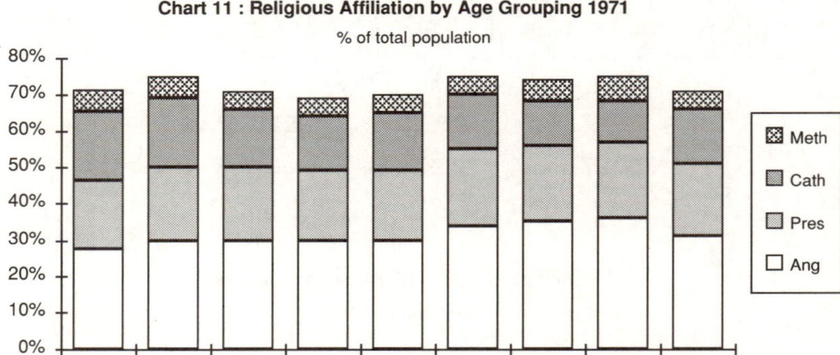

Chart 11 : Religious Affiliation by Age Grouping 1971

% of total population

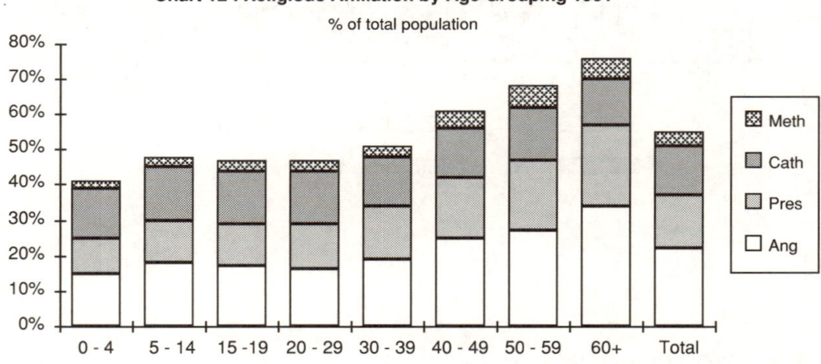

Chart 12 : Religious Affiliation by Age Grouping 1991

% of total population

A comparison of Charts 11 and 12 shows dramatically the aging of the traditional mainline denominations. In the 1970s there was some evidence of decline, but note the high level in the 1971 statistics of adherents aged 5-19. If these people had all retained their church links, there would be a high level of support in the 20-30 age group in the 1991 figures. This is not the case: the churches clearly did not hold their teenagers. There is decline in most age groups. The exception is those who were in their 40s in 1971. In their 60s today, they have maintained similar levels of religious affiliation since then. Overall the chart for 1991 suggests that in 20 years time the nominal adherence of the churches will be significantly lower than today, as those in their 50s and 60s die. Nor is there anything in the figures to make us think that those who are today's teenagers will be retained at their present level.

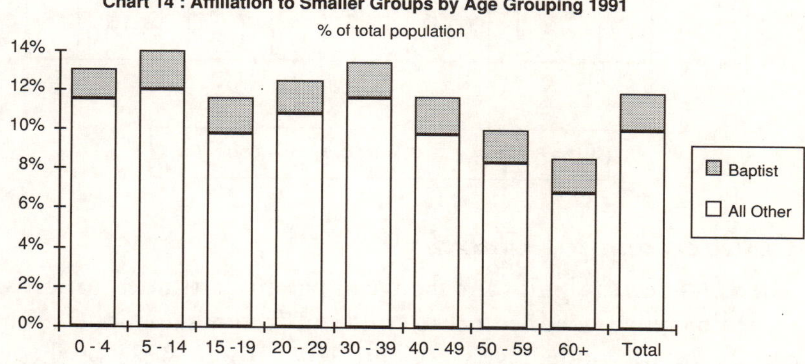

There are some significant age patterns evident in Charts 13 and 14 in regard to affiliation to smaller groups (generally evangelical). The major impact of these groups is with school-aged children (5-14). Older teenagers have either high levels of rejection of religion, or an inability to state their affiliation. Curiously the Baptist impact is most marked among the young, and among the 40s age range of males.

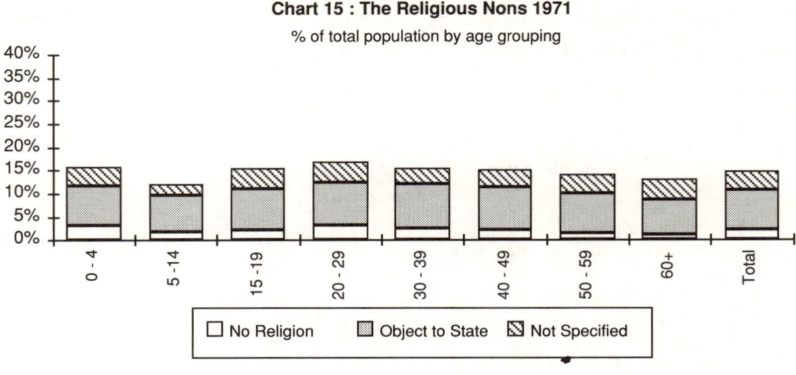

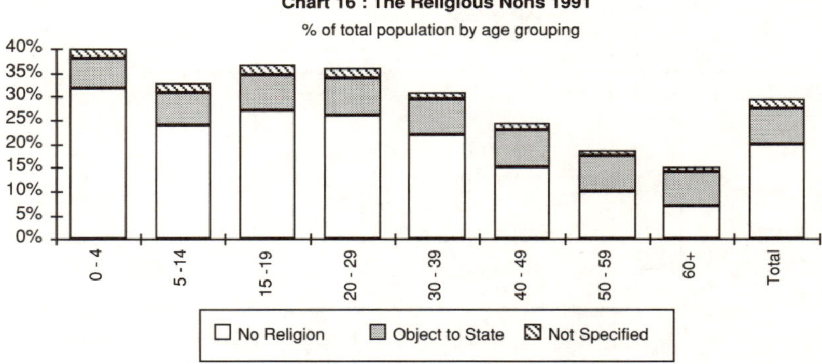

Children and the Church

There has been a significant change of parents' attitudes, towards recording religious adherence of children. It shows up in the 1991 census for the under 5s (see Chart 16). About 32% of these children (40% if the other 'non' categories are included) are described by their parents as having no religion. This is markedly higher than for any other age group. Moreover this level has increased over 20 years, though even in 1971 (see Chart 15) the level of no religion was high (nearly 16% compared with the average of 14% for all age groups). In one sense children are far more open to the gospel now than they ever were before. "My child can make up her/his own mind," is a comment one sometimes hears. On the other hand a person raised with no religion may never find one. Churches need to adopt strategies in response to this change.

Not all groups are failing to reach children. Baptist results deserve special attention. In the age range 5-14 they do remarkably well, particularly among males, considering that their proportion of the under 5s is not remarkable. The combined figures of all other religious groups are also significant. One may hypothesize that churchgoing people with young children often transfer to churches which will provide peers for their children. Another factor may be the increasing freedom of children to make their own choice of church.

If churches are concerned for children, and if children can be attracted to church, then the results of Hugh Dickey's research into children must be of particular concern.[2] Dickey shows that 12.7% of the nation's children are on Sunday school and children's church rolls, although on average, only 73% of this number attend. Of the children in Sunday schools, 19% have parents from outside the church. This compares with figures from a survey in 1978 which indicated that the proportion of children from non-church homes in Sunday church activities at that time was 36%. Other church activities for children probably attract many more children, and according to the Churches Education Commission 50% of all children are participants in Religious Education at school. Dickey suggests that Sunday schools in 1960 attracted 169,000 students in the primary age band; by 1970 this had fallen to 137,000, and by 1992 to 19,600. This sharp drop is evident in the three largest Protestant denominations. The weakness of the churches' adherence in the 20s to 40s suggest that there are fewer potential church parents and potential Christian education teachers.

Young People

The figures for youth deserve careful consideration. Most of the active outreach over the past 30 years has focused on youth. In the 70s the churches benefitted from such ministries. Today the evidence suggests that the churches fail to retain the late teens, while the religious nons do better in this age range than among children (see Charts 15 and 16). This suggests some significant issues which current strategies fail to solve. The churches must consider why so many young people choose not to identify with them.[3]

Church Attendance and Involvement

Several significant surveys help us understand and identify the scale of the believing and involved Christian community. Webster and Perry[4] examined the evidence from a survey of religious attitudes. They showed an average overall attendance of about 29% attending "frequently" which they defined as attending at least once a month, a fairly generous definition. (They also noted a weekly attendance rate of 17%.) In the Gold and Webster 1990 survey[5] a different definition of frequent attendance was used, indicating 16% of the population were weekly attenders, while 49% attended at least once a year. These figures may be compared to the Heylen Poll of 1985. A census of the churches of Palmerson North which I conducted in 1982, weighted against national patterns of weekly attendance, suggested a national attendance pattern of about 14%. Unfortunately we cannot tell just how much gross church attendance has changed in recent years. There has probably been a decline in Catholic attendance, but growth in some other groups. Levels of regular attendance of different denominations are suggested both by my poll of Palmerston North churches, and Webster and Perry's research: 5% of all census Anglicans attend on any Sunday, 11% of Presbyterians and Methodists, and up to 75% of the Baptist and Brethren denominations. Today, although the census adherence of Baptist churches is about half that of the Methodist Church, Baptists have a higher total attendance. If attendance and membership figures are a clearer indication of strength than census figures, it may be time to review notions of which are the mainline churches.

Religious Values

Attendance is not in itself a sufficient measure of faith. The figures for church attendance need to be weighed against measures of values and behaviour such as patterns of regular prayer, and view of the importance of God. Webster and Perry note the levels of those who often pray at 27%, those who pray most days at 17%, and those who regard God as very important at 34%. They also seek to estimate awareness of the spiritual dimension or religious experience, and find that 15.1% of the population has a sense of the presence of God.[6] Webster and Perry estimate that 24% of those who think God is very important in their lives do not attend a church, 24% of those who attend regularly think of God only as a life force, and 12% of regular church attenders do not believe in God.[7] By comparing these factors they argue that the 'religious' in the community are around 12% of the population.[8] The proportion of Christians in our society is presumably something short of this level.

Mainline Protestants

Anglicans, Presbyterians and Methodists are usually identified as mainline Protestants. Over the past century these denominations have declined in census affiliation from more than 80% of the population to their present level of 40%. Their present rate of decline is so great that in this decade they may drop to about 30%. Attendance and involvement rates have also changed. These denominations do reasonably well among the 5-14 year olds. However statistics on the impact of religion on age groups show that these denominations suffer the loss of many people in their late teenage years.

The values of many nominal Protestants are seemingly uninfluenced by their religious adherence. This was shown strikingly by Gold and Webster's survey. Significantly less than half of the nominal adherents in these denominations believed that God was personal.[9]

There is an important new factor among mainline Protestants: the growing numbers of Pacific Islanders in New Zealand, many of whom are affiliated to either the Methodist Church in New Zealand, or to the Congregational churches planted by the London Missionary Society and now incorporated in the Presbyterian Church of New Zealand. The Reformed Church however grew at the expense of Presbyterian churches among those Dutch from more conservative backgrounds in the Reformed Churches of Holland. The emergence of the Cook Islands Congregational churches, Samoan Methodist churches, and Samoan Assembly of God churches indicates the strain such cultural groups face accommodating themselves within large liberal denominations, but when they remain they enrich and enhance those denominations. Cultural issues thus are matters of critical importance for the future of these denominations and for their evangelistic strategy.

The Evangelical Community

It is useful to determine the size of the evangelical community. It can be measured in various ways. The International Social Survey Programme (ISSP) found that 17% of those surveyed said they had had a "born again experience", and 9% said "the Bible is the actual word of God, and is to be taken literally, word for word."[10] Webster and Perry estimate the evangelical community at about 5% of the total population.[11] The census authorities' preliminary results grouped some 10% of the population into a category of "other religious groups." We have had to use this for some calculations, but it is not a unified group even though evangelicals predominate within it. The total number in evangelical and pentecostal denominations according to the census in recent years is shown in Chart 3. It has in this period ranged between 4-5% of the population. It gradually declined until 1976. Since the 1970s growth of the separate evangelical churches has simply balanced decline in the older evangelical churches.

In the evangelical community we need to distinguish several groups. There are traditional evangelical denominations (notably the Baptist, Brethren and Salvation Army), and there are evangelicals and charismatics in most if not all other denominations. Murray Darroch's work, *Everything You Ever Wanted To Know About Protestants ... But Never Knew Who To Ask*, usefully details many of the groups.[12]

The traditional evangelical denominations (see Chart 3 which covers only the figures to 1986) may be divided into Baptists and others. The census estimate of Baptist adherents in 1986 and 1991 indicates there has been no growth relative to the population. Among the others, Brethren, the Churches of Christ and the Salvation Army have been in decline since the 1950s. The 1991 census shows some change. The Brethren have remained stable at 0.6% of the population, the Salvation Army have risen nearly 20% to 0.6%, and the Churches of Christ have declined sharply to about 0.1%. Within these denominations there are charismatic elements, but the majority have been unsympathetic to the charismatic movement. In contrast a high proportion of Baptist churches are at least sympathetic to the charismatic movement. Other factors should be noted. Denominations, like congregations, need a certain size to be able to act effectively in a period of religious decline. The Baptist denomination has been able to put resources into church planting and to establish purposeful directions.

The Pentecostal and Charismatic Communities

Among these we number traditional pentecostal denominations (the Assemblies of God, Apostolic Church and Elim Church) which originated in the 1930s, the newer pentecostal congregations, (New Life Centres, Christian Fellowships), and a range of new churches in the 1980s. Beyond this it may be harder to identify or quantify the charismatic stream. Charismatic congregations or groups within congregations can be found in most denominations, as can evangelicals. Songs, styles of worship, and beliefs all illustrate this. Among the pentecostal denominations there are clear differences. Gains by some groups, notably the Apostolic Church and some of the newer groups, have been balanced by some decline in the New Life movement. In 1991 a "Declaration of Unity in the Harvest" was affirmed by the Associated Pentecostals, a widely inclusive grouping of over 600 churches that is growing through church planting year by year. The Declaration is focusing commitment on the evangelization of New Zealand.

The Catholic Community

Webster and Perry indicate that the active and believing Catholic community is about 5% of the total community.[13] Nominal Catholicism continues to increase, although not relative to the population. There are significantly higher numbers of Catholics in the 0-29 age range than in other age ranges. Probably the key factor is the larger size of Catholic families. The strength of Catholicism among some of the new immigrants is also important. This is perhaps the denomination whose age spread most satisfactorily reflects the general population. In 1971 however Catholics had a strong concentration among under 5s, and while this has declined today, it is still higher than for other churches. This may be a reflection of different values on birth control. In Charts 7 to 10 Catholic adherents for the over 60s age group are relatively less than in the general population. Questions about Catholic membership are difficult to answer. Many retain Catholic identity and census affiliation while their levels of practice seem to have declined sharply in the last few years.

Dropping Out and Dying Out

The two major factors involved in these changing patterns are first, the overall aging of the religious community, and second, declining levels of religious practice by the more nominal. Various patterns may be identified which are likely to result in declining involvement in the church. It is evident that people in transition, particularly those changing their location, do not always re-integrate into the religious community. One significant reason may be the domination of congregations' leaders, and exclusive relational networks, making them slow to assimilate new people. Aspects of lifestyle and culture may also be significant. Evidence from culturally specific churches shows that they are most effective where a minority culture feels under threat.

Decline may be balanced by patterns of growth. We need to trace those age groups and social groups most responsive to the gospel and those who find it hard to maintain their commitment. It is interesting to note in the ISSP that 27% of the population had gone through a turning point in their lives where they made a new personal religious commitment.[14]

Understanding Unbelievers

Webster and Perry provided an interesting study of the values of those who declared they have no religion. Rejectors of belief in God (undefined) number only 7% of the population according to Gold and Webster,[15] a percentage confirmed by the ISSP's figure of 8%. Those who reject belief in God are predominantly male,[16] although one of the signs of the growing respectability of unbelief is that today the gender balance of the "none" category has swung, like "object to state", from eight as it used to be, to six males for every five females (see Charts 5 and 6). However the age distribution of the religious nons deserves consideration (see Charts 15 and 16). In 1971 patterns of unbelief were consistently distributed except for the 5-14s where unbelief was at a lower level, and the 20s where unbelief was at its highest level (more than 16% of the population). By 1991, while the low level of unbelief for 5-14 remained, unbelief was generally concentrated among the young.

General Religious Values in the Community

It should not be assumed that the rejection of religion is inevitable. There is widespread general interest in religion in our society, but it is modifed by the characteristics of Western society: individualism, and a desire for personal satisfaction. Webster and Perry noted that 36% of the community preferred to describe God as "some sort of spirit or life-force." In 1989, refining the question, they found that 52% believed in "some sort of spirit or life-force, not a person," whereas 41% believed in a personal God.[17] The ISSP suggests that 29% have no doubts about their belief in God; another 34% believe with some level of doubt; 17% preferred to believe in a life-force; and 12% were agnostic.[18] This survey asked a number of interesting questions about attitudes to religious influence. The New Age movement, often talked about but little defined, accommodates views that are highly consistent with the above values.

General Attitudes to the Church

The Church is not fading out of view, in society's thinking. According to the ISSP most people think the church has about the right amount of influence. It is curious that 56-70% do not want church influence on voting or politicians, and only 11-16% want more Christian influence on those in office. In the past few years the character of the Church and its development have been a regular focus of media attention and of community interest. Isolated events, while easily forgotten, have a cumulative effect upon people's attitudes.

Perhaps most prominent has been the contribution of the churches to debates on moral issues. During the 1986 debate over the de-criminalization of homosexual acts, the churches were identified with a huge petition against de-criminalization. However, at that time the Methodist Church and the Presbyterian Church favoured the reform. Though it became evident the following year that a few evangelical churches had sympathies in this direction, the debate was portrayed by the media as liberalism versus fundamentalism dividing the churches. In 1991 first the Methodist and then the Presbyterian Church faced, but could not resolve, the issue of the ordination of openly homosexual clergy. Visits by controversial liberal clergy like Bishop John Spong and Don Cupitt of Cambridge were presented enthusiastically by the media. Different attitudes to such issues within the Church complicate attempts to convey a strong image of the Church. The churches have come across as having no clear moral stance on issues on which the community has a sharp conservative-liberal split.[19]

There is a common impression that moral standards within the church have been sullied by a number of cases of the fall of clergy over sexual ethics. Some of these have been in America, but the New Zealand media has focused on the fall of evangelical leaders, clergy and lay. It would be hard to establish that there were any more or less than at any other time, but a bad impression is conveyed. Despite this the image of the clergy remains fairly high.

The media gives plenty of attention to the more evangelical wing of the church, but evangelicals have few voices in the media. Curiously, the media sometimes feature notable evangelical Christians in the public eye, and try to find evidence of lowering levels of personal commitment. "He is still involved in his church," comments the journalist with faint scandal. We are subjected to a fascinating range of images of the cruder forms of pentecostal faith-healing in all its drama, with critical commentary. Most of the community is vaguely aware that there is a charismatic movement, that it is labelled fundamentalist along with other groups of believers, and thereby that it is somehow a bad thing.[20] If there is any media coverage of large public evangelistic events such as the Luis Palau Mission to Auckland and the Leighton Ford Mission to Wellington (both in 1987), it is cool. One senses journalists' suspicion of evangelists.

Ethical and religious debate are in many ways more important than ever, but the Church must learn to contribute in a more creative and less authoritarian way than in the past. Massey University's student newspaper *Chaff* is not the only paper carrying raging debates in its correspondence columns between Christians and 'Anti-Christs'. There are some new elements. Debates now abound in crudity of language and expression. Traditional public moral constraints have been replaced by competition for explicitness in sexuality and violence.[21] These factors colour society; indeed they also colour the Christian community.

A further crucial factor in the public tone of society has been the abandonment by the state of some aspects of its traditional patronage of the church. This has made the position of Bible-In-Schools far more precarious, a hot topic of debate in decisions which have been thrown even more directly back into the local community. The ISSP, asking rather American questions, found that 43% wanted prayer in schools and 47% did not.

The Secular and the Religious

New Zealand has never had a state church. Although in the 19th century the Anglican Church occupied a place of social prominence, no church received much government aid. Denominational suspicions inhibited general assistance. Secularization of education by the 1877 Act was an inevitable and early consequence of this. In the 1940s denominational tensions eased, making possible state aid to church schools, church social work and church youth work. The current decline in state participation in community care gives opportunities for explicitly church social work, where the churches can afford it.

Secularization means the separation of Church and state. This is a marked feature of the New Zealand experience. The Protestant tradition in New Zealand has reflected and assisted individualism within society at large. Religious toleration, combined with the evangelical emphasis on the need for conversion, helped to create the secular society.

We need a theoretical model to understand such factors in times of religious change. This is generally provided by the notion of secularization. This concept is explained in very different ways by different sociologists, but common features seem to be an increased separation between Church and state, an increasing differentiation between religious and secular functions, and declining levels of participation. Attempts to explain why this has happened, and how far it will go, provoke controversy. However, the churches must address these deeper issues lest much effort be relatively fruitless. A stimulating model of a way forward is a form of evangelism which challenges the worldview of the person being reached. A person with a secular framework will require a new framework of thinking to understand the full dimensions of the gospel. This approach offers important insights for our current situation. It is essential that we know the inherent assumptions and religious values through which people filter religious options. These are the issues which churches must themselves resolve and to which they must respond in appropriate ways. We may not see dramatic changes in our generation, but we must work for long-term change. It may be that a new generation will make sense of our views. We do not start from a position of defeat. If the Christian gospel is true then the people of our generation are suffering from deep spiritual hunger. Our cleverness and our strategies alone are not sufficient. God is anxious that they should find the bread of life.

BIBLIOGRAPHY

Murray Darroch, *Everything You Ever Wanted To Know About Protestants ... But Never Knew Who To Ask*, (Wellington: Catholic Supplies, 1984).

Hugh Dickey, *What's Happening With The Children? A Nationwide Stocktake of the Church's Ministry in 1991,* (Auckland: Congress on Children and Families, 1992).

Hyam Gold and Alan Webster, *New Zealand Values Today: The Popular Report of the November 1989 New Zealand Study of Values*, (Palmerston North: Alpha Publications, 1990).

Peter Kaldor, *Who Goes Where? Who Doesn't Care?*, (Homebush West: Lancer Press, 1987).

P.J. Lineham, *Church Attendance in Palmerston North: Report of a Survey*, (Palmerston North Inter-Church Council, 1992).

P.J. Lineham, *New Zealanders and the Methodist Evangel: An Interpretation of the Policies and Performance of the Methodist Church of New Zealand*, (Wesley Historical Society (New Zealand), Proceedings, no. 42).

Arnell Motz (ed.), *Reclaiming A Nation: The Challenge of Re-evangelizing Canada by the Year 2000*, (Richmond, BC: Church Leadership Library, 1990).

Nationwide Initiative in Evangelism, *Prospects For The Eighties: From a Census of the Churches in 1979*, (London: Bible Society, 1980).

Ralph Neighbour et al., *A City that Rejects its Religious Institutions... Auckland ... Resistant and Neglected,* (Auckland and Houston: Touch Ministries, 1988).

New Zealand Government Department of Statistics, *New Zealand Census of Population and Dwellings 1971* (vol 3) *Religious Professions*, (Wellington: Department of Statistics, 1974).

New Zealand Government Department of Statistics, *New Zealand Census of Population and Dwellings 1991: Provisional Report*, (Wellington: Department of Statistics, 1992).

Alan C. Webster and Paul E. Perry, *The Religious Factor in New Zealand Society: A Report of the New Zealand Study of Values*, (Palmerston North: Alpha Publications, 1989).

FOOTNOTES

[1]For simplicity the term "religious nons" will be used for those who identify in the census with the three categories: No Religion, Object to State, and Not Specified.

[2]Hugh Dickey, *What's Happening with the Children: A Nationwide Stocktake of the Church's Ministry to Children in 1991*, (Auckland, 1992), pages 7-8, 18-19. This report is highly recommended.

[3]Compare this paragraph with the information in Chapter 12, "Who Responds to the Gospel?" that people in their late teens and early 20s are the most responsive group in New Zealand society.

[4]Alan C.Webster and Paul E. Perry, *The Religious Factor in New Zealand Society: A Report of the New Zealand Study of Values*, (Palmerston North, NZ: Alpha Publications, 1989), page 38.

[5]Hyam Gold and Alan Webster, *New Zealand Values Today: The Popular Report of the November 1989 New Zealand Study of Values,* (Palmerston North, NZ: Alpha Publications, 1990), page 64.

[6]Webster and Perry, ibid. These percentages are found respectively on pages 45, 74, 124, and 46.

[7]Ibid., pages 57 - 59.

[8]Ibid., page 22.

[9]Gold and Webster, ibid., page 67.

[10]*The International Social Survey Programme*, Massey University Department of Marketing, pages 2 - 3.

[11]Webster and Perry, ibid., page 47.

[12]Wellington, 1984.

[13]Ibid., page 47.

[14]Ibid., page 3.

[15]Ibid., page 66.

[16]Gold and Webster, ibid., page 68.

[17]Ibid., pages 66-68.

[18]Ibid., page 1.

[19]Gold and Webster, ibid., pages 25-27.

[20]"Fundamentalist" is an epithet commonly attached to committed Christians by media people and politicians which conveys an impression that all such believers are unreasonable religious fanatics whose zeal is in inverse proportion to their Intelligence Quotient. Most Christians reject such a caricature (editor).

[21]It is noted that the government is initiating steps to limit the range and possession of pornography.

[22]Ibid., page 2.

Who's Growing, Who's Not

by Alan Withy

*"To understand God's thoughts, we must study statistics,
for these are a measure of his purpose."
(Florence Nightingale)*

Florence Nightingale reminds us with these words that though some are suspicious of numbers, we must identify, analyse and ponder them if we are to know God's will for our time. Many pastors and ministers suffer from survey fatigue. Their responses to approaches from VISION New Zealand researchers have been predictably mixed. The establishment of a national research agency could streamline the collection and maintenance of statistics and reduce the flow of questionnaires and other requests for information which frustrate many church leaders.

A well-established business practice is to do a SWOT analysis[1] as a basis for planning and managing effective use of resources. It identifies strengths and weaknesses of an organization, and the opportunities and threats in its market. The All Churches Survey conducted through 1992 has identified many strengths and weaknesses in the Church in this country. It has revealed opportunities to establish new cells, congregations or churches for identifiable ethnic or cultural groups or for given geographical areas. Some of the threats have become apparent in the form of aggressive cults and insidious secularism.

A Season for Evangelism

Parts of the body of Christ have identified the 1990s as a decade of focused evangelism.[2] Many of these have set goals for attendance growth, development of new leaders, and planting new churches. It is hoped VISION New Zealand research data will be used by leaders to background their decisions as to how and where those leaders will be deployed and churches will be planted. The overall picture painted by the data should also lead to sensible coordination and cooperation in church planting.

Who Goes Where

The primary purpose of this chapter is to highlight which sections of the Church are growing and to seek to understand how and why. One group need not emulate any other group, but it would be foolish to ignore lessons that may be learnt. How may churches evangelize more effectively, and better fulfill their Great Commission responsibilities?

Four categories of church have been identified for the purposes of this analysis. They are mainline, baptistic, pentecostal and catholic.[3] Though not all may agree with the divisions used, it has been necessary and helpful to categorize and group denominations. Table1 gives a summary and analysis of the results for these four main categories. A fifth group has been added to indicate the relative sizes of Ratana and Ringatu, the burgeoning independent house group movement, other non-aligned Christians, other religions, and those who indicate no religion or object to state (as recorded in the 1991 census). Information has come from two sources: religious affiliation from the census, and attendance figures from denominational head offices.

Table 1 : Who Goes Where

	1991 Census	1991\2 attendance	Attend/ Census	Attend/ NZ popl'n
GROUP A: mainline				
Anglican	732,000	44,500	6%	1.4%
Methodist	138,700	16,000	12%	0.5%
Presbyterian	540,700	54,300	10%	1.7%
Other	19,800	6,000	30%	0.2%
Sub-totals	1,431,200	120,800	8%	4%
GROUP B: baptistic				
Baptist Union	70,200	31,000	44%	0.9%
Churches of Christ	4,900	2,800	57%	0.1%
Seventh Day Adventist	13,000	7,000	54%	0.2%
Salvation Army	16,800	7,500	45%	0.2%
Brethren	20,000	15,000	75%	0.5%
Other	400	3,200	800%	0.1%
Sub-totals	125,300	66,500	53%	2%
GROUP C: pentecostal				
Assemblies of God	17,200	22,000	128%	0.7%
Apostolic	6,800	9,700	143%	0.3%
Elim	2,400	5,800	242%	0.2%
Other	21,500	20,800	97%	0.6%
Sub-total	47,900	58,300	122%	2%
Group D : catholic				
Roman Catholic	497,700	124,500	25%	4%
Other	4,300			
Sub-total	502,000			
Totals A - D	2,106,400	371,600	18%	11%
Group E: other				
Ratana and Ringatu	56,000			
Other "christian"	105,200			
Other religion	122,400			
No religion or object	979,900			

Subtotal 1,267,500 plus A - D above = 3,373,900

Group A (mainline) includes Anglican, Presbyterian and Methodist, and under Other, the various Congregational, Lutheran and Reformed Churches.

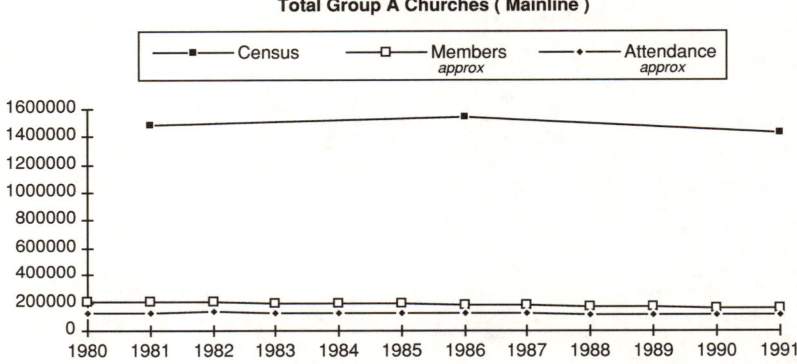

Group B (baptistic) includes Baptist Churches (formerly Baptist Union), Churches of Christ, Brethren and Salvation Army, and under Other the various independent and reformed Baptist churches and the Christian and Missionary Alliance. The Churches of Christ category includes the Associated, Life and Advent and independent churches.

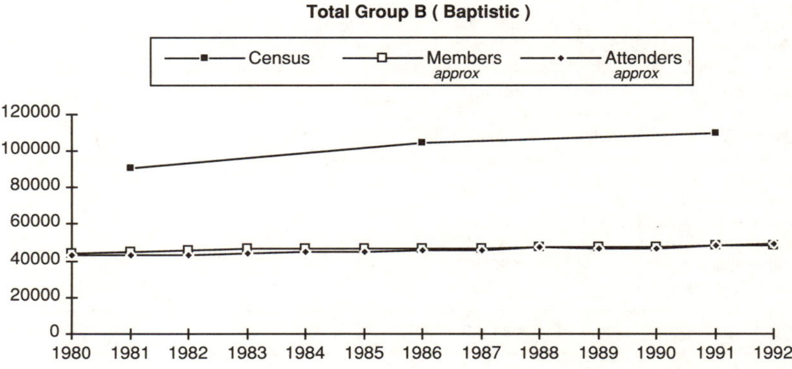

Group C (pentecostal) includes Assemblies of God, Apostolic, Elim, and under Other the Christian City Churches, Christian Revival Crusade, New Life, Nazarene, Indigenous Pentecostal, United Pentecostal and South Pacific Fellowship Churches. The census figure includes pentecostal nod. (not otherwise designated) and indigenous pentecostal.

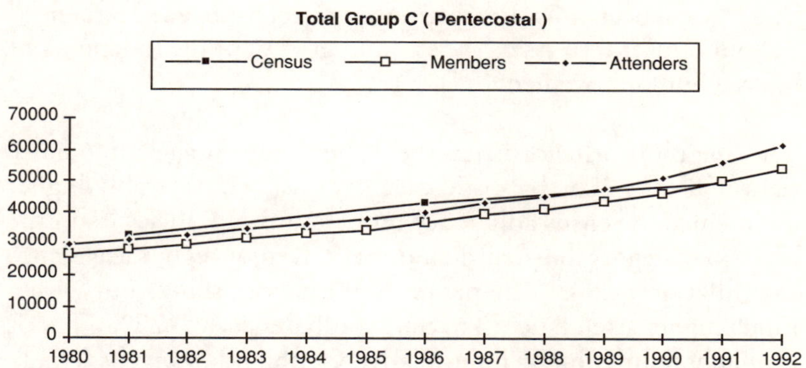

Group D (catholic) includes Roman Catholic and the various other Catholic and Orthodox Churches under Other. Roman Catholics comprise 99%.

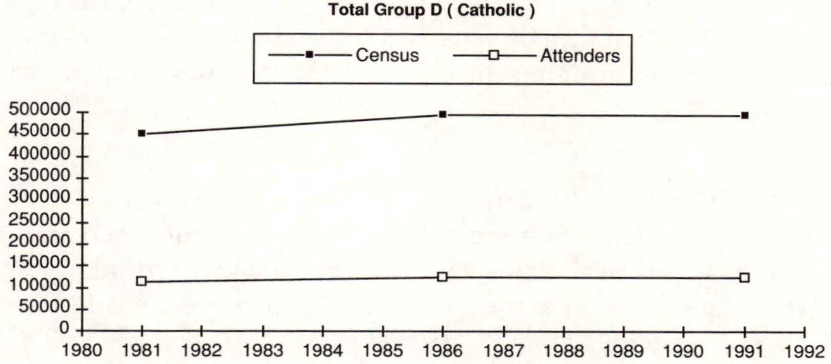

Group E (other) includes under other Christian the several categories in the census such as Christian no denomination, and born again Christian. It also includes various small groups such as the Exclusive Brethren, Christian Scientist and Commonwealth Covenant Churches. The other religion category includes Judaism, Buddhism, Taoism etc. No religion includes agnostic, atheist, uncertain, freethinker, and object to state. None of this fifth category has been fully surveyed but a project has been commenced by John Fulford, to assess the size and growth of the independent house church movement.

The mainline category has the lowest percentage attendance figures at 8%. The baptistic category has a considerably higher attendance to census adherence ratio, at around 50%. As in the mainline category the small denominations enjoy higher attendance to affiliation ratios. The pentecostal category stands out with a much higher attendance than census adherence, ie. 122%. This is probably a function of their relative youth and evangelistic zeal, and applies particularly to their three largest denominations. It is highly influenced by their phenomenal recent growth rates, not yet reflected in census figures. The catholic category, which is mostly the Roman Catholic Church, has a 25% attendance ratio to census adherence. Each of the sub-groups under Group E are less than 1% of the population, except no religion and object to state, which is a massive 29% of the population. Of even more note is the rapid increase in this group, from 15% in 1971 to almost double that figure today.

The Anglican Church

The Anglican Church attracts the greatest number of adherents in the census. When measured by Pakeha attendance it is third largest (after Roman Catholic and Presbyterian).[4] The post World War II decline in popular church attendance has had great effect. The charismatic movement has been of recent stimulus within the Anglican Church, bringing some tensions but also new diversity.

The bishops have confronted the government about its social and economic policies in recent times, protesting over the plight of unemployed and the poor. The Church has not published specific targets or plans for evangelism, but in the context of the Decade of Evangelism some dioceses are actively encouraging evangelism. One way in which this is being done is through contemporary expressions of church planting relevant and appropriate to the needs of local communities.

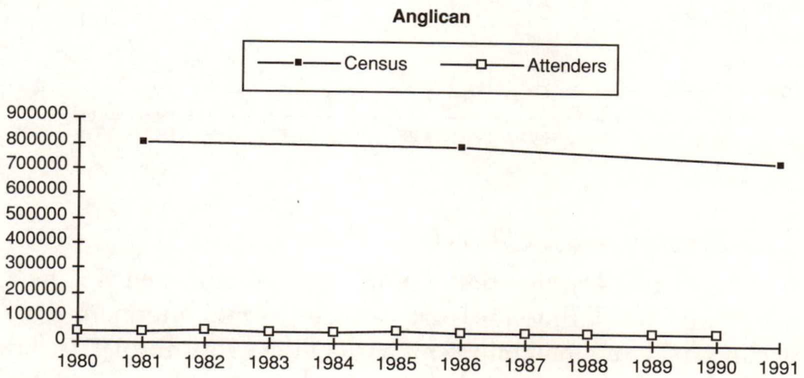

The Methodist Church

The Methodist Church began with great evangelistic zeal in 18th century England. It grew especially among the poor and powerless. Methodism came to New Zealand early last century and grew until the 1950s, when along with other mainline denominations, it began to decline in membership and attendance. It gave vigorous support to the church union movement of the 1960s and 1970s and is committed to close cooperation with other mainline churches. Methodists stress social care and involvement in many areas of society, from political participation and minority rights issues etc. to support for the casualties of redundancies and marital breakdown. A sizeable group of Methodist Pacific Islanders is having an increasing effect on the Church. Samoans, Tongans, Fijians and others originally evangelized in their homelands by Methodist missionaries, have established congregations here numbering over 6,000 people.

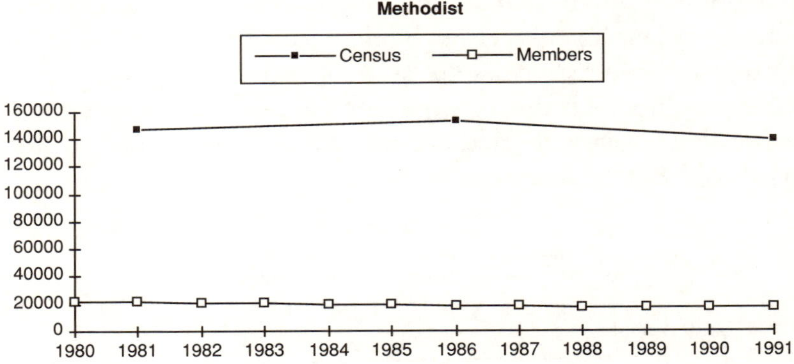

The Presbyterian Church

Although the Presbyterian Church has established 29 new congregations during the past decade, overall numbers have declined. The church union emphasis of the 1960s and 1970s has resulted in over one third of all Presbyterians now being in cooperating ventures with Anglicans and/or Methodists. The Presbyterian Church chooses to define its mission more in terms of people served in the community than membership numbers.

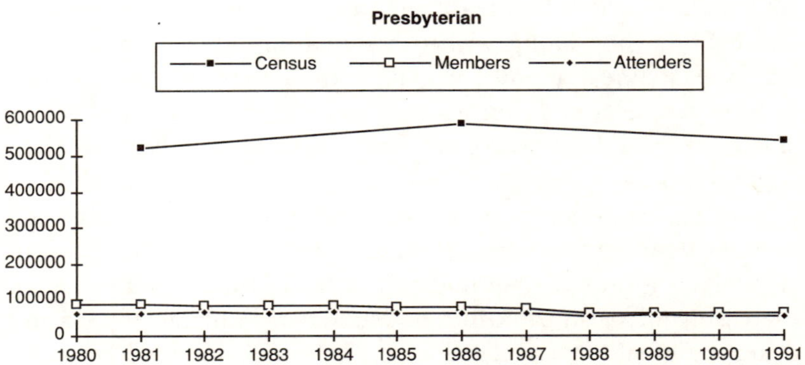

The national office of the Church identifies four main aims: proclamation of the kingdom of God, nurture of and teaching followers of Jesus, loving service to people in need, and working towards a just and peaceful society.

The church also emphasizes concern for the Treaty of Waitangi, vigorous participation in the Decade of Evangelism, and belief in corporate responsibility for the body of Christ.

Cooperating Ventures[5]

Membership and attendance figures for Anglicans, Methodists, Presbyterians and Associated Churches of Christ (but not Congregational) all include their own participants in Cooperating Ventures. These include Union Churches and all types of cooperating parishes. Across quite large areas of New Zealand, some of the participating Churches in the union movement of the 1960s and 1970s have been completely absorbed within cooperating ventures. These had a total of 16,000 members and about 11,000 attenders in 1991-92.

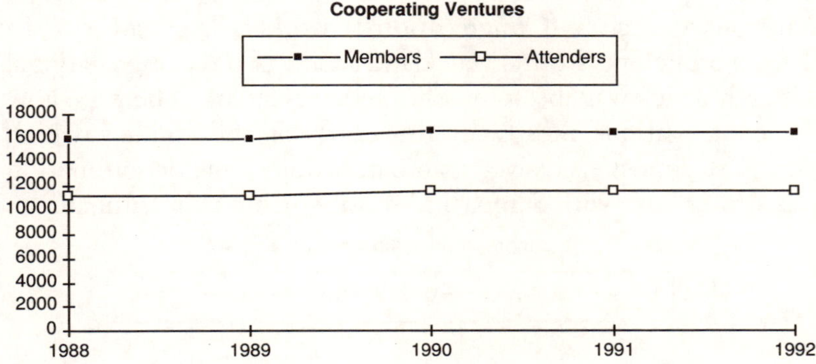

The Congregational Union

The first Congregational Church began in New Zealand in the 1840s. In 1969 over 90% of their members joined the Presbyterian Church. A strong missionary work last century by the London Missionary Society has resulted in a large following amongst

Pacific Islanders. Only eight congregations remain, most of which are multicultural. These have struggled through the 1970s and 1980s. However the Union has seen some growth in the last few years particularly amongst Pacific Islanders in Auckland. Five new churches are under consideration and courageous goals for 20 churches and 2,000 members have been set for the year 2000.

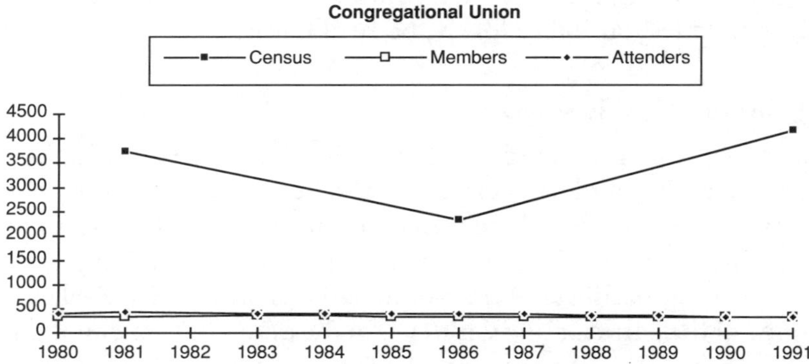

The Congregational Christian Church of Samoa

This is a part of the Church in Samoa established by London Missionary Society (Congregational) workers last century. In 1964 it broke away from an Auckland Pacific Island Congregational Church which was about to become Presbyterian. There are now 55 congregations mostly in the north of the country which comprise almost exclusively Samoan people. The denomination has strong links with Samoa and most worship is in Samoan.

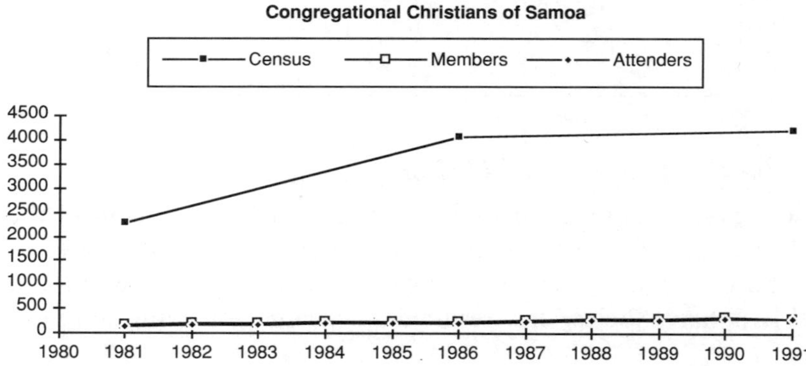

The Lutheran Church

The Lutheran Church ministers primarily to people of Germanic ancestry through 33 congregations, particularly in the lower North Island. In 1992 goals of planting seven new churches and of fostering a new emphasis on mission during this decade have been established by national and local leaders. Membership is presently about twice their average attendance.

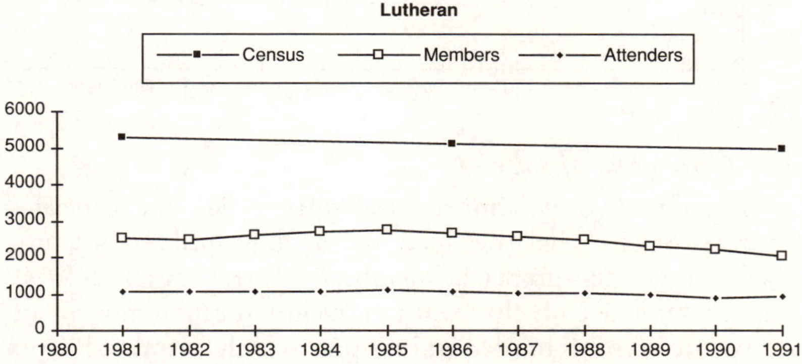

The Baptist Churches (formerly Baptist Union)

The BCANZ has shown a constant rise in membership since 1900 when there were 3,600 members, with the exception of the two decades in which World Wars occurred. Growth in all other decades has been remarkable, showing decadal increases in membership ranging from 9% upwards. The rate of growth peaked in the 1950s when it was 46%. In 1985 when there were 22,500 members in 163 churches, the annual Assembly of Baptist delegates set goals of having a total of 300 churches and 40,000 members by the year 2000. By 1992, 36 new causes had been established and membership had risen to 24,000. The denomination attracts about 7,000 non-member attenders at worship, by far the greatest number of any non-pentecostal denomination.

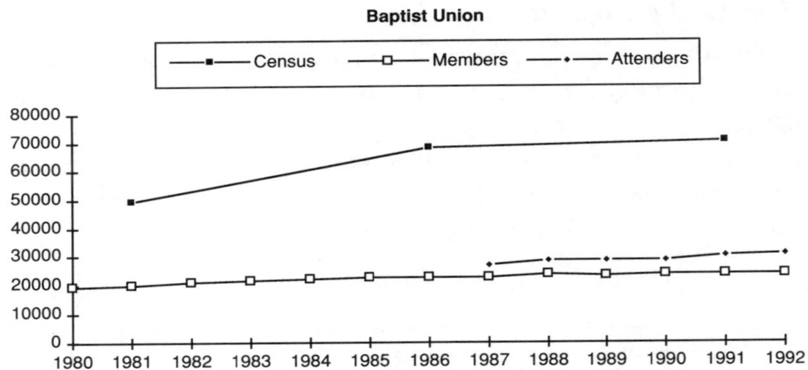

The Churches of Christ

Following steady growth from the 1840s to the 1940s the Associated Churches of Christ have declined considerably until very recently. They lost a large number of members in the 1960s and 1970s during their active involvement in the church union movement. Many transferred to denominations which refrained from involvement in the unsuccessful union negotiations. There are currently about 2,000 members in 43 congregations.

The Associated Churches of Christ has recently reconfirmed its commitment to the evangelical and biblical message and has seen a return of confidence, with modest growth in the last few years and renewed commitment to church planting. The first national Convention of Elders held in 1991 set goals for strong eldership in all congregations by the year 2000. The Church of Christ (Life and Advent) was formed last century in this country on a doctrinal distinctive. It has declined in recent years. In 1992 a majority of its congregations are planning to join the Baptist Union. There are about 300 members in seven churches. There are a further dozen or so independent and non-aligned Churches of Christ estimated to have about 1,500 members. The largest of these is the Church of Christ (New Zealand) in Mount Roskill Auckland, with up to 1,000 attenders.

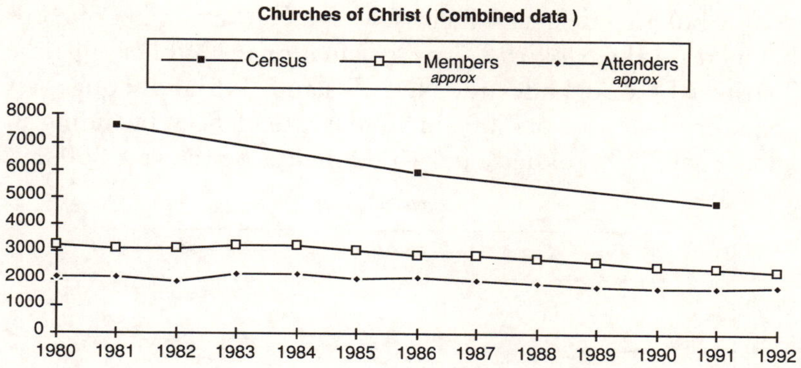

The Christian and Missionary Alliance

This denomination was founded in Canada and established its first congregation in Auckland in 1973. It has grown to eight congregations, the newest and largest of which is primarily Chinese. Goals have been adopted to increase to 16 churches and 2,000 attenders by the year 2000.

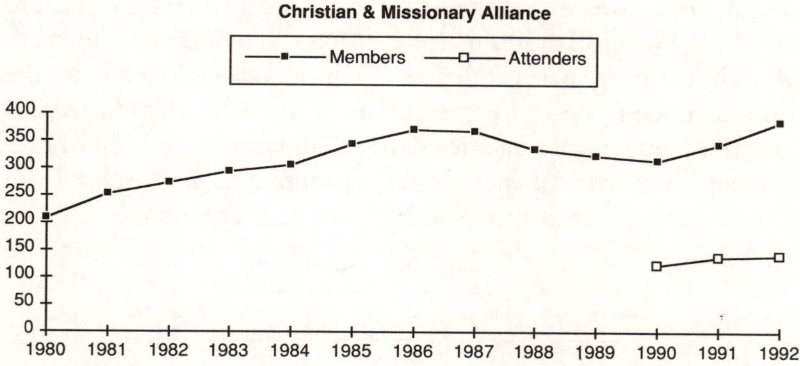

The Salvation Army

The Salvation Army was established in Great Britain last century and quickly spread throughout the Western world and beyond. It has a strong dual mandate for the saving of souls and social action. The number of soldiers in this country has declined in the last decade but attenders have increased slightly; the number of corps has increased by two to 94. By proclamation in October 1991 the Territorial Commander for New Zealand, Fiji and Tonga, set goals for an increase of 4,000 in Sunday attendances, including an additional 3,500 soldiers, and 15 new corps by the year 2000.

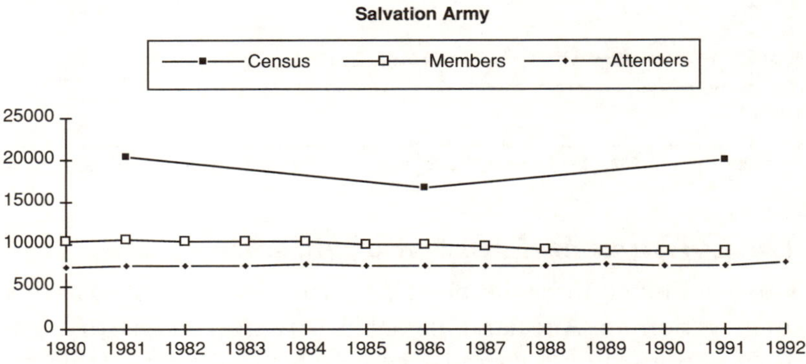

The Seventh-day Adventist Church

The Church was established in New Zealand in 1886 and has steadily grown to 10,500 members today. Their commitment to church planting has produced a considerable increase in the number of congregations, from 69 to 94 in the last decade. About half the members are Pacific Islanders and a further 12% Maori. An important part of the Church's programme is its schools, of which there are 18 primary and three secondary schools.

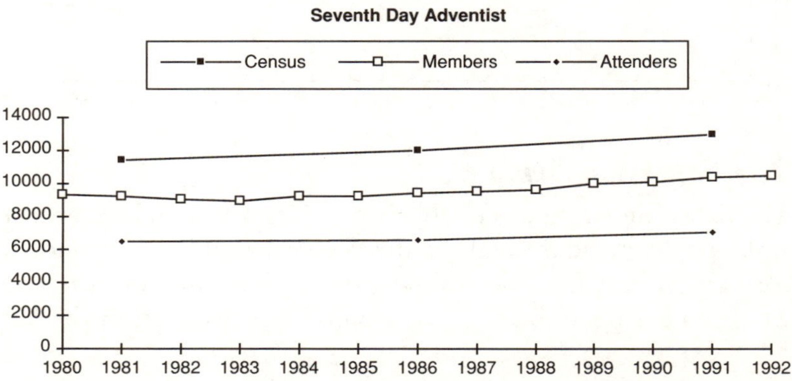

The Open Brethren Assemblies

It is difficult to obtain overall information about the Open Brethren because of their strongly independent and congregational form of government. They have assemblies throughout the country which cooperate for research, leadership training and overseas missionary work. Under 20,000 people identified themselves as Brethren in the 1991 census, down from 24,000 in 1981. It has been variously estimated that between 12,000 and 15,000 are regular attenders.

The Assemblies of God

Few statistics have been collected by the Assemblies of God in the past, and figures are mostly estimates. However, it is clear that the Assemblies of God have seen growth over the past decade or so which, in comparison with other denominations, is phenomenal. This growth is partly a result of mainline people transferring after experiencing charismatic renewal. However, even the most critical observer would have to concede that the figures represent a substantial influx of previously unchurched and nominal people. Since 1980 the number of assemblies has jumped from 85 to 180. Some of these are language and ethnic congregations, including 54 Samoan Assemblies with 5,000 attenders, nine Tongan, seven Fijian, two Korean and one Hindi.

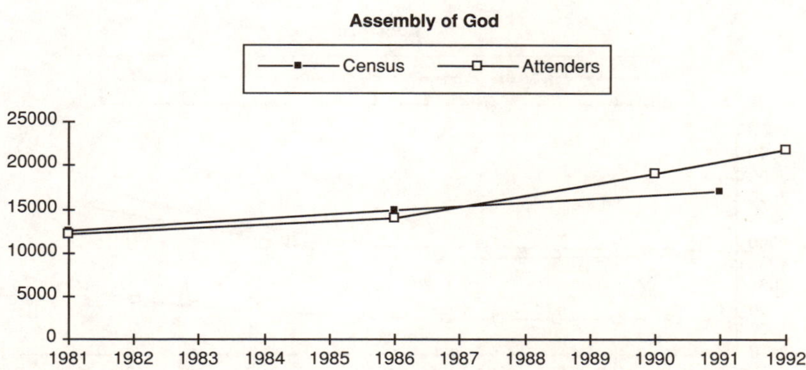

In the English speaking assemblies there is a considerable presence of non-Europeans, particularly Maori. The denomination set goals in 1988 to increase from 118 congregations to 218 by the year 2000. A higher goal is under discussion because progress is well ahead of target. Goals were also accepted for 200 more pastors and leaders in full-time ministry, and 20,000 new disciples, by the year 2000.

The Apostolic Church

The Apostolic Church was established in New Zealand in 1934 by the parent body in the United Kingdom. By 1985, 37 churches had been established. The major factors thought to inhibit growth through this period were centralized government and financial management, and greater emphasis on pentecostal distinctives than reaching the lost. Over the last five years major changes have been made. Church government and financial management have been devolved to local churches along with bold sharpening of focus on the Great Commission. Strong commitments to leadership training and church planting have resulted in dramatic growth in the last five years. The number of churches has increased from 49 to 85 and the number of regular attenders has doubled from about 5,000 to nearly 10,000. Such has been their growth that goals set in 1987 were doubled in 1992. They now plan to add another 30,000 regular attenders, establish 214 new churches and train 400 new pastors by the year 2000!

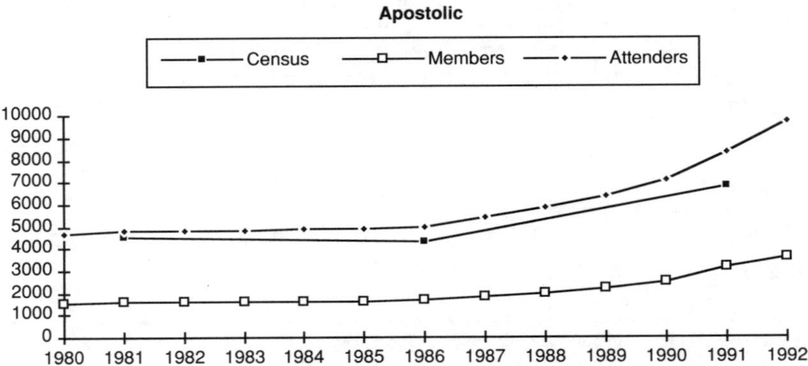

The Christian City Church

This denomination was established in New Zealand in 1987 as a branch of CCC International. It seeks to be evangelistic in non-traditional ways, particularly through coffee bars and rock concerts. Over half the attenders are in Auckland. In sharp contrast to the mainline churches, 60% of attenders are under twenty years of age. Only 10% of its people are over forty. CCC targets the baby-boomers[6] and their children, and has quickly grown to eight congregations with over 1,600 regular attenders. Goals of the leadership include planting 42 new congregations by the turn of the century.

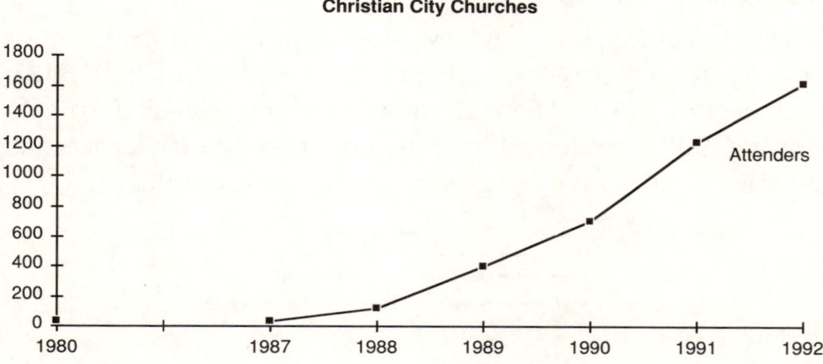

The Christian Revival Crusade

The CRC began in Napier in 1944 and had grown to ten congregations by 1988. In that year the leadership established goals to train new leaders and plant new congregations. These goals for the year 2000 include growth to 40 congregations. Each congregation was challenged to plant a daughter church and set aside 2% of income for growth. By 1992 attendance and number of pastors have grown by 50%, and the number of congregations has increased from 10 to 18.

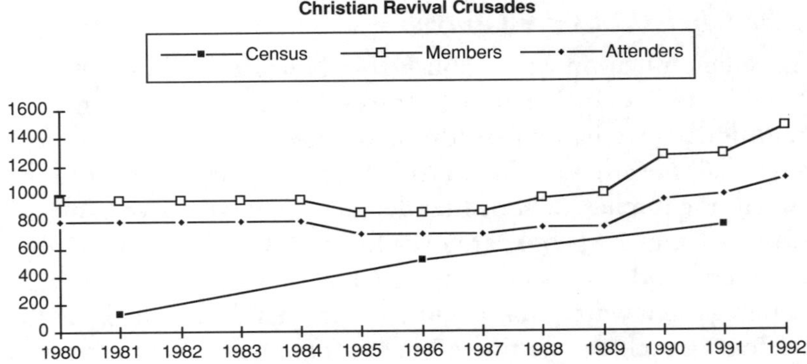

The Elim Church

The Elim Church began in New Zealand in 1952. There were six congregations by 1970 and this grew to ten with over 1,000 regular attenders in 1980. There are now 45 Elim congregations with nearly 6,000 attenders. Goals include training new leaders and planting a further ten congregations by the year 2000.

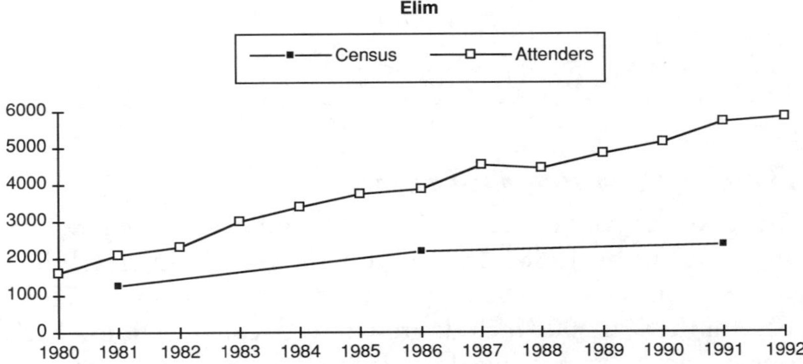

The Church of the Nazarene

The New Zealand district of the Church of the Nazarene had 12 congregations with 400 members in 1980. By 1992 this had grown to 600 members in 13 congregations.

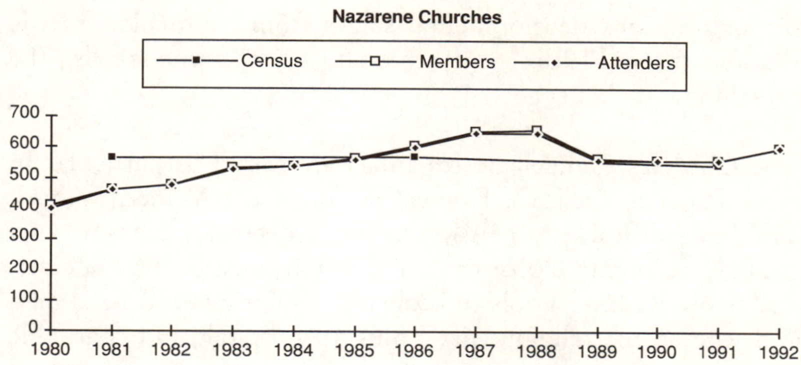

The New Life Churches, & South Pacific Fellowship

The New Life movement was established in this country in 1942. The first national meeting of leaders of what was then known as the Indigenous Churches of New Zealand took place in 1959. In the 1980s the group appointed national and regional leadership. In 1980 there were 8,000 regular attenders in 70 congregations. By 1992 that had grown to 15,000 in 108 congregations.

The South Pacific Fellowship was established in 1987 when 18 congregations with about 1,800 members linked together. Many came from what was then known as the Indigenous Churches of New Zealand but became the New Life Churches. Some were previously not aligned to any group. The South Pacific Fellowship is a loosely associated group with both full members and associates. In some cases these are also affiliated to other groups. There are presently 39 congregations with some form of affiliation with the fellowship. They have nearly 5,000 regular attenders.

The Roman Catholic Church

Since Vatican II there has been growing encouragement of ecumenism and respect for other denominations. However the leaders of the Roman Catholic Church decided not to participate in the VISION New Zealand project. The Church has gone through various developmental stages from its mission to the Maori in the mid 19th century, to what Father Simmons calls, "the present era of challenge".[7]

The Church's evangelistic teachings are found in particular in three Papal Encyclicals: Evangelization in the Modern World; The Lay Faithful; and Mission of the Redeemer. It has its own Evangelization 2000 project. The Church consists of 6 Dioceses, 287 parishes, 220 schools and colleges, 680 priests and 1624 men and women in "religious life", plus 49 hospitals and charitable institutions.

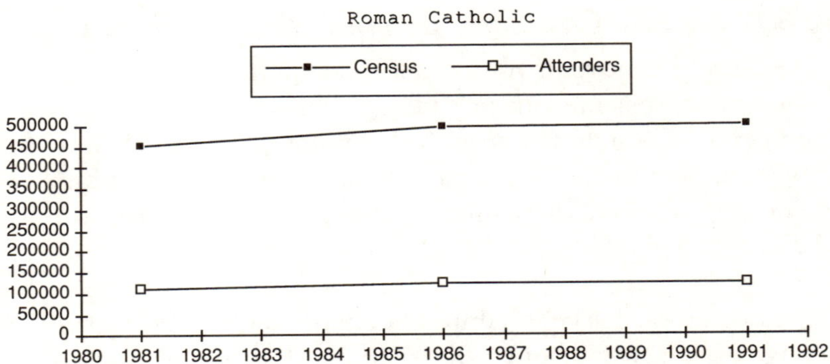

Who's Growing and Who's Not

Before looking at the growth/decline rates of denominational attenders, consider the numbers and growth/decline of other groups. Table 2 gives some figures from the census for 1971 - 1991. Ratana and Ringatu have grown substantially in recent years, and have an increasing appeal for young Maoris who are disaffected with Pakeha society and churches. Interestingly, there are movements within both of these groups to come closer to mainstream Christian beliefs in a Maori way.[8] Mormon and Jehovah's Witness figures have almost doubled. The large increases in adherence to eastern religions can be linked to increased immigration from Asian countries. Those who indicate no religion or object to state, are nearly one third of the population. Those who formerly showed up as nominal adherents now declare themselves as of no religion, a helpful clarification.

Table 2 : Other Groups

Breakdown of Group E (other) in Table One from the 1971/1981/1991 Censuses.

	1971	1981	1991
Denominations	2,349,618	2,247,015	2,106,400
(A-D above)	82%	71%	66%
Ratana	30,156	35,766	47,595
Ringatu	5,635	6,114	8,052
Mormon	29,785	37,431	48,009
Jehovah's Witness	10,318	13,689	19,182
Spiritualist	1,015	2,403	3,084
Christadelphian	1,668	1,683	1,845
Worldwide Church of God	33	915	825
Christian Science	816	447	321
Hindu	3,845	5,940	17,661
Buddhist	1,423	3,936	12,765
Islam	780	1,701	5,772
Ba'hai	350	1,440	2,868
Sikh	380	597	2,058
	----------------	----------------	----------------
	86,204	112,062	170,037
	3%	4%	5%
No religion & Humanist)			
Atheist and Agnostic)	426,809	784,230	979,908
Pagan and Pantheist)	(15%)	(25%)	(29%)
Object to state)			
	----------------	----------------	----------------
Total population	2,862,631	3,143,307	3,373,926
	=========	=========	=========

The denominations may take comfort from the increasing honesty of the nominally Christian populace. However, the challenge to reach fringe or nominal members before their honesty breaks whatever links remain should spur mainline Churches to re-evangelize their adherents.

Table 3, which gives Annual Average Growth Rates[9], makes it very evident that of the denominations, the:

mainline are static or declining
baptistic are plateaued or slow-growing
pentecostal are growing, and in some cases spectacularly.
catholic remain a substantial proportion of the churchgoing
population.

Table 3 : Who's Growing And Who's Not

Average Annual Growth Rates for Denominations where the data is available.

	Churches			Attendance		
	76-81	81-86	86-91	76-81	81-86	86-91
Anglican Church	0.1%	-1.0%	0.0%	1.2%	1.0%	5.3%
Methodist Church	-0.3%	-0.3%		-3.2%	-3.2%	-0.4%
Presbyterian Church	-3.2%	-1.0%		-0.9%	-0.1%	1.9%
Baptist Union	0.4%	2.7%	1.4%	3.5%	3.0%	3.3%
Seventh-day Adventist	0.4%	3.8%	1.6%	1.0%	0.4%	2.1%
Salvation Army	0.4%	0.2%	-0.8%	3.7%	-1.0%	-0.1%
Assemblies of God	5.4%	5.1%	10.6%	17.6%	2.9%	10.7%
Apostolic Church	1.6%	8.4%	13.2%	11.2%	7.7%	9.8%
Elim Church	14.9%	24.6%	5.0%	27.0%	21.3%	10.5%

International figures confirm that these are world-wide trends. It
is estimated there are now about 300 million pentecostals world-
wide, out of a total Christian community of about 1,800 million.
Awareness of the significance of their growth rates is one factor that
has led to increasing acceptance of pentecostals, as signalled for
example by the Lausanne II Congress in Manila in 1989. The body
of Christ is seeking to learn from pentecostal effectiveness, as the
need to awaken the sleeping giants of mainline denominations is
recognized. As has been said, the greatest mission field in the
Western world is the nominal fringe of the mainline churches.

The proportion of pentecostal growth that comprises transfers
from other denominations is often debated. Only the transfers of
active members should be of concern. If pentecostals (or any lively
caring churches) are reaching nominal adherents who are unreached
by the denomination of their background, no one with a kingdom
perspective can object. Experience here and in other parts of the

world indicates that where denominations will not or cannot meet the contemporary challenge, new groups spring up to carry the torch.

It is undeniable that there is increasing interest in spirituality in the Western world, including New Zealand. In spite of the reportedly pervasive influence of the New Age movement, it probably has no more support than one of the smaller Christian denominations. The challenge to the whole Church is to present the gospel to those who need Christ. Mainline and baptistic churches are challenged by pentecostal growth to learn how they may have an increased share in the harvest. Pentecostal churches have other challenges, including the challenge to multiply and conserve long-term the fruit of their ministries, and to be part of a more unified Church.

Goals and Style

Preliminary analysis of the VISION New Zealand survey of all churches seems to confirm the findings of earlier research regarding the relationship between church growth and attitudes to Scripture, the Spirit, and styles of ministry. Beasley-Murray and Wilkinson[10] found from a survey of 350 English Baptist churches that growing churches are most likely to have a pastor who has married conservative evangelical theology with an open attitude to the Holy Spirit (calling themselves "charismatic"), and well developed leadership skills. Thong Ng[11] in a survey of the 20 fastest growing Baptist churches in New Zealand, and Dick Holland[12] in a recent survey of the 20 fastest growing Presbyterian churches in this country came to similar conclusions. It is my personal conviction, arising from research for this book, the research of others, and general observation, that if the Church in New Zealand is to grow we will need more church leaders who:

> have a love for and respect for the Scriptures as authoritative
> are actively seeking the person and work of the Holy Spirit
> in their ministry, and
> have good leadership skills.

Leadership skills include visionary goal-setting, ability to inspire a team, delegation and monitoring, good personal time management and adherence to priorities, and well developed interpersonal skills and supportive attitudes, These qualities may be even more important than others often more highly regarded, such as preaching and pastoral care gifts. Researcher George Barna makes a strong point when he writes, "In every one of the growing, healthy (ie. user friendly) churches I have studied, a discernible link has been forged between the spiritual and numerical growth of those congregations and the existence, articulation, and widespread ownership of God's vision for ministry by the leaders and participants of the church. Conversely, visionless congregations fail to experience spiritual and numerical growth."[12] Barna emphasizes the black and white nature of this finding. Those who are leaders of these local leaders will need a national vision and readiness to cooperate in meeting the challenge of the Great Commission, encouraging the whole Church to take the whole gospel to the whole nation.

FOOTNOTES

[1] SWOT is an acronym which stands for Strengths, Weaknesses, Opportunities, and Threats.

[2] Anglicans and Presbyterians: Decade of Evangelism; Baptists: Decade of Mission; Apostolics: Decade of Release; Assemblies of God: Decade of Harvest; Salvation Army: Growth 2000.

[3] Three categories have been adopted, mainline, baptistic, and pentecostal, as used by Hugh Dickie in his research for the Congress on Children and Families 1991. Catholic has been added.

[4] For detailed information about the Anglican Church and Maori, see the second part of chapter 16.

[5] Cooperating Ventures is the generic term given for Union Parishes and various other congregations which comprise members of the Churches which were party to the Act of Commitment 1967. They are Associated Churches of Christ, Anglican, Congregational, Methodist and Presbyterian Churches.

[6] Baby-boomers are people born between 1946 and 1961.

[7] E.R. Simmons, *A Brief History of the Catholic Church in New Zealand*, 1978.

[8] See Lionel Stewart's comments in Chapter 16.

[9] Average Annual Growth Rate (AAGR) is defined as the average annual percentage increase during the period.

[10] Paul Beasley-Murray and Alan Wilkinson, *Turning the Tide*, (London, UK: Bible Society of Great Britain, 1981).

[11] Thong Ng, *A Focus on the Fastest Growing Baptist Churches in New Zealand,* (Baptist College Thesis, Auckland, NZ: 1984).

[12] Dick Holland, *Breakthrough For Growth,* (Study Leave Report, Te Puke, NZ: 1991).

[13] George Barna, *The Power of Vision,* (Ventura, CA: Regal, 1992).

What Is Our Gospel?

by John Hitchen

What is our gospel? This is perhaps the crucial question in Christian mission today. Certainly it is the crucial question if we are to have an adequate vision for Aotearoa New Zealand.

Strangely, we Christians are slow to define the gospel. We often act and speak as if our good news is self-evident. Our evangelism often assumes the good news is already understood in our society. If that were ever a fair assumption it is sadly misplaced today. General awareness of biblical concepts, teachings, or even personalities is so shallow that we are fools to think something as radical and unpredictable as the gospel is commonly understood. We must not ignore the task of defining our message. The good news is power, announcement, and summons.

God's Power in Action

Our Christian gospel is fundamentally *God's power in action.* Our modern world lusts after power. This lust drives political ambition. Its energy is blatantly exploited in the business world. Our best brains pursue the lure of power in every field of human enquiry. Many of our most emotive words focus on this theme. Just think of the images conjured up by these words: the powerless; abuse of power; empowering the exploited; the corridors of power. Vast financial resources are poured into achieving power across the spectrum of human achievement. Most pointedly, we are all too conscious of our lack of power over ourselves. Helpless, we are haunted by our inability to cleanse our own sense of inner failure and guilt. We know all too well the sheer frustration of having great hopes and good intentions but lacking the moral fibre to achieve them. We feel our own powerlessness as we watch families disintegrate and personal lives crumble under the pressure of modern lifestyles. And where we do see power at work, it is often the kind that destroys or further undermines the fabric of our society.

Into this context the gospel comes as a radically different power. "I am not ashamed of the gospel, for it is the power of God," wrote the apostle.[1] Unlike other modern forms, this power alone picks up broken bits and makes them whole again. The gospel re-integrates personalities torn apart by drug abuse. The gospel cleanses the sense of failure and self condemnation left in the wake of incest and teenage promiscuity. The gospel releases the middle-aged man frustrated with no higher purpose for living than the accumulation of possessions and gadgets; it involves him in strategic community service and building bridges across ethnic divisions in our society. The gospel turns the street-kid brought up without parental contact into a generous and thoughtful mother, wife, and homemaker. The gospel changes introspective, inhibited, shame-ridden young men and women into quietly confident courageous innovators who grapple with ethical standards in the New Zealand business world; who offer serious assistance to members of the gay community; who develop aid, community leadership and spiritual welfare services in needy countries globally; and who cross socioeconomic barriers in our own country to provide fresh opportunities to those still reeling from the latest economic downturn. The gospel takes ordinary decent Kiwis, whether Pakeha, Maori, Pacific Islander or Asian, and loosens the grip of their endemic selfishness, complacency and preoccupation with material things. This gospel gives them new ability to face up to their own inner needs, to begin to let go of crippling pride and prejudice, and become honest citizens with a worthwhile value system and sense of direction in today's world. You say, it is easy to write like that. But I am thinking of particular people in each of these categories, people with names who have crossed my path since I arrived back in New Zealand six years ago.

Yes, the good news of Jesus Christ is all about changing lives. It is a dynamic which restores and renews dysfunctional persons and sets them on the path to wholeness. That is the point of Paul's, "the gospel is the power of God for salvation".[2] Salvation is wholeness of life; it is becoming integrated, wholesome people again. Through this gospel the living God shares his own life among us. He demonstrates he is here and available with his own reconstructive touch to renew our lives today. The gospel is the igniting power which releases love, faith and hope to penetrate our needy society in person, through renewed women and men discovering the way to full-orbed living. News of a good power in our day is good news indeed.

The Announcement of Good News

The gospel is announcement as well as power. The gospel announces and explains *God's action in Christ for us.* The good news declares what God has done. It interprets certain crucial events in a particular way.

The announcement is that in Jesus of Nazareth, God *came* into our human scene. God has broken into history in person. The originator and controller of all that is, has made a live appearance on planet earth. That is news. God so cares about his creatures that he came to us in person.[3]

He even *lived* a human life. And what a life it proved to be: a life lived totally for others, clean, kind and wholesome in every way. Ignoring the expectations of his stratified society he related to commoners and leaders alike, disregarding their national and religious backgrounds. Despite his efforts to conceal his true origin, his uniqueness shone through. His mastery over the powers of nature, his penetrating knowledge of human hearts, his awesome control over raw spirit powers and his intense hatred of hypocrisy showed he was no mere human. Yet he demonstrated his divine origins only to serve the needy. Displaying love as the hallmark of his true humanity, he accepted equally all those he encountered across the spectrum of society. So much so, he proved a popular hero for a time. And such an embarrassment to the religious establishment that he was disposed of, it seemed, by their plots.[4]

The way he *died* became the focal point of the news. He taught his followers to understand his death as God's answer to the basic needs and yearnings of the human heart. Conscience itself, as an inner reflection of the standards of our unchanging God, demands satisfaction, punishment, and restitution for wrongs done. The law of God declared it indelibly. The Jewish sacrificial system reflected the universal human need for forgiveness through an atonement. God presented Jesus as that sacrifice of atonement. Christ died to deal with the global sin problem. As both perfect sacrifice and high priest, strange though the combination may seem, Jesus personally dealt with the human defilement which banished us from our maker's presence. His death re-opened direct access to the upright, holy God. His perfect life, offered up in willing death, is a pardoning ransom, as he taught. He died on behalf of self-opinionated, sinful humans. He thereby satisfied totally the legal condemnation rightly barring proud rebels like us from enjoying the presence of God. This death therefore frees, cleanses and renews all who will admit their broken relationships with God. By humbly accepting Jesus Christ's death as God's judgement on our own disobedience, we find the only adequate basis for re-admission into family fellowship with God. Moreover, this death portrays vividly the depths to which the yearning heart of God would go to reclaim us for his intended purposes. In this death, true love has been displayed and redefined once and for all.[5]

Powerful though this death would have been on its own, it does not stand alone. As the life and character of the person who died would lead us to expect, the good news is that Jesus the Christ *rose* from the dead.[6] The unembellished historical facts have withstood the critical scrutiny of 2000 years. The apostles' recorded testimony, the fact and endurance of the Church, and the personal experience of the risen Christ by successive generations of Christians are best accounted for by the fact of the resurrection. It rewrites our understanding even of death. Good news indeed.

But the good news is no antiquated message. This same Jesus of Nazareth, by the express action of God, now *rules* the universe as Lord. The forces released through his death and resurrection have impacted not merely our globe but the whole universe. A person, the Lord Jesus Christ, now sits in control of the affairs of the universe. This is good news. The ultimate authority in the cosmos is not some impersonal force, not blind fate, and certainly not inexorable law. Rather, the living, loving, accessible person, our Lord Jesus Christ, has final control.[7] The gospel presents Jesus Christ as our king waiting in sovereign majesty for us, his subjects, to acknowledge his rule.

This announcement goes one step further. Jesus Christ, the active Lord of creation, will *return* personally to our globe. History is heading to God's pre-determined goal. All the details are not spelled out. Jesus himself warned of our continuing ignorance about such details. But he spoke often and clearly about the fact. Jesus will return in person to wrap up God's present purposes for planet earth. His return will confirm the seriousness of human accountability. If God never holds us accountable for our actions he is treating us as less than free responsible beings. At Christ's return our dignity as humans will be finally validated. We shall each account for the way we have lived our lives. It is unthinkable that all accumulated human evil should never be brought to justice. Christ will return as judge. Only thus will patience and hope be shown in their true colours, as essential to human life. Only thus will God be finally vindicated. The role of his grace and forbearance underpinning the very structures of human existence will finally be made clear. On the basis of the work of Christ thus far in human history, his return is eminently rational. It is integral to the apostolic gospel.[8]

These, then, are the constituent ingredients of the announcement we call the gospel. God in Christ came, lived, died, rose, rules, and is returning as our Saviour, Lord, Prophet, Priest, Judge, Advocate and King.

A Summons to Respond

But the gospel is more than an announcement. It also *summons us to enjoy the benefits of this action.* The gospel is God's active power, an invitation calling for response. Once we have heard and understood this news, we become freshly accountable to God. He summons us to enter his kingdom. He calls for ongoing commitments as his loyal subjects. Good news brings great responsibility.[9]

The gospel summons us to change in every aspect of life. It invites us first to a radically *new understanding of God himself.* We now know God as Jesus Christ explained him. God is not the exclusive property of one especially religious nation. He is equally accessible to all peoples. He yearns for intimate personal relationships with people of every cultural background. We can enjoy knowing him. This gospel revelation of God as our loving Father reclaims and reinstates the categories of love and family life which are so abused in our human experience. The gospel demonstrates their intended fulness as Jesus Christ sets forth through his life and death the essence of God as love.[10]

The gospel also summons us to embrace the *news about human purpose.* We who had lost our way, who had become alienated from our intended goals and purpose, have now been found. The gospel opens for us a renewed sense of direction. We can rediscover our true identity as God's pilgrim people en route to an eternal appointment with him. Here is a new world view. Time takes on new importance in the light of the eternal. Values are determined from an other-worldly, not merely this-worldly, perspective. Possessions lose their depth of attraction in the light of their transience. Relationships, and people as persons, take on a new sense of ultimate permanence and priority. Too often our evangelism fails to summons people to a new world-view. But ultimate meaningfulness is good news indeed.[11]

At its heart the gospel invites us to discover the *good news about human sin.* Christians need not highlight that we humans have 'blown it' in our modern world. Newspapers give daily coverage of that reality. Our gospel does however offer a radical reinterpretation of our dilemma by tracing its roots back to our disrupted relationship with God. Any adequate analysis of human need must take into account mankind's basic rejection of God, which the Bible calls sin.

God now offers cleansing from sin's pollution. Christ's in-depth forgiveness deals with our fundamental human bias towards evil. The distorting, corrupting effects of habitually choosing our own selfish way can at last be corrected. Christ's inner clean-up and moral restoration renews us as whole persons. But it goes further than that. Christ has bridged permanently the awful chasm our sin created between ourselves and our holy God. We have peace with God. Our rebellion and enmity have been dealt with. We are reconciled through trust in Christ.[12]

The gospel also summons us to demonstrate the n*ews about human society.* The Christian gospel creates new social relationships. Jesus' love in us immediately reinstates a healthy social concern. Love becomes the distinctive hallmark of believers. The gospel constantly reconciles enemies. Its very nature challenges social divisions. This open secret had never dawned on God's people in previous ages. But now the gospel makes the hope of Christ available to every cultural group world-wide. Any 'gospel' which does not involve its adherents in cross-cultural friendship was publicly condemned by the apostles.

The gospel's inherent concern for people also releases *power for social action.* Christ's zeal for justice and social righteousness now infuses his followers. For all their apparent conservatism in regard to moral values, those who drink the new wine of Christ's gospel create a ferment for social structures which restores sanctity and dignity to human life. History warns of the short-sightedness of political powers which under-estimate the social impact of the death and resurrection of Christ.[13]

The biblical gospel contains other components often overlooked in the West. It includes unexpected *news about spirit powers.* During his earthly life Christ Jesus demonstrated his authority over demonic powers. He proved his right to establish the kingdom of God by freeing those dominated by the powers of darkness. Even more, Christ's death and resurrection have permanently affected cosmic good and evil forces. Angelic powers now serve the interests of believers. Christ's peace accomplished at Calvary has finally subjugated evil powers. Through the cross all the powers of wickedness have been disarmed and publicly displayed in their true weakness. Though rearguard actions abound, Christ has dealt the decisive blow. This is good news indeed for those living in fear of spirit powers, including increasing numbers of men and women in the Western world. Those who open their lives to the living Christ through his Spirit are rescued from the dominion of darkness and transferred to the kingdom of God's Son. As we share the summons of the gospel we must reinstate these cosmic aspects of Christ's great redemptive victory.[14]

The gospel also includes *news about our global environment.* Our understanding of the universe is reinterpreted in the gospel. Creation is a household inheritance gifted by God to his 'first-born', Jesus Christ. This transforms our attitude to the world around us, which is intended to glorify Christ. Creation awaits and participates significantly in God's eternal purposes, sharing somehow in our redemption as children of God. Thus serious environmental concern becomes a gospel duty.[15]

The gospel includes radical *news about human suffering*. Christ's suffering at Calvary transforms our understanding of suffering. God brings love, faith and hope into human suffering. Christ's shouldering of human suffering in person means God is available, in *love,* to relieve human suffering. Moreover, God transforms suffering through *faith*, to make it productive. Perseverance, character and *hope* are generated specifically in the furnace of suffering. Far from expecting every hurt to be immediately relieved, gospel resources enable us to rejoice even in suffering as one way in which God prepares us for the ultimate consummation of the kingdom.[16]

Yet the gospel is not merely "pie in the sky when you die". We Christians certainly have plenty to look forward to. But our good news is that *God comes right into our present daily experience* too. The kingdom which will be completed at Christ's return is accessible already. Our faith link with Christ the King is a living reality now. We experience his presence bringing us courage and peace to face the pressures of modern life. He delights to do the unexpected to demonstrate his power and gracious concern for his wayward creatures. He does heal. He does demonstrate his victory over evil forces. He miraculously works to confirm his role as Lord in his own universe. Most amazing of all, he condescends to share with us on a daily basis. Each of his followers experiences the Holy Spirit of God living within his or her own life and personality. He renews our lives and equips us with previously unrealized gifts to serve him. His kingdom is already available, but not yet here in its fulness. There is no contradiction in the gospel between our present experience of both suffering and the indwelling Spirit. After all, our miracle-working Saviour willingly submitted to the awful suffering of the cross.[17]

The Whole Gospel

Initially, different aspects of such a comprehensive biblical gospel appeal to different people. We all run the risk of trying to reduce and domesticate both its scope and impact. We are prone to take the personal aspects of the gospel and ignore the social and world-view implications. Or, once alerted to the broader social implications, we can overlook the depths of personal integrity upon which they are based; we can work for bland social betterment without calling for personal commitment through repentance and conversion, which is the gospel's essential cutting edge. Or, in our zeal for personal evangelism and social change, our western materialistic worldview can remain largely unchanged; we can hold back from the costly process of bringing our value system and thought patterns into line with the demands of the gospel.

The real challenge is to grasp this good news ever more fully, more adequately, and therefore more humbly. This is the vision-imparting news our nation needs as we move into the 21st century. Thanks be to God for his indescribable gift![18]

FOOTNOTES

[1] Romans 1:16.

[2] Ibid.

[3] See for example John 14:10-11, 17:21-24, 2 Corinthians 5:19, Philippians 2:5-9.

[4] See for example John 11:47-53, Acts 10:36-40.

[5] See for example Mark 10:33-34, 45, Luke 24:44-47, Romans 3:21-26, 1 John 4:9-10.

[6] See for example Acts 2:23-24; 1 Corinthians 15:3-7.

[7] See for example Ephesians 1:20-22, Colossians 1:15-17, Hebrews 1:2-3.

[8] See for example John 5:25-29, Romans 14:9-12, 1 Corinthians 5:10, 1 Thessalonians 1:9-10, Titus 2:11-14, Hebrews 9:26-28.

[9] John 3:3-5, 12:47-50, Romans 1:18 - 2:16.

[10] See for example John 1:18, Galatians 4:4-7, 1 John 4:7-16.

[11] See for example Luke 19:10, Ephesians 2:1-13, Hebrews 11:13-16.

[12] See for example Romans 3:21 - 5:21, Colossians 1:19-23, 1 John 1:5 - 2:2.

[13] John 13:34-35, Ephesians 2:11ff, Colossians 1:3-8, Galatians 2:11-16, James 2:1-12, 1 John 4:11, 19-21.

[14] Colossians 1:16-20, 2:9, 15, Ephesians 1:20-22, 3:10, 6:11-13, Hebrews 1:14, 1 John 4:1-4.

[15] Romans 8:22-25, Colossians 1:15-17, Hebrews 1:2-3, 10-12.

[16] Romans 5:1-5, 8:18-39, 1 Peter 1:6-7, 4:12ff.

[17] See John 1:11-13, 14:17-27, 16:33, Acts 1:8, 1 Corinthians 6:19-20, 12:4-13, 2 Corinthians 5:17.

[18] 2 Corinthians 9:15.

10

Being and Telling the Gospel

by Barry Tetley

Deafening speakers blasted the U-shaped complex of multi-story flats with a 'gospel in a nutshell' harangue. I felt sorry for the flat-dwellers, their peace and privacy so offensively infringed. People had been invited to view the Hollywood film *The Love Bug*. A modest Bangkok crowd had seated themselves before the platform and screen. But first came the programme of gospel preaching. I wondered how much they could understand. When eventually the film was shown, the whole sound track, every speaking part plus accompanying sound effects, was reproduced vividly in Thai by the earlier preacher.

"Could such methods do more harm than good?" I thought. That question also crops up in discussion about evangelism in New Zealand. How can we evaluate the methods used in our evangelism?

Evangelism centres in a message of good news. But McLuhan's famous phrase is also true: "The medium is the message."[1] In a wander up Auckland's Queen Street on a Friday or Saturday night, whatever message might be heard, the medium will certainly have spoken loud and clear: that Christianity is fragmented and at odds with itself, that the church owns a disturbing number of 'strange' people, and that many of the self-appointed spokespersons of the church do not understand the first principles of communication. Are these the messages we want to convey? So one test of evangelism is to ask: does the method convey and clarify the gospel message? Or does it confuse and even contradict the message of Christ? Jesus Christ has not left us in the dark as to his intentions.

Linked in two sections of Matthew's Gospel dealing with Christian witness in our world (5:13-15 and 10:16) are five interlocking pictures of how it should be accomplished. They apply more than ever to evangelism today. The first metaphor is salt: "You are the salt of the earth."

In The World Like Salt, in Direct and Sustained Contact

Salt was a preservative and a savour. The use by Jesus of this metaphor indicated not only the kind of impact Christians should have, but also how it should happen. Salt works by direct contact. The Gospels portray Jesus himself in direct personal contact with all kinds of people. As "the friend of sinners" he was continually in their homes. "He went into the house" is a frequent and often overlooked New Testament phrase. He affected people by the quality of his presence, just as salt has its effect by direct contact. Sustained contact is also implied by the danger of the salt "losing its saltiness". It is a picture of an ongoing process of influence, not simply of momentary encounter. And so it should speak to us of evangelism.

We frequently think of evangelism in terms of a spiritual encounter, an hour of decision, a powerful moment of encounter between an evangelist and a stranger. We are thinking of an encounter that radically transforms, perhaps like the conversion of Paul, as we imagine it. Evangelists themselves often speak and report of their ministries like this.

More than we may realise, our understanding of conversion has been affected by the 18th century Evangelical Awakening inspired by George Whitefield and John Wesley.[2] Their preaching tried to add a "heartfelt" faith to what was often lifeless knowledge.

Though already a clergyman, John Wesley dates his conversion from the day his heart was "strangely warmed". George Whitefield's favourite theme in all his preaching was the new birth. And in many camps still, Christians are expected to describe a born again experience as central to their testimony of Christ.

But questions arise. While the Bible speaks clearly about regeneration or the new birth,[3] is this how conversions are described in the New Testament? Conversions are usually described as a change of allegiance. The words used, repent, receive, believe, turn to, be with, have faith in, be baptized into the name of, all express aspects of a change of allegiance. Clearly knowledge, emotion, and will are intertwined in any life-changing decision. And undoubtedly Peter, Matthew and Mary Magdalene all felt the charisma of Jesus, just as after Pentecost the Holy Spirit replicated his presence within people. But the outcome is expressed in terms of allegiance: "They left all and followed him". Even when a heart-warming experience is described, it culminates in an open profession of allegiance. "They have received the Holy Spirit just as we have", Peter said of Cornelius' household. "So he ordered they be baptized in the name of Jesus Christ."[4]

If in the 18th century the message of a heart strangely warmed was necessary to supplement religious formality, today a message of clear-cut allegiance is needed to supplement wishy-washy emotion. The evidence of conversion and the test of evangelism is not the report of an emotional moment. It is the evidence of a new and whole-hearted allegiance to Jesus Christ, understood, declared, and lived out.

Jesus taught (to a crowd apparently drawn by his charisma) that converting is a matter of a considered decision, a decision reached on a basis of adequate information and understood implications. In Luke 14:25-33, Jesus likens converting to a man considering a large building project: "Will he not first sit down and estimate the cost...?" Or a king weighing up whether to resist or yield: "Will he not first sit down and consider...?"

The way Jesus drew people into discipleship accords with this teaching. The early acquaintance of the disciples with Jesus recorded in John chapters 1 to 4 happened "before John was put in prison"[5]. It was "after John was put in prison"[6], with that message of cost, that they responded to Jesus' renewed invitation to follow him.[7] It was no sudden thing, without time to "sit down and consider". It was a process. And in each important part, the preceding teaching, the ultimate summons and response, and the ongoing discipleship, at all stages they were in contact with the savory and sustained influence of the person of Jesus. With John's and Luke's help we can also track the Jerusalem hearers who sat at Jesus' feet during the three feasts preceding his crucifixion[8] and their eventual conversion at Pentecost when they became part of the apostolic church.

In describing his own evangelism, Jesus regarded the good soil as those who hear the word, retain it, and persevere to produce the fruit.[9] Understanding is crucial.[10] The seed, growing gradually into fruit-bearing maturity, well illustrates conversion as seen in Jesus' ministry. Viewing conversion, and evangelism, as a process therefore makes our understanding of it clearer. People usually move gradually from one position of understanding and acceptance to another. This is not to say it happens at a given rate in a particular time-frame, nor that there are not exceptions. (However we do not base principles upon exceptions.) Statistics from modern evangelism often give unhappy evidence of the 'fall-away' factor. Modern methods that pressure people in the heat of the moment often do not work. People who swing from one position to another in a short space of time are susceptible to the pendulum effect.

Paul's conversion, like many others, hinged on a momentous encounter with Jesus Christ. But even in this conversion there was a process. There were other influences associated with the names of Gamaliel, Stephen, Ananias and Barnabas.

All major life decisions such as marriage, divorce, emigration, a changed career path, and converting[11] involve complex personal transactions. The vortex producing a major decision often swirls with emotional pulls and pushes. But when any major decision has been made, a period of post-decision re-evaluation is inevitable. Unless, in the cold light of day, the decision can be justified upon the facts of the matter, it will not hold. The now famous Engel Scale[12] (modified below) helps by showing evangelism and conversion as a process.

-7	Awareness of a supreme being
-6	Some knowledge of the gospel
-5	Knowledge of the basics of the gospel
-4	Grasp of personal implications
-3	Positive attitude towards becoming a Christian
-2	Recognition of personal need and intention to act
-1	Decision made to follow the way of Christ
0	Act of allegiance to Christ as Lord
+1	Post-decision re-evaluation
+2	Incorporation into a local church
+3	Growth in Christian mind-set and lifestyle.

For emphasis, only the "human steps" are identified. But conversion is not just a human process. We are "born of God". We assume here that God is active in every step of the process. If then conversion is usually a process, and God is active throughout the process, evangelism, the range of Christian activity designed to promote conversion, must also be viewed as a process. Sustained direct personal contact with Christian influences will be required. Elsewhere in this book is reported the frequency and variety of contact with the Christian gospel that is common in the conversion process.

With the salt metaphor Jesus was emphasizing the sustained direct personal contact that characterized his own ministry. When as evangelists we use encounter techniques rather than cultivate relationships we are neglecting an essential feature of evangelism as salt in the world. How often have we been encouraged to fire off a shot of gospel truth in a way that wounds rather than heals, in a way that alienates rather than cultivates, in a way that damages a relationship rather than develops one? In doing so we have done more harm than good. That is not acting as salt.

Churches evangelize like salt when they invest in the nurture of their contacts. The whole range of Christian education from catechizing to apologetics may be involved. Evangelists must learn to view their role in this context. Anglican evangelist Michael Green describes his method after an evangelistic address in his new book *Evangelism Through The Local Church*. He closes the meeting with an off-hand offer to talk with anyone afterwards about joining a "Discovering Jesus" group so that interest awakened can be pursued. As people discover Jesus they are helped towards a considered decision.[13]

Likewise, in his book *Lifestyle Evangelism* Joseph Aldrich emphasizes the variety of ways we see the gospel presented in the New Testament.[14] He describes evangelism as "a process that begins with the specifics of the individual's life. During the process, the evangelist finds himself doing at least five things:

1   **Relating** to the person's humanness and uniqueness with a view to helping the person solve a problem.
2   **Discovering** the person's problems and needs for which the gospel will prove to be good news.
3   **Sharing** how the gospel relates to that particular felt need and ultimately solves the underlying real need.
4   **Advocating** a commitment which will make the gospel solution operational through the Holy Spirit.

5   **Supporting** the person's feelings and thoughts as he or
         she moves through the commitment process."[15]

Here is the genius of Christian evangelism. Essentially it relies on ordinary frail people relating to one another, in continual personal contact, adapting and applying the truth, advocating a commitment with support and encouragement. This is salty evangelism, an indispensable part of Jesus' kind of evangelism. But there are other aspects too. If this metaphor stood alone, we might misread it. Salt works secretly, hiddenly. Is evangelism to be secretive and surreptitious? Not at all! Jesus counters this mistake with a second metaphor.

Like a Lighted City on a Hill, Shining Forth Openly

Correcting any idea that the Christian message should be hidden or secretive, Jesus uses a second image: that of a lighted city set on a hill that cannot be hidden (Matthew 5:14). Clearly this calls for the openly stated proclamation of the Christian message, the public presentation of the teaching and summons of Jesus. Seldom is the unchurched public in New Zealand able to see or hear a plain statement of what Jesus taught. Often the lunatic fringe gains public attention. Often a 10-second disjointed news-clip is all that is heard of an overall Christian world-view.

For Jesus there were not two competing approaches to evangelism: the presence of salt, or the proclamation of the lighted city. Both approaches are to be seen in evangelism. This was the underlying rhythm of his own ministry: his intimate personal presence ministering to individuals, and his public proclamation of the kingdom's teaching. Visits to the Jerusalem temple are always associated with his public and open teaching of the way of the kingdom.[16] The Apostles followed the same rhythm: more personal contact in homes, and public evangelism in the temple.[17] Here was a balance that Paul observed in his ministry.[18]

Instinctively Christians desire the good news to be openly and boldly proclaimed. Jesus is the way, the truth and the life, the route to God. The evangelist is the agent of this good news. He or she will necessarily be gifted in communication, able to answer the questions people are asking, explain the Christian perspective, promote the Christian response. As someone has said, "Every evangelist should be a theologian and every theologian an evangelist." Credible public voices for the gospel of Christ are desperately needed in New Zealand today, as are gifted communicators able to hear and answer the questions thrown up by a nation now largely ignorant of biblical Christianity.

Often however Jesus and his gospel seem to be represented by superficial stereotypes. There are those who thoughtlessly parrot answers to questions no-one is asking, who lack the skill to listen and to deliver Christ's answers in Christ's way. New Zealanders are aware of American televangelists who have used the media for raising money from gullible viewers, damaging the integrity of the Christian enterprise. Attitudes have attached to evangelism which, going unchallenged, have hindered our cause. Plainly, Jesus saw that Christians could not be light in the world unless the world could see their good works and give glory to God. The Church must return to the character of evangelism practised and taught by Jesus.

Like Sheep Sent Amongst Wolves, With Winsome Vulnerability

Moving on from the two primary strategies of evangelism, presence and proclamation, in Matthew 10:16 Jesus sets the benchmarks of quality for all Christian evangelism with three further metaphors.

If a city on a hill depicted the openly visible nature of Christian proclamation, it also spoke of a fortress. City walls were often 5 to 10 metres thick. Strong and invulnerable, they were designed to provide a safe sanctuary in threatening times. Since the 3rd century Christians have built sanctuaries, and with them has often grown a fortress mentality. A sanctuary-centred mind-set has made us want to evangelize from a position of strength and safety. In fact, we prefer to evangelize on our own terms, on our own territory. Viggo Sogaard has said, "Effective evangelism takes place on the premises of the recipient, the place where he is in control. We do not like that; we therefore invite him into our church. We rent an auditorium where we are in control. But Jesus said to go out, be involved in society, let them be in control, and you evangelize them, communicate with them".[19]

When Jesus sent out his apostles to evangelize they had no illusions about their vulnerability. He used the most graphic picture of vulnerability imaginable: the lamb sent into the midst of wolves. We cherish and celebrate our sense of mission. Unfortunately we have forgotten the winsome vulnerability that should characterize Christians in mission. The 12th century Crusades exemplify militant Christianity, and the results remain as memories in the Muslim world. Militancy still pervades our evangelism. Words like crusade, campaign, invasion, rise-up (uprising), army, blitz, armed and dangerous, which draw on military images, appear in the names of various New Zealand programmes and organizations. An approach is embraced which engenders militancy in attitude and action.

A student new to Auckland University felt the militancy of several campus groups and complained in the student paper *Craccum*: "A lot of my friends are religious, and I have respect for their beliefs as I know that they do for mine. I suggest you people try to do the same. After being set upon last week by your group, I lost all respect for you. The next time you people decide to approach someone you don't know, and begin to give them advice on how you think they should be living their lives, take a little time to think; you know nothing about them and how they live, and you could be doing more harm than good."[20]

The use of force has also been recognized at formal evangelistic meetings. Affirmation Six of the 1983 International Conference of Itinerant Evangelists in Amsterdam states, "In our proclamation of the gospel we recognize the urgency of calling all to decision to follow Jesus Christ as Lord and Saviour, and to do so lovingly and without coercion or manipulation".[21] Billy Graham says, "I am convinced that a high-pressure invitation cannot be the call of God the Holy Spirit. By such methods we are guilty of giving people a false assurance of salvation. That is leading them astray, and leaving them in a worse situation than before. Also we may build a great resentment against the gospel."[21]

One of my neighbours speaks of an evangelistic meeting when his arm seemed to have a mind of its own. "I didn't want it to, but up in the air it went. I tell you I got out of there as quick as I could afterwards." He was trapped into a profession he was not ready to make and now believes Christians are manipulative, not to be trusted. The gospel is about human dignity, an offered path of atonement, and a considered allegiance to the living God. Evangelism that forces, manipulates, and coerces betrays the gospel. In any case forceful evangelism is counter-productive. It produces wariness, defensiveness and resistance. Consider a wolf entering a flock of sheep. An evangelistic force entering a community or even someone's home, invokes a wary resistance. But what hackles rise when a vulnerable lamb enters a pack of wolves? The lamb's very vulnerability is the key to being received. And this was the spirit of evangelism Jesus commended in Matthew 10. Be vulnerable! Accept offered hospitality! If your sandal thong breaks, accept the help of others, for they might accept yours too. Live by faith in God, not by the force of your resources, and others might catch your faith from you, for that is the goal of the evangelistic enterprise.

Evangelism causes us discomfort. If the discomfort arises from being part of a force that manipulates other people, then the discomfort should warn us of the damage we are causing Christ.

On the other hand, if it is the discomfort of feeling vulnerable, take heart! For this is the hallmark of apostolic evangelism; they were sent like lambs into the midst of wolves, and so are we.

Like Serpents, With Skilful Proficiency

Like other images, the sheep image is invoked to teach one particular attitude, in this case winsome vulnerability. Jesus was not commending the stupidity of sheep. Quite the opposite. In his next image the proverbial skill of the serpent becomes his benchmark for ministry proficiency. Be as wise as serpents. The word he uses emphasizes both the wise mind and the trained muscle; both thoughtful well-judged action and skilful accomplishment. In a way this metaphor explains the three years' training Jesus gave his apostles. It also explains the need for comprehensive training of men and women for ministry, routine in established churches.

We can only be ashamed of the ineptitude of some Christian witnessing: of the outdoor preacher talking to an invisible audience; of packaging the good news in meaningless jargon; of presenting a canned gospel which presses a person to make an uninformed decision about a life-changing allegiance after fifteen minutes. In numerous writings, Jesus is portrayed as a model of excellence for his skill as a teacher, communicator, pastor, and as trainer of the twelve. He made them fishers of men, forming their attitudes, developing their knowledge and perfecting their ministry skills, readying them to undertake their post-Pentecost mission, which was marked with such success.

It has been said that "Christianity won over the Roman Empire in the first three centuries because they out-thought, out-loved and out-served their contemporaries". Not only does this describe effective evangelism, it hints at the meaning of skilfulness in a Christian context. Skilfulness is not slickness. It is skill that addresses with commendable proficiency the intellectual, emotional and social needs of our contemporaries. They out-thought, they out-loved, and they out-served.

In science, medicine and education, Christians have demonstrated the excellence of their skills. This excellence is essential in public evangelism. The best message in the world deserves the best presentation. A cluster of Christian musicians spring to mind who employ their gifts to convey the spirit of Christianity with style and grace. Others have excelled as apologists. The Oxford scholar C.S. Lewis could present the gospel with concise logic in his *Mere Christianity* or with childlike charm in *The Chronicles of Narnia*. By and large the record in New Zealand hardly matches the criterion of Jesus. Occasionally a quality presentation is seen. But public evangelism often seems to be left to amateurs, and the standards of Jesus are not met. With the skill of serpents we must find ways of upgrading the way the gospel reaches our society.

Like Doves, With Transparent Sincerity

It was difficult in Jesus' day, as in ours, to distinguish craft from craftiness. The serpent image was a limited image, speaking of skill. But it also implies deception. Another metaphor was needed to teach the Christlike quality of sincerity. Opposite to a serpent's deceitfulness was the guilelessness of the dove. This picture speaks powerfully in a day when Christianity is considered by some as a sham to cover up self-interest. Recognizing that modern evangelism has contributed to this reputation, Billy Graham has led in the formation of the Evangelical Council for Financial Accountability. Another of the Amsterdam Affirmations says, "We will be faithful stewards of all that God gives us, and will be accountable to others in the finances of our ministry and in reporting our statistics".[23] These are praiseworthy steps. Accountability to the Church as the wider body of Christ is laudable, though in America it was the civil courts that eventually had to deal with the recent misdeeds of televangelists. Transparent honesty needs to go deeper than the handling of finance and statistics. We must also be accountable for how we handle people and how we handle God's word.

Again Jesus is our model of the transparently open, honest, and sincere evangelist. He abhorred people coming to him under false pretences.[24] No guile was found in his mouth. Paul stood in the tradition of Jesus against some people who "peddled the word of God for profit". "In Christ, we speak before God with sincerity, like men sent from God"[25] having "renounced secret and shameful ways, we do not use deception, nor do we distort the word of God. On the contrary, by setting forth the truth plainly, we commend ourselves to everyone's conscience in the sight of God".[26] A recovery of principle is needed today. We will each need a readiness to be accountable to one another as we are accountable before God. These essential characteristics of Christian evangelism, as taught and modelled by the Lord who sent us, must be seen in all we do. Nothing less complies with the intentions of God the Evangelist.

Conclusion

The purpose of VISION New Zealand is to mobilize the Church in the re-evangelization of New Zealand. It is a new and changed New Zealand. It will need new and changed forms of evangelism. Our present methods sometimes bear little resemblance to the ways or words of Jesus. The above guidelines are offered as a measure for judging present methods, and as principles for shaping new ones.

FOOTNOTES
[1] Marshall McLuhan, *The Medium is the Message*, (New York: Random House, 1967).
[2] Discussed by H.S. Stout in *The Divine Dramatist: George Whitefield and the Rise of Modern Evangelicalism*, (Grand Rapids: Eerdmans, 1991) pages 206ff.
[3] The key verses are John 1:13, 3:5, James 1:18, 1 Peter 1:3, 23, 1 John 3:9.
[4] Acts 10:47-48.
[5] John 3:24.
[6] Mark 1:14.
[7] Mark 1:17.

8 Tabernacles, John 7:31. Dedication, John 10:24, 41. Passover, John 12:12, Luke 19:47-48.

9 Luke 8:1, 4-15.

10 Matthew 13:19-23.

11 The KJV translated the active verb in Matthew 18:3 as the passive "unless you be converted". It would have been better to have rendered it "unless you convert", or as it is rendered in more modern terms, "unless you turn" (RSV) and "unless you change" (NIV), which captures the active human responsibility involved.

12 Popularized through the writings of James F. Engel in books like *What's Gone Wrong with the Harvest?* (with H. Wilbert Norton, Grand Rapids: Zondervan, 1975) and *Contemporary Christian Communications* (Nashville: Nelson, 1979).

13 Michael Green, *Evangelism Through the Local Church*, (London: Hodder, 1991) page 247.

14 Joseph C. Aldrich, *Lifestyle Evangelism*, (Portland: Multnomah Press, 1981).

15 Slightly adapted from Aldrich, pages 88-89.

16 John 18:20.

17 Acts 2:46, 5:42.

18 Acts 17:17, 20:20.

19 "Information Bulletin No. 19" (Wheaton: Lausanne Committee on World Evangelization, June 1980).

20 *Craccum* (Auckland: Auckland University Students' Association, 2 April 1990) page 10.

21 Billy Graham, *A Biblical Standard For Evangelists*, a commentary on the 15 Affirmations made by participants at the International Conference for Itinerant Evangelists in Amsterdam, Netherlands, July 1983 (Minneapolis: Worldwide, 1984) page 57.

22 Ibid.

23 Ibid., page 89.

24 Luke 9:57, 14:25ff.

25 2 Corinthians 2:17.

26 2 Corinthians 4:2.

11

Bridging Where Society Hurts

by Brian Hathaway

Graham has been unemployed for 18 months and is the father of two pre-school children. He and his wife are struggling to make ends meet. Some of their furniture has been repossessed and Housing Corporation has been on their backs about their mortgage. They approach a budgeting agency for help and Dawn visits their home. They wrestle with hard decisions about what to go without to make the money cover their outgoings. A local church gives them an interest free loan to enable them to repay high interest credit card spendings. One morning Dawn arrives at their doorstep and asks Graham to come with her to a local Christian Medical Centre where there is a supply of emergency food. There on the table is a box overflowing with nutritious groceries and vegetables. She hands the box to Graham. He takes it home, places it on their kitchen table, and bursts into tears. "I didn't think there were people who cared like this," he sobs. Within a few weeks Graham and his family commence attending the local church who had offered this care and love.

Peter and Jill are waiting at the bus stop after shopping in the city. They start a conversation with Ling, a Chinese woman waiting for the same bus. Ling arrived in New Zealand from Singapore four weeks ago and is very lonely. They talk together as they travel home. Jill is also Chinese from Singapore and so they have a lot in common. As they part they exchange telephone numbers. Later that week Peter and Jill telephone Ling and arrange to take her sightseeing and out for a meal. A friendship develops. Ling starts asking questions about why Peter and Jill have shown such a love for her. They explain they are Christians and share their faith in Christ. Ling is a lapsed Buddhist and asks many questions. She starts to read the Bible and gradually the truth about Christ dawns. Peter and Jill have the privilege of seeing her come to faith in Christ. Later she returns to Singapore and shares her faith with her family.

Barbara is a sales representative for a greeting card company. She visits a regular client at a Christian craft and book shop. Barbara's brother is very sick and Joyce, who manages the shop, spends some time talking with her and offers to pray for her brother. Barbara is not a Christian but agrees. They bow their heads and Joyce prays both for Barbara and her brother. At the end of the brief prayer Joyce notices there are tears in Barbara's eyes. Some weeks later Barbara visits the shop again and tells Joyce that her brother improved dramatically after her prayer. They talk further about Christian faith. The dialogue continues.

Rangi is a street kid. Well, he is on the streets when the weather is favourable, but he returns home during the winter months. One day he walks into a small T-shirt shop in the city. He knows there is something different about this shop; many of his friends have been talking about it. The people in the shop welcome the shy Maori lad and invite him to have a meal with them. He comes back the following week and the week after, never staying long, just enjoying the hospitality. One evening the shop owners invite him to come to their home. To Rangi's surprise there are several street kids staying in this house. The home owners invite him to stay and he accepts the offer. They do strange things like praying at meals, singing with guitars around the fire and talking about God's power to break habits such as drug addiction and alcoholism. Soon Rangi puts his trust in Christ. As the years roll by he becomes involved helping other street kids come to Christ. He even goes to Hong Kong for three months and works with drug addicts there.

Each of the above reconstructions illustrate one simple fact: ministering God's love and care to people in need regularly creates opportunities to share about Christ. Sensitivity and patience are called for, and opportunities must be grasped when they occur. Many New Zealand churches are seeking to bridge where society hurts by creating relevant caring ministries for their communities. We must recognise the dignity, worth and value of each human being and seek to minister in love to their needs. At the same time we must also be prepared to bring the message of hope in Christ.

> Billy Graham, commenting on his goals for a 1992 crusade in Philadelphia USA said, "There has been a change in our ministry. I think we have broadened it. Not only is there a vertical dimension in our ministry in calling people to receive Christ but there is also a horizontal dimension in that we are addressing the social and physical needs of people as well." He then outlined plans to provide practical assistance to homeless in the area.[1]

Evangelism and the Whole Gospel

If the gospel is really what we claim it is, it should impact and affect all aspects of an individual's life and all areas of our society. Human beings are not just souls that need saving; they are people with emotions and relationships which need restoring, bodies which often need healing, finances which may need sorting out, and minds which require a new perspective from which to view life.

Sin has penetrated the whole human race. It has penetrated all systems, structures and relationships established by men and women. It has penetrated our financial systems, educational systems, social systems, our media, arts and political systems. If sin has gone this far then God's saving and healing grace must be capable of reaching to a similar extent. God's intention is to reverse all the consequences of the Fall.

We need to return to the life of Jesus to see his integrated approach of feeding and healing both body and soul with no apparent dichotomy or sense of strain. In the ministry of Christ on earth we see him coming against all the evidences of sin: disease, death, hunger, demonic activity, separation from God, discrimination and spoiled human relationships. At his death he destroyed the power of sin and Satan, thus ensuring the ultimate goal of the Father: to restore to his Son everything that sin and Satan has damaged.[2] An understanding of the present yet incomplete kingdom of God on earth leads us to the conclusion that this process of restoration has started now, and as followers of Christ we are called to engage in it just as Christ did.

Thus evangelism is the good news that God is committed to reconciling everything to his Son and undoing all the effects of sin on this planet. The good news is that sin, disease, discrimination, death and oppression are never the last word. Jesus is Lord and King. He brings forgiveness, healing, dignity, life and release. Evangelism must not be seen just as the bringing of women, men and young people to saving faith in and obedience to Jesus Christ. This is only part of the good news. The implications of the work of Christ are much more than personal salvation from sin and obtaining eternal life.

> Why is Mother Teresa one of the most respected Christians to the non-Christian world? Is it that her form of Christianity is credible? Is credibility a factor in effective evangelism?

People to Whom Jesus Ministered

The mandate for the ministry of Jesus is found in Luke 4:18-19. He had been anointed by the Holy Spirit at his baptism in Jordan and had confronted Satan in the wilderness. Then he entered the synagogue in Nazareth to read Isaiah's messianic prophecy: "The Spirit of the Lord is on me, because he has anointed me to preach good news to the poor. He has sent me to proclaim freedom for the prisoners and recovery of sight for the blind, to release the oppressed, to proclaim the year of the Lord's favour."

His evangelism was in the power of the Spirit, to the poor, those who had no work and had to beg. His proclamation was freedom to prisoners: those in prison for conscience sake or debt, recovery of sight: an essential faculty for employment in those days, and release for the oppressed: those down-trodden or broken by the calamities and the circumstances of life. Clearly the evangelism in which Jesus engaged was in words, in deeds, and in the evidence and power of the Holy Spirit (signs).

For some in Jesus' day, the starting point for understanding the good news may have been through his spoken word. For others it might have been his compassionate deeds. For still others it may have been through a power encounter as he stretched out his hand to heal sickness or deliver from demonic oppression. The good news is that Jesus is Lord over all human philosophies, all human need and all spiritual oppression.

Neither signs nor deeds explain the gospel by themselves. They need the word of explanation. Faith is ignited in the human heart by words. People cannot believe in someone about whom they have not heard, and they cannot hear unless they are told. "Faith comes by hearing and hearing by the word of God."[3] But nor do words by themselves demonstrate the gospel. Words need to have flesh on them, they need to be incarnated just as Christ became the incarnate word. He is the model and example when it comes to evangelism.　Words need to be validated and demonstrated by deeds and signs.

The New Testament writers use an interesting Greek word to describe how Jesus felt about people in need: the word splanchnizomai.　It literally means 'to be moved in your stomach'. It can be translated as 'to yearn with compassion'.　This word is used twelve times in the New Testament.　Eight of these instances record how Jesus felt when faced with those displaying physical needs.　In each of these cases[4] he reaches out and meets those physical needs: healing the lepers, the blind, an epileptic, feeding the 4,000, the 5,000, or raising a widow's son.　Three times this word is used by him in parables[5], where he describes the responses of people to human need: the master to a servant in debt, the good Samaritan to the injured man at the side of the road, and the father as his prodigal son returns.　Only once is it used when Jesus responded by teaching and preaching.[6]

For many of us from evangelical, pentecostal or charismatic backgrounds (EPC) our compassion for the needs of people has often been shown primarily by a response of preaching to them. Should anyone misunderstand this point I hasten to add that such a response is not wrong, it is just incomplete.　In Acts 6, the preaching and prayers of the apostles needed supplementing by ministries of serving and caring.

The New Testament indicates that Jesus ministered to a wide range of people.　Many of these came from the lower socio-economic end of the society of the 1st century.　As we examine the categories of people to whom Jesus ministered, we see most of these represented in our New Zealand society today (see Table 1).

Table 1 : Categories of People to Whom Jesus Ministered

Category	Jesus Ministry	NZ Society Today
Sick	Menstrual problem Fever Epilepsy	Sick
Disabled	Deaf) Blind) Crippled) Lame) Paralysed) Dumb)	Invalids Elderly Disabled Handicapped
Economically poor	Beggars	Unemployed
Children	Luke 18:15	Child abuse Abortion
Women (widows)	Luke 8:1-4, 8:43	Abused women Solo mothers
Different culture	Greek woman	Alien/Refugee
Different religion	Samaritan	Hindu, New Ager, etc.
Different politically	Roman	Any oppressive power
Social outcasts	Prostitutes Tax collectors Lepers Criminals Demonized	Sexual deviancy Radicals/gangs Aids victims Those in prison Psychiatric care & deliverance

To these people Jesus was the good news in flesh. He loved them, he showed compassion to them, he taught them about God. He went to where they were and ministered out of who he was, giving what he had. We also need to minister to people out of who God has made us and what he has given us. It may be sobering for us to ask the question, "If Jesus was in New Zealand today how would he evangelize and to whom would he go?" The answer to this question must be a key to the re-evangelization of New Zealand in this decade.

It seemed quite legitimate for Jesus to teach, preach, heal bodies, restore sight, raise the dead, set the demonized free and feed the hungry, without having to demand or expect that people follow him or obey his teachings. In fact he clearly taught that we should "let our light shine before men, that they may see our good deeds and glorify our Father in heaven."[7] Good deeds are legitimate in their own right. They glorify the Father and are an evidence that the good news of God's love for a fallen and fractured humanity has indeed broken into human society.

Christians sometimes worry about being 'ripped off' by those they are seeking to help. No doubt this happens from time to time. Maybe it also happened for Jesus. How many people took what he gave just to satisfy their own somewhat self-centred needs, without even stopping to return thanks? He healed ten lepers and only one returned to thank him.

> A Vineyard Church in Cincinnati, USA (Vineyard churches are associated with John Wimber and his Signs and Wonders ministry) is heavily involved in ministering to the practical needs of people and has grown from 35 to 1,600 in six years.[8]

The New Zealand Scene

As we survey the New Zealand scene in the 1990s what do we see? In a word, almost unlimited opportunities to convey the truth, love and power of Christ to people around us. We have a government committed to decentralization, thrusting responsibility for a wide range of activities back into local communities. We have financial policies that are cutting budgets and creating turmoil among those dependent on government money to survive. We have disintegration of the family as we have known it. We have escalation of violence with many people becoming the victims of wanton crime. We have sexual perversion and promiscuity being blatantly offered as alternative life styles. We have mounting problems with drug dependency. We have unemployment standing at 11% of the total work-force. We have businesses failing and mortgagee sales of family homes.

Such events in society create many human needs. Every human need is a bridgehead for the gospel of Jesus Christ presented in truth (words), love (deeds) and power (signs). We will now examine some of these opportunities.

> **Why has it been acceptable for Western missionaries to the Third World to minister to the practical needs of people but not for churches located in the Western world that send them?**

Opportunities

Abortion. With one abortion for every six pregnancies in this country there are opportunities to counsel those considering abortion and those who have had a child aborted. Demonstrations outside abortion clinics may have a place, but Christians must be careful not to be seen as those who only criticize on social issues. They need to roll up their sleeves and actively become part of the process of healing and restoration for those being destroyed by our society.

AIDS. AIDS is on the increase around the world with little immediate hope of a permanent cure. The Church should be involved in the area of support for victims and their families.

Christian groups in the UK have been to the forefront in AIDS education and support.

Budgeting. With so many people facing major financial worries, many churches are offering budgeting advice or encouraging their people to be trained and join reputable budgeting agencies. Some churches are linking budgeting advice to monetary loans or the provision of food. In these ways they seek to help remedy what is often the source of the need, financial mismanagement, while also recognizing that many who are poor are good managers, yet lack adequate resources.

Business mentors. Individuals often have ideas for creating work or developing small businesses but they may lack the skills to get them up and running. There is an opportunity here for successful Christian business people to offer their advice, expertize and experience in helping others establish themselves in business enterprises. Groups of Christians could provide interest free loans to help such endeavours get underway.

Child abuse. "Recent figures point to disturbing increases in Pakeha, Maori, and Pacific Island communities."[9] The number of reported cases of child abuse has jumped by 133% in the past 5 years, from 10,663 in 1988 to 24,861 for the year to June 1992.[10] This symptom of familes in need signals an opportunity for Christian care by individuals at the neighbourly level, and by churches caring for families in their communities.

Clothing. Opportunity shops providing second-hand clothing have long been a way for church groups to minister within a local community. Some churches run clothing exchanges or swap meets.

Citizens' Advice Bureaus and Community Houses are places where Christians can make a valuable contribution in serving those within their community.

Drug and alcohol support are areas where specialist help is often required. Churches should set people apart for this and encourage them to receive the training they need. Christians involved in Alcoholics Anonymous have many opportunities to point people to a source higher than themselves as they seek to overcome their addiction.

Elderly. Those aged 60 and over currently make up 15.4% of our total population and this percentage is rising. Many rest homes have been established by denominational groups. The 60s plus programme offers opportunities for those with the right caring skills to offer practical help to older people.

Family needs. Many family needs are apparent in our local communities. Christians have an enormous number of opportunities to share sound Christian principles as we build genuine caring relationships, and as we offer seminars, videos, parenting courses and retreats, counselling, support groups and good books. Churches should be aware of the opportunity to donate good books on family issues to their local libraries.

Pressures on young families. Young mothers always need support with the heavy loads they face in their home responsibilities. Those with experience could offer training and guidance to first-time mothers, thus sharing their skills, insights and practical support.

Pre-marriage and marriage counselling, and marriage enrichment offer openings to care, and to share positive Christian values.

Parent-teenage strife occurs in the best of families and sometimes for no apparent reason. Both parents and teenagers need support, advice and encouragement. Many Christians have attended Tough Love groups, and learnt how to blend faith and works in such situations.

Solo parents have their own particular needs. Churches need to be aware of the needs of both the solo parent and child/

children, and to look for opportunities to relieve the pressure on the parent and provide role-models for children.

Reconstituted families have their unique strains. Those in the church who have successfully surmounted this situation have a lot to offer those struggling with the difficulties and challenges it presents.

Finance. Several churches are now offering interest free loans to those with genuine financial needs. Others have paid debts for those imprisoned through failure to pay their own small debts. Some Christian groups are establishing interest-free societies to help people get free of home mortgages. The Christian Church in New Zealand has incredible resources when it comes to finance. We have not yet realized the full potential of this resource to help either members of our own Christian communities or those in the wider community. Christ's words to "turn worldly wealth to our advantage thus gaining friends who will welcome us into eternal dwellings"[11] offer an evangelistic tool that the Church by and large has yet to discover.

Food and meals. Many people in our communities worry about where their next meal will come from. Children go to school without beakfast and have very little for lunch. Churches have long been involved in providing soup kitchens and food banks. Others have been working with schools to provide lunches for needy children. Some Christian care centres have frozen meals available to take to a solo parent who is forced to go home to bed because of illness. Meals-on-wheels have been offered to the elderly and shut-ins.

Grief counselling. At the death of loved ones or friends many people are prepared to question and consider life's values. There is greater sensitivity to spiritual matters and often recognition that much of what our society counts as valuable is empty and transient.

At such times skilled Christian grief counsellors can have opportunity to care for and support grieving people.

Handicapped people. Various groups seek to help both the handicapped and those who care for them. Some churches have been exploring the provision of help in areas such as transport, relief for caregivers, and support groups for the handicapped.

Health needs. With the changes in our medical benefits and moves towards increased charges for doctors' visits, prescriptions, and time in hospital, many lower-income people are unable to receive sufficient care. Some churches are seeking to provide help for people in these situations. Christian health practices are springing up around the country. These provide an opportunity to offer support for a wide variety of needs. Many of the medical problems treated by general practitioners and other health professionals have deeper roots. Christian care and counselling may be able to address these roots. There are opportunities today for teams of skilled Christian people to support Christian health practitioners and provide a pool of resources they can draw on.

"We affirm God is both Creator and Judge of all men. We should share his concern for justice and reconciliation throughout human society... We express penitence both for our neglect and for having sometimes regarded evangelism and social concern as mutually exclusive. Although reconciliation with man is not reconciliation with God, nor is social action evangelism, nor is political liberation salvation, nevertheless we affirm that evangelism and socio-political involvement are both part of our Christian duty. For both are necessary expressions of our doctrines of God and man, our love for our neighbour and our obedience to Jesus Christ."[12]

Holiday periods can increase stress on families, especially families with solo parents. Many families are unable to get away for a break for financial reasons. Many innovative ideas are being explored by churches throughout our country. Events and ideas are being tried such as kids' holiday clubs and children's programmes, community family Christmas parties (one church ran such an event in a local supermarket carpark), families sharing their Christmas dinners with lonely people, several families sharing resources and going on holiday together (which is especially helpful for solo parents), financial provision for stressed people to enjoy a vacation, and many others.

Home and property needs can become a major source of stress for the differently abled, the sick, the elderly and the solo mother. At least one church has a team of young people who give Saturday mornings to help in such basic areas. Retired people with practical skills have an important part to play here. Teams of Christian unemployed people could use some of their time to cover basic needs for such people.

Housing. Particularly in the cities, housing has become a major source of concern. With cuts in benefits and high rentals many people are facing housing pressures. Some churches run emergency accommodation. Some have safe homes for abused women. Some Christians have been exploring the cooperative building of low-cost homes.

Hot lines. There are numerous telephone personal help or referral services offered around our country. Many of these are run by churches and provide emergency support and counselling. One of the best known is Lifeline. Such services require people who are available to receive calls, offering an opportunity for Christians who have the necessary skills.

Life skills. In these days many young people have no training or modelling from their parents in some of the basic life skills.

Churches could provide training in such areas as the preparation of simple nutritious inexpensive meals, simple home medical care, and other basics. Many other opportunities exist here.

Lonely and shut-ins. Some churches offer drop-in centres or care centres as a way of providing some social interaction for lonely people. The provision of church buildings for such services usefully employs the millions of dollars the Church has invested in its buildings, for the benefit of those living around them. Other groups hire neutral buildings for such support groups.

Overseas students face tensions as they settle into a new culture and environment. Some churches have effective ministries with them through offering homestay, private board, English tutoring, and social interaction. To send overseas students back to their own people with the gospel of Jesus Christ must be regarded as a successful evangelism strategy

Pre-school. Many churches now offer pre-school facilities. These range from registered kindergartens to occasional get-togethers of mothers who have pre-schoolers. Other variations on the theme include day-care centres for children of working mothers, baby-sitting services, and pre-schoolers' music groups. In some churches play groups are very fruitfully linked with the provision of Christian parenting courses.

Prison ministry is well-established in New Zealand and around the world, providing many opportunities for Christian service.

Psychiatric patients. With the decision by health authorities to place such people back into local communities the question must be asked, "Who will look after their special needs?" Obviously this is not an area that churches should rush into without adequate numbers of skilled people, though most ex-psychiatric patients have more normal than abnormal needs. Many ordinary caring church communities are ideal for providing non-dependent support systems.

Refugees. Much of the responsibility for the integration of immigrants into our society has been accepted by church groups. By offering help with language, employment, housing, our systems such as banking and schooling, and adjustment to a different culture, Christians can build bridges of love and support.

School boards of trustees. With the devolution of centralized control of our education system, boards of trustees have been given considerable autonomy. For those with the interest and skills, being a member of a BOT offers many opportunities to serve children and families in our local communities.

Sexual abuse. Counselling and support in this area quite clearly requires considerable expertize and should not be entered into lightly. The hurt, anger and brokenness that sexual abuse produces in victims requires a lot of skill, wisdom, love and patience on behalf of the one seeking to help the victim. It is not an area for well-meaning Christians with glib answers or instant cures. It is encouraging to see a number of Christian counsellors around New Zealand becoming skilled in this area.

> "We believe that the kingdom of God affects the whole of a person's being. Therefore we are concerned about physical, cultural, social, spiritual, intellectual and emotional wholeness in human lives.

> "We believe that the kingdom of God addresses all the needs that women and men experience. Therefore we are concerned to minister to the needs of: the rich and the poor, the imprisoned and the free, the oppressor and the oppressed, the over-fed and the hungry, as well as all others in need.

"We believe we must respond to all people in need, especially sisters and brothers in the kingdom of God. Therefore we will give from our material abundance to assist the economic and spiritual transformation of the lives of people in poverty in other parts of the world."[13]

Sexual deviancy. This is another area where considerable expertize and experience is necessary.

Transport. Our mobile society often demands we travel considerable distances to receive essential services. Many people require help with transport. There are opportunities for ministry here but financial costs need to be considered and covered. A group of local churches could fund a retired person willing to offer such a service to the local community.

Unemployment. With 11% of our total work-force unemployed, and decline in this figure likely to be negligible or small over the next few years, unemployment will continue to create many problems in our society. In the past churches have been heavily involved seeking to provide work opportunities for people. Many employment programmes have been funded by the Government and much good has been done. With cut-backs in Government spending the rug unfortunately has been pulled from under some excellent schemes. There are churches that have attained New Zealand Qualification Authority standards and commenced the new "Training Opportunities" programmes. One challenge for the Church is to free up the finance in its own control to support and train those who are unemployed.

Victim support. This service is modelled on similar support networks operating overseas and provides support for victims of crime. The police are training citizens for it.

Youth at risk. Young people are found in many of the above-mentioned categories. Youth are the future New Zealand. Time and effort put into seeking to support and help those at risk may prevent lifetime habits and lifestyles becoming established in early years. Many groups within our society seek to cater for youth, and churches have traditionally been to the fore in this area.

Some Cooperative Responses

In these areas of social concern, there are some significant developments occurring around New Zealand. In some regions churches are cooperating to provide care for people in their communities, rationalizing the provision of support and removing competition between local congregations. These are healthy signs.

In one area about 40 churches cooperated to produce booklets listing all of the support services they offered to the community. They covered the cost of publication and distributed these to government departments, schools, doctors' surgeries, community groups, Citizens' Advice Bureaus and other agencies.

Another significant recent development has been the establishment of Christian Love Link in at least 15 local communities, involving a total of over 350 churches. Christian Love Link's primary goal is to link people in need with caring people from local churches. It coordinates the combined resources of groups of churches, and relates positively with local welfare agencies to identify unmet needs and seek ways of meeting those needs. A group of churches sets up a clearing house to field and screen calls from people within the community requiring help. These calls are then redirected to people from local churches who can provide the help required.

Industrial chaplaincy also offers many openings for Christians to support those in the work-place. Chaplains are recruited from the churches and trained to care and counsel those requiring help.

Christians can achieve a measure of unity by a combined commitment to minister to the needs in our communities. Surely this will speak much more to the non-church community than all of our best schemes to promote church unity through doctrine or liturgy.[14]

How do people see the love of Jesus unless we care?

Priorities for Care

There is little point in churches being involved in the care of those within their local communities if they do not care for their own members first. Essentially local congregations are designed by God to be communities of love, care and mutual support. It is God's intention that his people become colonies of heaven reflecting the values and lifestyle of his kingdom.

Many of the regulations given to the nation of Israel at its formation indicate that God's desire was that his people should be notably different from the surrounding nations. The 1st century church was known for its love and care of its members. It may be that the greatest miracle of the early chapters of Acts was not the 3,000 converted on the day of Pentecost, nor the speaking in tongues or miracles of the Apostles. Perhaps it was the way the early church cared for its own. There was no needy person among them. They sold property and gave the money to the church leaders for this purpose. This touched the early Christians in the area of their possessions and cut right across their self-centredness, truly a miracle.

The Biblical record is clear. We must care for the members of our biological family first.[15] Then we care for those of our church family.[16] Then for those of our world family: "Let us do good to all people, especially to those who belong to the family of believers."[17]

The Cost

It would be wrong to leave a topic such as this without commenting on the cost of providing caring ministries. Much of what Christians do in seeking to bridge into a local community is activity of the 'seed sowing' or 'salting' variety. The effect of this is often difficult to measure. Most of the time it is neither very glamorous nor high-profile. Many EPCs reared on principles of church growth, and living in a society that puts a premium on measurable goals, feel the need to measure what they are doing in terms of numbers and results. This is especially so if they think of what they are doing from a narrow understanding of evangelism.

We possess only three commodities in life. These are time, abilities (skills and gifts), and physical resources (money and possessions). Jesus depicted the Good Samaritan using these three commodities to help the man lying in the gutter, and said this is what it means to "Love your neighbour as yourself."[18] To minister to those in need in our communities will involve us in using all three of these commodities. This will mean cost and commitment.

Those considering establishing caring ministries must consider this cost carefully. It is counter-productive to commence such ministries only to have them collapse through lack of commitment or resources. Church leaders need to provide adequate care, support, and opportunities for rest and relaxation for those involved in helping others. With mounting pressure and need around us in society, stress levels and burn-out may take their toll on those seeking to help others.

FURTHER READING
Joseph Aldrich, *Lifestyle Evangelism*, (Portland, Oregon: Multnomah Press, 1981)
Fran Beckett, *Called to Action*, (London: Collins Fount, 1989)
Larry Christenson, *A Charismatic Approach to Social Action*, (Minneapolis: Bethany Fellowship, 1974)
Evangelical Fellowship of New Zealand, *Kingdom Manifesto*, (Auckland, 1988)
Consultation of the Evangelical Fellowship of New Zealand, *Findings of the Theological Commission*, (Auckland, January 1987)
Evangelism and Social Responsibility, (Grand Rapids; CRESR, 1982)
Brian Hathaway, *Beyond Renewal the Kingdom of God*, (UK: Word, 1990)
Bruce J. Nicholls, (ed.), *In Word and Deed*, (UK: Paternoster Press, 1985)

John Perkins, *With Justice for All*, (Ventura: Regal Books, 1982)
Richard Randerson, *Hearts and Minds*, (Wellington: SRC, 1992)
Howard A Snyder, *A Kingdom Manifesto*, (Downers Grove, Ill.: IVP, 1985)
John Steward, *Where God, People and Deeds Connect*, (Melbourne: World Vision Australia, 1990)

FOOTNOTES

[1] *Challenge Weekly*, Auckland, 2 July, 1992.
[2] Colossians 1.
[3] Romans 10:14-17.
[4] Matthew 9:36, 14:14, 15:32, 20:34, Mark 1:41, 8:2, 9:22, Luke 7:13.
[5] Matthew 18:27, Luke 10:33, 15:20.
[6] Matthew 9:36.
[7] Matthew 5:16.
[8] *Equipping the Saints*, Volume 6, No. 2, Spring 1992.
[9] *New Zealand Herald*, Saturday 17 October 1992.
[10] Ibid., Friday 16 October 1992.
[11] Luke 16:9.
[12] *Lausanne Covenant*, Lausanne Congress for World Evangelization, 1974.
[13] *Kingdom Manifesto*, Evangelical Fellowship in New Zealand, 1988.
[14] The New Zealand Council of Christian Social Services provides a vehicle for common representation of concerns to government and to the community at large.
[15] 1 Timothy 5:8.
[16] 1 John 3:16-18.
[17] Galatians 6:10 (NIV).
[18] Luke 10:27.

12

Who Responds to the Gospel?

by Ray Muller

As a teenager I remember the excitement of being part of a special bus trip to Wellington to hear Billy Graham. We left from my parish church in Wanganui after the early Sunday morning communion service. Some of my friends were persuaded to join us at the last minute, peers for whom I had been praying intensively for some time. The trip was itself an adventure but paled significantly compared with the excitement of being part of the thousands of people who packed Athletic Park that Sunday afternoon. The choir, the music, the message all combined to make the event memorable. The most joyous part of all was watching the people move forward to express their willingness to receive Jesus Christ as their personal Saviour. It began slowly at first but soon momentum built up as the choir sang "Just as I am" and as hundreds of people moved from their seats and out on to the grass in front of the platform. My friend Barry Kissell was beside me and I asked if he wanted to receive Christ He nodded and I went forward with him and there had the joy of leading my friend to Christ. Barry was the first of many.

Has Evangelism Changed?

Many churches are celebrating a Decade of Evangelism and there is wide commitment to it. The proclamation of the gospel is a priority for many Christians, but while the gospel of Jesus Christ remains a message of unchanging good news, the way it is communicated is changing dramatically. No longer can we recreate the halcyon days of the 60s and 70s and expect thousands to turn out to public parks and hear big name speakers. The influences of secularization, materialism and competing ideologies challenge the relevance of the Church and of the Christian faith. It is a different world. Maybe evangelism today has to be different too, if we are to communicate in a relevant way and change the lives of secular people.

While we would all affirm that the Church has an unchanging gospel in a changing world, just how do we communicate the gospel in order to enable people with different perceptions and needs to respond as disciples of Jesus Christ? Is there a change in the reasons and ways in which people respond to Christ in the 1990s compared with earlier years?

This Survey

To help us grapple with these issues a survey was conducted among some 130 churches throughout New Zealand. The churches were chosen by their respective denominational executives as being evangelistically effective. Major urban, provincial urban and rural churches were selected.[1]   People in the congregations of these churches were invited to complete a questionnaire, indicating when and how they came to personal and active commitment as Christians. More than 10,000 questionnaires were completed and from them we selected those who stated they had made a commitment to Christ since 1980. This gave us a sample of 1488 females and 1,208 males, making a total of 2,715 people.[2]

In order to discover whether the trends of the 1990s were different from those of the 1980s, we took 1987 as a pivotal point, comparing 1980-86 with 1987-92. 1987 was chosen not only because it was near the centre of the range of the survey selection but because it was the year of the sharemarket crash, an event which significantly altered New Zealand's economy and lifestyle. Massey

University research has identified changes of attitudes from this year. [3]

In assessing changes in evangelism, some key questions are raised: Are there trends, indicators or hints which can give us direction as we move through the 1990s towards the year 2000? Can we discern the working of the Holy Spirit as we evaluate the ways in which people are responding to Christ today? Are the churches reaching only those who have previously been influenced by a Christian church or are people with no previous religious background becoming Christians?

Religious Backgrounds

QUESTION A: What church did you belong to or attend before your commitment to Christ?

14.3% of the 1980-86 group and 15.7% of the 1987-92 group said that they did not attend any church. Approximately 85% said they did have connections of some sort with a church. Anglican 17%, Presbyterian 14%, Catholic 10%, Baptist 7%, Methodist 6%, Salvation Army 5%, Assembly of God 3%, Apostolic 3%, etc. The range approximates to the national census figures.

We can have two reactions to this. First, we can regret the relatively small percentage of people who have made commitments to Christ who had no previous church background and resolve to find ways of communicating with unchurched people.[4] Secondly, we can note the pre-evangelistic role churches have played in preparing people for a commitment to Christ. This highlights that evangelism is a process and that a person's previous church involvement can contribute to that journey of faith discovery and development.

If previous experience or connection with a church through attendance at worship, Sunday school or youth group is significant and aids the evangelistic process, then the declining numbers of people involved in such activities is cause for concern.[5] The responses in the following table show this declining trend.

	1980-1986		1987-1992	
	None	Some	None	Some
Sunday School	25%	74%	37%	63%
Youth Group	59%	41%	62%	38%
Church Attendance	30%	70%	33%	67%

Turning Points

QUESTION B: Were there any major turning points experienced
in the year before you came to Christ?

Research has shown that people are more open to new values and willing to consider new options for their lives, during periods of transition or stress.[6] A period of transition is a span of time where the normal behaviour patterns of an individual or family are disrupted by some unusual event. These can become turning points which stimulate the process whereby a person is receptive to the forgiveness and new life which is available in Jesus Christ. One research project showed that more than 90% of those who remain within the fellowship of the church following conversion were dissatisfied with their non-religious lifestyle before anyone shared the gospel with them.[7] The support of a sensitive Christian friend or church at such times can provide opportunities for expressing God's love and healing.

The survey offered such major turning points as: move to a new town; major career change; got married; marital conflict; major illness in the family; new child in the family; death in the family; long period of unemployment; separation or divorce; leaving Home; rejection by friends; inner turmoil.

The greatest response was to inner turmoil, followed by moving town, marital conflict, separation/divorce, and death in the family.

The following chart shows the percentages and compares the two groups.

Chart 1 : Major Turning Points

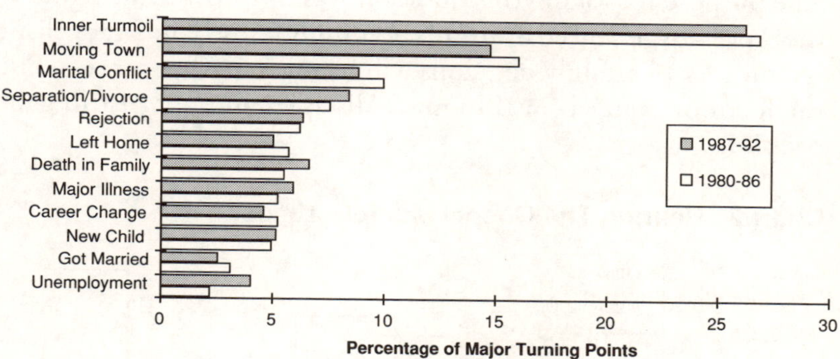

Some significant trends emerge from comparing the two groups. First, each one of these turning points continues in the 1987-92 group. Second, the rating or frequency of each turning point within the two groups remains the same. Third, some of the turning points are increasing in the 1987-92 group at a greater rate than others. For example: while unemployment has a low percentage on the chart numerically, its percentage increase between the pre and post 1987 groups is higher than any other.

Here are the top six indicators which showed an increase between the two groups: Unemployment increased by 78%, death in the family up 20%, major illness up 14%, separation/divorce up 12%, new child up 4%, rejection up 1.5%, inner turmoil went down 2%. All others decreased. These indicators suggest that people and churches who are able to caringly minister in these areas will be able to enrich the lives of people who respond with these needs. The warm support and faith of a caring friend, person to person, will be more welcome than a formal programme from an organized church.

Hearing the Gospel

QUESTION C: How many times had the need for personal
commitment to Christ been explained to you?

The purpose for asking this question was to throw some light on
the process experienced by people becoming Christian. Evangelism
is a process. Certainly decisions will be made in that process, but
the focus of evangelism is to make disciples and not just to gain
decisions.

Chart 2 : Hearing The Gospel Multiple Times

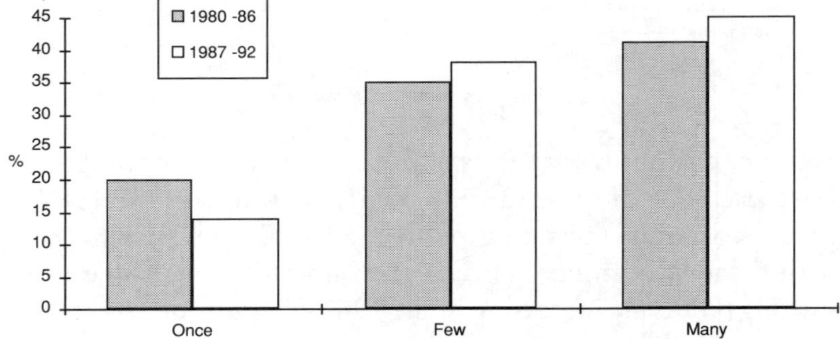

The responses show that while 20% of people in the pre 1986
group said they responded to the gospel on a first hearing or
explanation, only 14% did so in the post 1987 group. This
suggests that the trend in the 90s is for people to weigh up and
consider the implications of what is being presented, before
deciding to respond. This is also supported by the increases among
those who said they heard either a few times or many times before
responding. Those who said they heard several times were 35% in
the pre 1986 group and 38% in the post 1987 group. For many
times, there were 41% in the pre 1986 group and 45% in the post
1987 group. Research has shown that converts who have had
multiple exposures to the gospel are more likely to continue in the
Christian walk than those who have one or few. In an age when
it seems unfashionable to make commitments, especially life-long

commitments, to anything or anyone, it is not surprising that people wish to ponder and consider important life issues raised by the gospel. If commitments to Christ are to be genuine and express true discipleship, it is essential that people should be able to count the cost beforehand.[8]

QUESTION D: From what sources had the need for personal commitment to Christ been explained to you?

The questionnaire offered such possible sources as: in a church service, at an evangelistic meeting, discussion group or short course, radio, television, video or film, a book or other written material, personal explanation. Personal explanation was the most frequent source from which people had commitment to Christ explained to them. This was followed quite closely by in a church service. Both of these rate around 30% and could well interrelate. The third highest was an evangelistic meeting. When comparing the two groups it should be noted that the sources which remain the same or show an increase in the 90s are personal explanation, church services, radio/television/video/film, book or written material. Evangelistic meetings and discussion groups declined as a source.

Chart 3: Personal Explanation is Primary Source

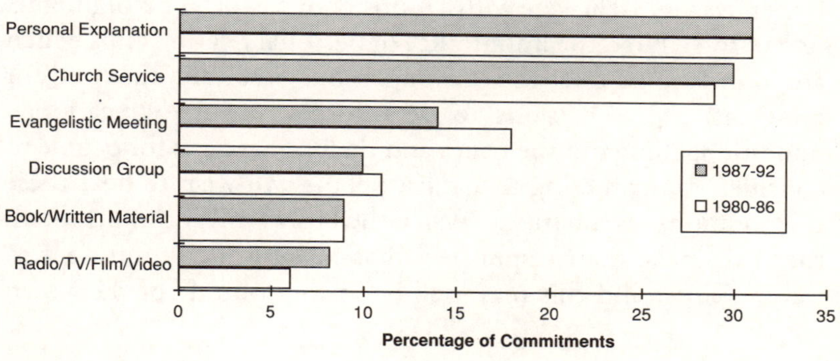

Chart 4 : Location

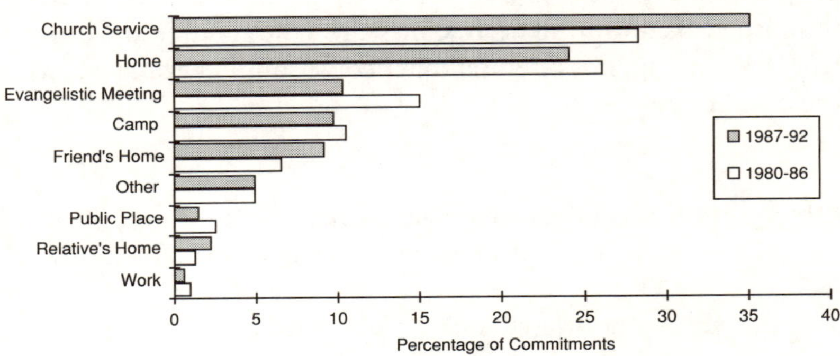

QUESTION E: Where were you when you made your
                        commitment to follow Christ?

In the 1987-92 group, the only three locations which have
increased are a relative's home, a friend's home and church services.
All other places rated less frequently.

QUESTION F: Was anyone with you when you made your
                        commitment to follow Christ?

Of the total survey, 45% indicated that a family member, a friend
or group of friends were present, 25% were alone, 13% were in a
large meeting, 10% were with a minister or pastor. This highlights
two points. First, the importance of personal relationships which
are foundational to effective evangelism. Secondly, the need for
evangelistic presentations to be informative and educational,
honestly spelling out the issues and the implications for people to
consider; remembering that most people will wish to hear these
presentations several times. When the Holy Spirit prompts them,
they can make their responsive steps towards a commitment to
follow Christ and this may well be in the solitude of their own

home. The Holy Spirit is the evangelist. The gift of new life, new birth is a work of the Spirit.

Two areas show an increase in the 1987-92 group. They are friend and group of friends, pastor/minister is slightly up, but the other categories are down. The following chart shows the comparisons.

Chart 5 : Who Was With You?

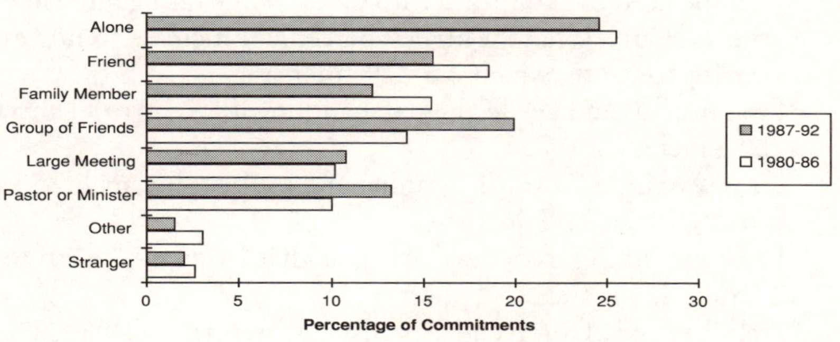

Why do people respond?

QUESTION G : Which phrase best describes why you decided to trust Christ as your Saviour?

"I became convinced about the truth of Christ," was the most frequent reason given for their response. "I was afraid of death without Christ," received the least response.

Here are the phrases ranked in order of frequency from the total survey responses:

I became convinced about the truth of Christ.
I was searching for some meaning and purpose for my life.
I felt the need for a friendship with Jesus.
I saw something in other Christians that I wanted.
I felt the need of forgiveness for my sins.

I was in crisis and needed help in handling it.
I was dissatisfied with my life.
I felt the need to have peace with God.
I was afraid of death without Christ.

The percentages of responses in the two groups are shown on the chart below, but note the five reasons showing an increase in the post 1987 group :

"I felt the need to have peace with God," while rating quite low in the total survey, has the highest percentage increase. It moves from 4% to 7.1%, which is a 77% increase.

"I was in crisis and needed help in handling it," is up to 11.8%, a 53% increase.

"I was searching for some meaning and purpose for my life," is up to 19.1%, a 21% increase.

"I saw something in other Christians that I wanted," is up to 11.2%, a 4% increase.

"I felt the need of forgiveness for my sins," is up to 11.1%, a 2% increase.

These all relate to the major turning points identified above, especially: inner turmoil, marital conflict, separation, divorce, death in the family, which rated so highly. Again, this highlights personal and relational factors in communicating of the gospel.

Chart 6 : Why I Decided to Follow Christ

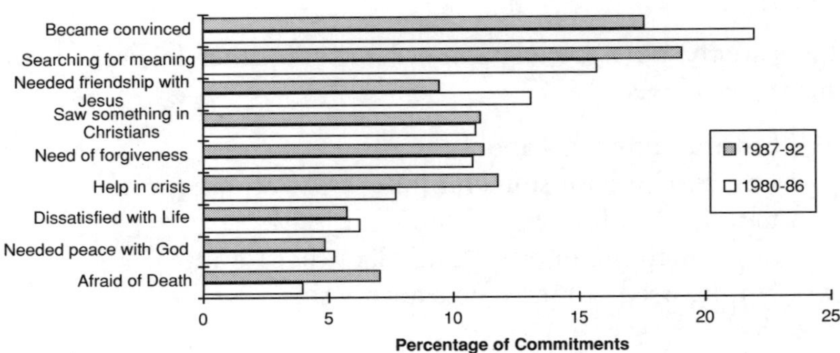

On analysing the responses of those who came from no church background, the following reasons:

> "I became convinced about the truth of Christ,"
> "I was searching for some meaning and purpose in life,"
> "I saw something in other Christians that I wanted," and
> "I was in crisis and needed help in handling it."

These rated more highly than for the total sample or from those with a church background. They are key issues which open doors for the gospel.

It is also gratifying to note that the witness of some Christians is seen as effective and causes others to want it. Communication of the gospel is not a matter of words only, but also of deeds. Show and tell were two commands of Jesus and it is both, not one or the other. John is surely right, "Our love should not be just words and talk; it must be true love, which shows itself in action."[9] Our lives should reflect the love of God we have received. "I cannot hear what you say because I am deafened by what you are," is a serious judgement. The caring actions of Christians and churches in response to human need give credibility to the gospel we seek to proclaim.

Primary Influence on Commitment

Seeking to evaluate the amount of influence that various factors, programmes or people have as part of the evangelistic process enables us to further determine effectiveness. In comparing the main influences in the two groups, trends again emerge. The greatest percentage increase was for friends, up 9.3%.

An analysis of those who had no church background clearly shows that friendship was the primary influence in them deciding to become Christian. It is highly significant that friends were rated as being almost twice as influential as any other person or factor.

The friendship factor cannot be underestimated. Both as a means for sharing faith and for seeing the new convert become a mature disciple in the fellowship of the local church, friendship and personal relationships are paramount. Those who continue in the church have established significant contacts before their conversion and also developed significant friendships within the church following their conversion.

In contrast to the friendship factor, crusades showed a major 41% decline in influence, as did non-church or para-church ministries with a 16% decline in influence. Many people who indicated Christian literature in the survey, made a particular note in the margin that the Bible had been a major influence. Church programme can mean a range and variety of things from an organized evangelism programme to a caring or social programme.

Chart 7 : Friends and Family are Primary Influence

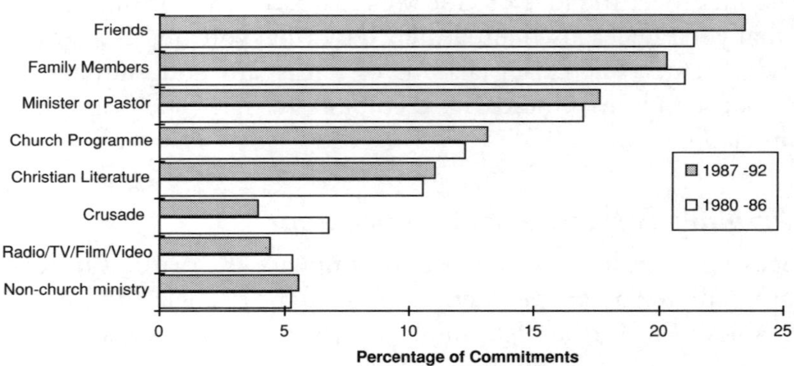

**Chart 8 : Friends Continue as Primary Influence in
1987-92 Group**

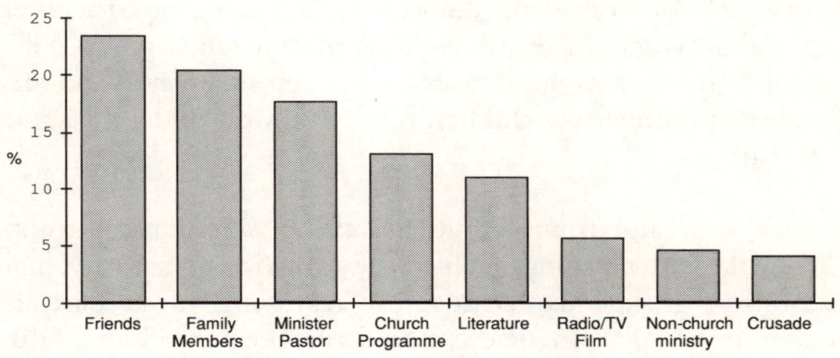

Age When Coming to Commitment to Christ

The data on the age of people when they make a commitment to
actively follow Christ, shows little difference between the two
groups . The 1980-86 group showed a peak at age 15 years and the
1987-92 group peaked a little later at between 16 to 19 years.
Those making commitments in the 30-35 year age group were
slightly more in the latter group too, otherwise the profiles are
almost the same. For this reason, the chart shows the profile of ages
for the total sample and is not separated into groups.

Chart 9 : Age When Coming to Christ

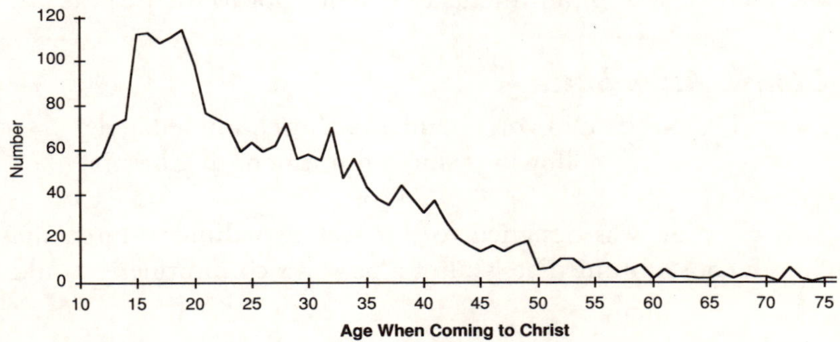

The ages which stand out above all others as the most responsive, are those in the 15 to 20 year age group. The majority of those who made commitments to Christ were aged between 15 and 40 years and were 65% of the total. Almost half, 48.2%, were aged between 15 and 30 years of age and are a significant target group. The numbers decrease as age increases. 7% of those surveyed said they made commitments as children when they were under the age of 10 years.

Older teens and young adults are clearly a responsive group. Wrestling with meaning and life issues, growing to maturity, high mobility, gregarious friendships, searching for a partner, determining a place in society, considering the purpose and future of the world, these and similar issues for this age group, highlight the stressful periods of change which we identified in the major turning points above. Evangelistic effectiveness will be enhanced as churches and individuals build on responsiveness to these issues of this age group.

What about the age groups that are not well represented and would appear to be less responsive? It is vital that ways are found of empowering Christians in those groups to reach out in an intentional way to the networks of relationships around them. Sharing the gospel may not be easy in those circles, but ways must be found; they must not be overlooked or ignored.[10] Pastors and chaplains note that elderly and terminally ill people do have time to reflect and many make commitments to Christ prior to their death.

Church Attendance

QUESTION H: Did you attend any church immediately following your commitment to Christ?

This question was designed to discover two things. First, the church chosen immediately after a person's commitment would probably show a preference based on either their personal experience or their background. Secondly, it could also show which churches are being evangelistically effective. Making a comparision between the 1980-86 group and those in the 1987-92 group helps to highlight that.

Chart 10 : Church Attended Following Commitment to Christ

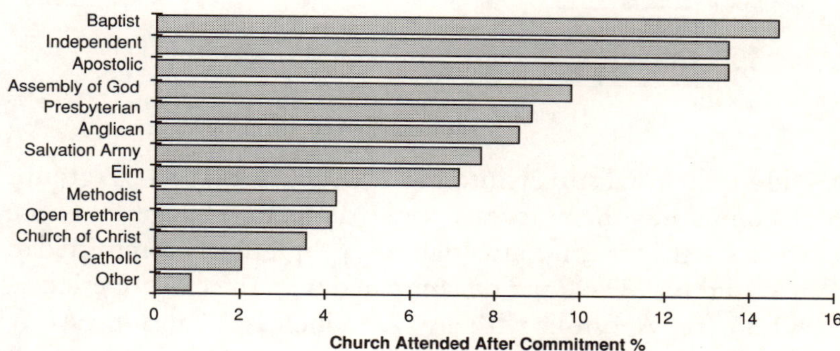

This chart of total survey responses speaks for itself and needs little comment. The Baptist church has the highest response, followed by Independent Pentecostal churches, and the Apostolic church. A second group consisting of Assembly of God, Presbyterian, Anglican, Salvation Army and Elim churches are next with a close range of between 9% and 7% of the responses. The third group of Methodist, Open Brethren and Church of Christ churches are around 4%.[11]

**Chart 11 : Church Attended Following Commitment to Christ
Comparison of 1980-86 and 1987-92**

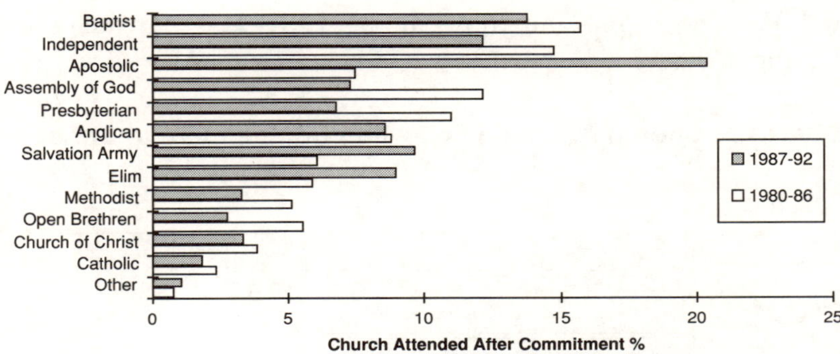

Dividing the total survey into the 1980-86 and 1987-92 groups and comparing them reveals some dramatic changes. Those churches with increasing attendance of people newly committed to Christ in the 1987-92 period compared with the earlier period of 1980-86 are: Apostolic with an 172% increase, Salvation Army with a 59% increase, Elim with a 52% increase, and Other with a 37% increase.

The churches which show a decline in this factor in the 1987-92 period compared with the earlier period of 1980-86 are: Anglican with a 2% decline, Baptist 12%, Church of Christ 12%, Independent Pentecostal 17%, Catholic 20%, Methodist 36%, Presbyterian 38%, Assembly of God 40%, Open Brethren 50%.

While this comparison does not exactly measure evangelistic effectiveness, it does give an indication of a church's evangelistic influence at least as it is perceived by those responding to the survey. It is not possible without further analysis to say whether these people are still attending these churches. However, this comparison does provide indications of trends as it has in the previous charts.[12]

Conclusion

The survey of 2,700 people who have made commitments to Jesus Christ since 1980 have highlighted a number of features concerning Pakeha church life and evangelism in Aotearoa New Zealand. It shows us that the highest percentage of those who made commitments had either an Anglican church background or no church background at all. Not surprisingly, this reflects the 1991 census figures for the New Zealand population.[13]

Inner turmoil was the major turning point preceding a person's commitment to Christ, although unemployment, death in the family, major illness and separation or divorce are increasing factors. Personal explanation rated as the most significant way people heard the gospel, with 84% saying they either heard the explanation several times or couldn't remember how many times. 34% responded in a home and 30% in a church service. 25% were alone and 45% were with one or more friends or family. The importance of personal relationships as the foundation for evangelism was highlighted continually in the survey, with friends and family members being the major influence in people becoming Christian. The most responsive people were in the age group between 15 and 30 years.

While becoming convinced of the truth about Christ was the primary reason people gave for becoming Christian in the survey as a whole, for those in the later period searching for meaning and purpose in my life became their primary reason. A significant challenge facing the Church therefore, is the training of Christian people to express their belief in Jesus Christ in clear and convincing ways and to be apologists for the faith both in what they say and in what they do. As George Hunter says, we need to recognise that "post-enlightenment people have doubts, questions, and challenges that must be honestly addressed before an experiment of faith is possible."[14] The sharing of one's personal faith story with those seeking for meaning to life can be the means of opening up dimensions of faith for them which will lead to salvation. Churches seeking to be effective and sensitive in an endeavour to reach New Zealanders for Christ, will need to consider this profile and these indicators if they are to succeed in a fruitful evangelistic and apostolic mission towards the year 2000 and beyond.

FOOTNOTES

[1] 12 churches from each of the following denominations were invited to participate in the Survey; numbers in brackets indicate actual participation: Anglican (9) Apostolic (11), Assembly of God (7), Associated Churches of Christ (9) Baptist (9), Elim (6), Methodist (9), New Life Churches (4), Open Brethren (6), Presbyterian (5), Salvation Army (8). All churches surveyed were predominantly Pakeha churches.

[2] A copy of the Evangelism in New Zealand Questionnaire is available from the writer.

[3] See *New Zealand Values Today* by Hyam Gold and Alan Webster (Palmerston North: MUP, 1990).

[4] A church's involvement in the community will be a determining factor in reaching non-church people. (See next chapter). See *How To Reach Secular People* by George G Hunter (Nashville: Abingdon, 1992).

[5] The Congress on Children and Families in January 1992 reported that only 9% of all primary school children in New Zealand attend a Sunday school and that Sunday schools are only reaching 3% of children from non-church homes.

[6] A Receptivity/Stress scale has been developed for various age groups. See *The Pastor's Manual for Effective Ministry* by Win Arn (Monrovia: Church Growth Inc, 1992).

[7] Quoted by Joseph C Aldrich in *Gentle Persuasion*, (Portland: Multnomah, 1988) page 99.

[8] Bill Hybels, Senior Pastor of Willow Creek Community Church in Chicago, estimates that on average, seekers will attend their services for six months before they are ready to make a commitment to Christ.

[9] 1 John 3:18.

[10] One programme for reaching the over 60s is based on Win Arn's *Live Long and Love It*, a book, video and kit.

[11] Catholic = those who indicated their attendance at a Catholic church immediately following their commitment to Christ but who now attend one of the churches surveyed.

[12] Growing churches do not necessarily grow through conversion growth but often through transfer growth, sometimes called "the re-cycling of the saints" or "kingdom re-alignment"! See also Chapter 13.

[13] Anglicans are 22% of the population and No Religion are 20%.

[14] *How To Reach Secular People*, page 129.

You are NOW entering the Mission Field

How Are Churches Doing Evangelism?

by Ray Muller

The task of bringing people to faith in Christ and of making disciples belongs solely to the Christian church. Evaluating the effectiveness of churches doing that task is very difficult. Many do not keep records of biological, transfer and conversion growth and others are defensive when questions are asked.[1] The increasing numbers of those who census by census declare themselves to be no religion, combined with declining numbers of some mainline churches, would suggest that New Zealand churches on the whole are not effectively reaching our population for Christ.

Thankfully there are some exceptions and the question is, can we discover insights from evangelistically effective churches which could help us all?

In June 1992, the clergy and pastors of 130 churches from eleven denominations in New Zealand, were sent a questionnaire inviting information and reflections on evangelism in their church. The churches were chosen by their denominational executives for being evangelistically effective. Sixty-seven churches from eleven denominations responded to the questionnaire. [2] In order to gain a cross section of Pakeha New Zealand church life, churches in urban, provincial and rural areas were invited to participate. Of those who responded, 33% were from major urban areas, 57%

were situated in provincial urban areas, and 10% in rural areas of New Zealand.

Some of the obvious questions to ask are: do churches need to make their Services evangelistic? Does evangelism happen in the church building or outside of it? Does the minister or pastor need to be gifted as an evangelist in order for the church to be effective? What priority needs to be given to evangelism by the pastor or minister? What priority needs to be given to evangelism by the church itself? What engagement does the church have with the community and how extensive is that? How does the church respond to human need? What are the strategies churches are using which seem most effective in reaching Kiwis in the 1990s?

Priority for the Leader

What is the role of the pastor or clergy leader in evangelism? Can the church be evangelistically effective without pastoral leadership in this area? Peter Wagner has frequently asserted that the role of the pastor is a critical factor for growing churches.[3] It seemed important to assess what priority the clergy of our churches gave to evangelism. 18% said it was their top priority and a further 63% said it was one of their top priorities. In other words, 81.5% of the pastors rated their personal commitment to evangelism as a high priority. Only 1.5% said that evangelism had a low priority for them in their ministry.

While evangelism can happen without the minister being personally involved, if a church is to have an evangelistic edge to its life, and worship and ministry which will find fruition in effectively making new disciples, then the lead has to be given and modeled.

Chart 1 : Pastor's Priority in Evangelism

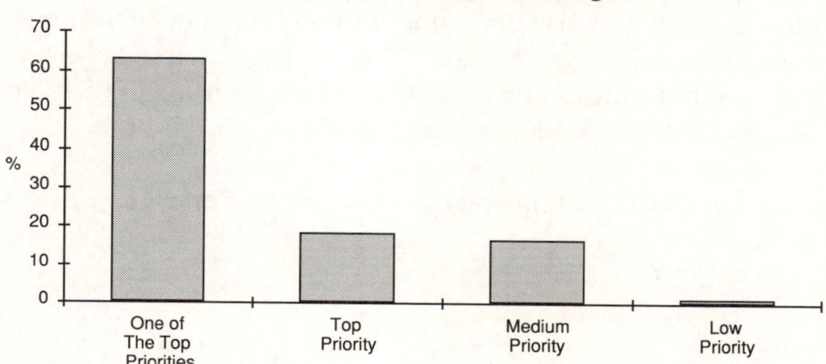

We also asked the question: What priority does evangelism take in your church? It is not surprising to note that 12% said that it rated top priority and a further 67% said that it was one of the top priorities for their church. Therefore 80% of the churches gave a high priority and place to evangelism in their life and ministry. This obviously reflects the priorities and ministry emphasis of the pastoral leadership.

Evangelistic Services

It has been the past tradition of some churches to have a gospel service on a Sunday evening, where it was anticipated that uncommitted people would hear the gospel and come to faith in Christ. Some churches carried this on Sunday by Sunday and year after year, even when it was quite unfruitful. My early church experience reserved evangelistic services for special occasions. For example, I made my own personal commitment to Christ in my home church at a parish mission led by evangelists of the Church Army. A special youth service is another example of a special occasion for evangelism. I vividly recall in 1970 preaching at a youth service and when I gave the invitation for those who wished to respond to Christ to remain behind, I was totally unprepared when the whole congregation stayed, not a single person moved to leave!

During the 1980s many churches gave up regular evangelistic services and for good reason. It is not very encouraging fishing in a pool where there are no fish. What has happened since? Does a church today need to have services which focus on evangelism and if so, what style and how regularly?

Chart 2 : Frequency of Evangelistic Services

The response to this question is surprising. All of the churches surveyed except one, said they held evangelistic services! 55% of the churches said they had a weekly evangelistic service, 19% said they held one monthly and 17.5% said they held one less frequently. When asked if an invitation was given for people to respond and accept Christ, all except one said yes. When asked at what point they gave the invitation, 67% said they did so at the end of the service, 16% gave an invitation during the address or sermon, 13% did so either during the address or after it. The physical response asked for varied with 28% asking the person to come to the front, 26% asked the enquirer to see someone who was identified, 25% asked people to raise a hand, and only 5% invited people to fill in a card. In my view the technique is not the issue, but the sensitivity with which it is presented surely is. I do affirm the concept that the gospel requires a response and that a sensitive and respectful invitation to respond is entirely appropriate. As William Abraham says "the announcing or gossiping of the gospel should include the invitation to respond in faith and repentance".[4]

It would be quite wrong to draw a superficial conclusion from this and assume that effective evangelism is solely a matter of evangelistic church services. The lively and clear presentation of the gospel, its content and challenge, in the context of celebrative worship does provide an opportunity for harvesting but only when preliminary pre-evangelism work has been done and relationships developed. Christians who are sharing their faith with their friends do invite them to church services which are relevant and oriented to the enquirer and the seeker. But they must be carefully designed with the non-church and secular person in mind. Evangelistic services then become part of the process towards a person's commitment to being a disciple of Jesus Christ.

Most Effective Ways of Reaching People

When asked to rate the most effective ways of reaching people for Christ, evangelistic church services ranked third. Friendship was clearly number one, followed in descending order by: small groups, church services, evangelistic messages, special events, pastoral counselling, crusades, social action group, public evangelism.

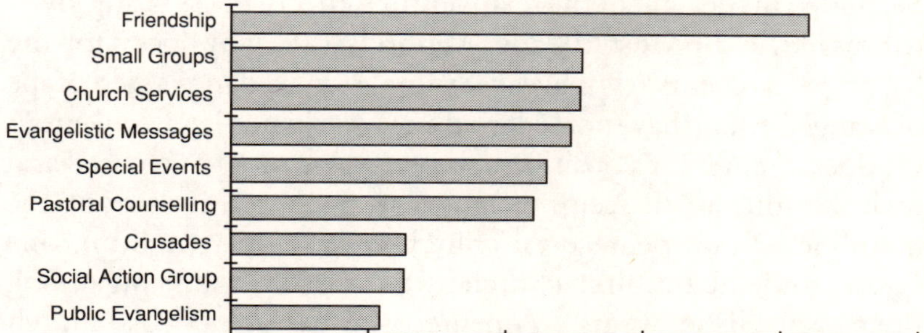

Chart 3 : Friendship Most Effective Method

Extensive research in many countries including New Zealand, shows conclusively that the majority of people (75% - 90%) who become Christians and join the church, do so because of the influence and invitation of a friend or relative. The relational and friendship factor is the primary ingredient for the majority of people who respond to Christ. Perhaps this is not surprising when we consider that a personal God sent Jesus Christ, who is the friend of sinners. The good news of God's love and forgiveness did not remain abstract but is revealed incarnationally in the person of Jesus. Relationship is at the heart of the Christian faith and is foundational for effective evangelism.

The response to the question, does your church hold any evangelistic events, is an intriguing one because the event most frequently offered was crusades or missions by the local church. Social events were in second place, followed by special services. Children's programmes and youth ministry rated fourth equal. Friendship events rated less than the use of the media. I wonder why?

Two questions are raised for me. First, if friendship is so important why is there not a greater focus on ways to enhance the building and development of friendships and relationships? Possibly the social events helped with this but it deserves much more attention.[5] Secondly, in the light of the relatively low effectiveness rating given to crusades in the Most Effective Methods scale, why does it top the list of special events?[6] Is it because some are locked into a stereotype of evangelism and have not reflected on, or evaluated its effectiveness? Or does it represent a position and practice from a pentecostal and revival tradition? It seems to represent the latter, for among the mainline or non-pentecostal churches, only one Anglican, one Baptist and one Brethren church listed crusade or mission among their evangelistic events. A pentecostal pastor said his church engaged in both personal evangelism and crusades but noted that there was a far more lasting response from personal evangelism! This is certainly consistent with the findings of world-wide research.

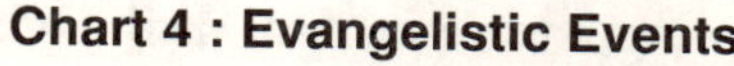
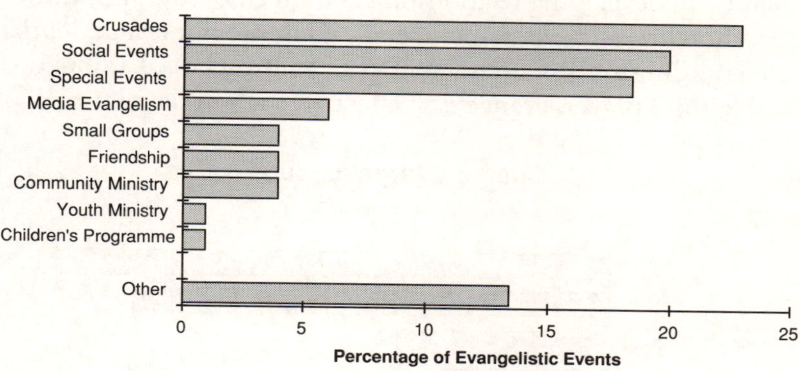

Among the creative variety of other events churches held were such activities as: car rallies, Guy Fawkes bonfires, letter box drops at Christmas and Easter, men's meetings, women's meetings, healing services, Christmas carol services, beach missions, professional quality dance, music, drama group presentations in prisons, schools and shopping malls, street parties, television advertising, musicals, youth and children's outreaches, friendship dinners, mothers' groups, groups for elderly, student outreach evenings, encounter groups for non-Christians, craft groups, videos, film series, door-to-door visitation with questionnaires, the Jesus video and planting new congregations.

Focusing on Special Groups

A key factor in evangelism in the 1990s is sector or target group evangelism. Church growth research shows that churches are most effective in evangelism when particular groups within society are identified and strategies are developed to reach them. What people groups within our society in Aotearoa New Zealand were the churches in the survey targeting? The top three groups were young people 32%, families 27% and friends and relations 12%. It is important to emphasize that equipping church members to identify and reach those within their special spheres of influence or personal networks of relationships, is a highly effective and productive investment of training and resources. Enhancing the friendship factor and developing relationships is both enjoyable and fruitful for churches and their members. This provides an essential undergirding for all church activities and outreaches. Without this and faithful prayer, evangelistic effectiveness will be minimal.

Chart 5 : Target Groups

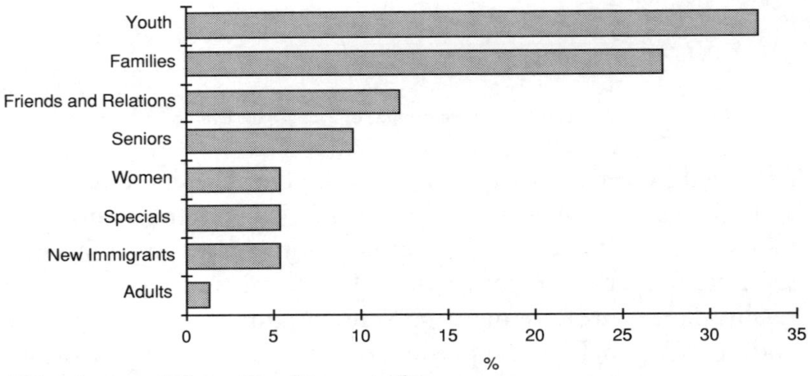

Having a Plan for Evangelism

The successful implementation of evangelism training and creative events to reach target groups within society requires a plan or strategy. The strategy must involve not just one way or method of doing evangelism but multiple ways and a variety of resources. Of the churches surveyed 25% did not have a strategy although some were starting to think about it. Most churches seeing effective evangelism happening with their people, have a strategy for motivating them to make friends, and to train them to share their faith, and for events which will help them do evangelism.[7]

What were the ingredients or components used by the 75% of the churches who did have a strategy for evangelism?

Prayer. While prayer was not mentioned more often than any other ingredient, I put it first. Hopefully those who did not actually specify it, do in fact pray. The first and essential priority for an evangelistic strategy is intercession. Some churches have weekly prayer meetings specifically for evangelism. Some regularly pray for their community by streets, others by target groups and their needs. One church sets specific prayer goals for evangelism. Many encourage their people to identify people, write their names, and to pray specifically for opportunities to reach them. A number of Christian authors are now writing about the strategic nature of prayer in effective evangelism, including C. Peter Wagner. In a previous parish, despite all the church growth knowledge, experience and professional training I sought to implement, it was not until we prayed specifically for converts that the Lord gave us any! Prayer underlines for us that God is the evangelist.

Identifying Personal Networks. The most frequent ingredient mentioned by churches was identifying their members' networks of personal relationships. This is often referred to as oikos, from the New Testament word meaning household or extended family. It speaks of the spheres of personal influence we have among family members and relations, the neighbours who live around us, the people we work with, and the folk we encounter in recreational and leisure activities.[8] This is the basis of friendship evangelism. By enabling church members to identify the spheres of influence God has given them, equipping them to reach out and share faith and providing opportunities for support and accountability, churches can develop a highly effective and intentional strategy. Many churches offered regular training for their members to do this. Some made it part of their new member incorporation programme.[9] Evangelistic events which reinforce opportunities for Christian people to extend and develop their oikos or networks, will be more effective than those which do not.

Groups. Many churches identified their small group activities as part of their evangelistic strategy. These included: home groups devoting one night per month to outreach, special interest groups, evangelistic home Bible studies, the use of videos in groups, (especially the Jesus video used as a four week discussion course), enquirers groups, Discovering Jesus groups, Christianity Explained groups. Groups provide a non-threatening and welcoming environment for people to question and explore the Christian faith, where personal needs can be met in a sensitive way. Some churches are beginning to implement an intentional redesign of church life based on cell groups and the development of lay leadership. Churches doing this are experiencing quite dramatic growth. It offers a very positive evangelistic edge to church life and is an important model for the future.[10] Churches averaged one group for every 17 people attending, which is a good ratio, although 1:14 or more is preferable for growth.

Church Planting. The planting of new churches and area congregations is a key strategy for a number of churches concerned with reaching specific groups of people. Chapters of this book are devoted to this strategy and there is no need to elaborate further, but they are commended to the reader.

Special Programmes. Many churches focused on ministry to children and the opportunities and bridges they provided to their parents and friends. Although different, this does relate to ministry to families which is another focus for a number of churches. Ministry to and with families is an area which will need major attention by the caring church of the 90s, and may even prove more strategic than youth work. Others identified ministry with youth as a focus. These target groups are highlighted by Chart 5. There were also a host of community programmes which met needs and built bridges to people in the community. Some of these included: pop-in for parents and pre-schoolers, residential homes for at risk teens, AIDS patients, and pregnant teenage girls, drop-in for youth, programmes for the elderly, ministry into hotels, ministry in rest homes, hospital visiting, craft groups, sports events, gymnasium, toy library, ITIM chaplaincy, parenting seminars, time out, clowning, drama and street and mall presentations, exercise groups, Maori language, singles ministries, concerts and musicals, seminars, evergreens, street dinners, young women's support group, healing ministry.[11]

Involvement in the Community. In addition to those activities mentioned above, all except five of the churches have significant ministries of community care and social action. Some express their commitment to mission in extensive and sacrificial ways. For many churches there is no pietistic escape from the real world of poverty, injustice and hurt in Aotearoa New Zealand. Here are some examples of the community ministries which represent a wholistic view of mission and evangelism: food parcels and food banks, budgeting services, opportunity shops, victim support, prison ministry, drug rehabilitation, recovery ministry, dependency and related therapy groups, emergency housing, soup kitchens, interest free loan finance, life chain, writing letters to government, love link, Bible in schools, gymnasium, liaison with Social Welfare, pregnancy support, home for handicapped accident victims, aged care, hospice care, hospital after-care, child care, foster grandparents, Access training schemes, unemployed, work scheme for the disabled, grief seminars, divorce recovery, marriage enrichment, firewood, horticultural unit, anger management, Taha Maori and language groups, work with periodic detention trainees, Mission to Seamen, refugee re-settlement.

Worship. Many churches specified their worship services as vital components in an evangelism strategy. Some gave examples of the use of music, video, testimony, preaching, advertising and follow up to show how important this was to them. Many churches are aware of the need to be sensitive to the enquirer, new person and especially to the non-Christian attending church. In many churches, the music, language and culture expressed on Sunday morning is mostly foreign to the average New Zealander. The experience of such Christian worship can just as easily turn a person away from Christ as attract them to him.

A large church in Brisbane was attracting many visitors but the number of visitors who returned was diminishing. After some months, the church leaders began to ask why. A researcher was commissioned to follow up those visitors who had not returned. As a result of the interviews it was discovered that one of the main reasons for the visitors not returning was the length of the service. One hour and twenty minutes was found to be the maximum time that people would happily tolerate; over that, the visitor retention rate declined dramatically.

A friend of mine was discussing recently his concern over people who arrived 15 to 20 minutes late for a service. It was discovered that with the church scheduling a considerable time of singing at the beginning, much of it repetitive, the latecomers had discovered how to control their time and shorten the service for themselves and not miss anything of importance! For most families, worship is not the only activity they engage in on a Sunday; there are many other demands as well, even for the most committed.

For many people the language of songs, hymns, readings and sermons is not only a different and foreign culture, with unexplained and unfamiliar biblical images, it is also often insensitive to gender issues. Through the use of inclusive language, greater respect for people is often shown in the secular market place than within churches. The message is not just the sermon; it is the whole service. Eddie Gibbs has said that people decide in the first few minutes whether or not they will return to a church for a second time. He also says we do not get a second chance to make a good first impression![12]

Worship services for specific groups were not held only on Sundays. Increasing use is being made of days and nights during the week in order to meet the needs of people unable to attend on Sundays.[13] When services are held, who they are for and the appropriate style for that service, are issues to be considered in an evangelism strategy.

Seeker sensitive worship needs to be a priority for all churches and for most services but special seeker targeted services are also necessary as part of an evangelistic strategy.[14] For this reason some churches are developing new services at different times for the benefit of unchurched people, some are weekly, some monthly and others less regularly. The use of special music, drama and topical sermons are part of this new strategy. Perhaps above all, the unchurched enquirer needs to sense the presence of God in worship. Even unchurched secular people can tell whether or not what is happening inside the strange world of the church is spiritually authentic or not. People are looking for integrity and meaning. "They are looking for clarity and guidance to know what is right, and for motivation and power to do the right. They hope to be lifted above themselves, to see a vision of a better world, of themselves as better people. Hope, acceptance, strength are desired. Is the worship real, or is it just for show?"[15]

Community service and worship are two sides of the coin of corporate witness which churches present to the public. Ideally they complement personal aspects of evangelizing by individuals and groups.

Incorporation. Several churches also indicated their visitor follow-up procedures as a part of their evangelism strategy. This raises the important dimension of the incorporation or assimilation of new members. Most churches can improve their effectiveness in this area. Too many churches assume that the incorporation process happens automatically. Churches who do not give careful attention to incorporating new people can be accused of being uncaring and unloving. Because church members of long standing have become thoroughly familiar with their church, they forget what it is like to be new and in an unfamiliar setting. Many sincere new Christians drop out, not because they were not really converted or do not really believe, but because we have failed to welcome, care, include and incorporate them.[16] Again, friendship is a major influence in the successful incorporation of new people. Recently I heard the ministry of evangelism described as the ministry of inviting and including. I like that.

Effectiveness and Growth

The churches in the survey were regarded by their own denominations as being evangelistically effective. In an effort to measure this, we asked how many converts the church had gained over the previous five years and for their average weekly worship attendance for all services from 1981 - 1992. Unfortunately, some churches don't keep any records or statistics for attendances and so it is not possible to evaluate whether they are growing and effective. In church growth research we use a calculation based on a church's figures over a ten year period. Decadal Growth Rate is an internationally recognised standard measurement. The scale for growth over a ten year period looks like this:

25	%	= marginal
50	%	= fair
100	%	= good
200	%	= excellent
300	%	= outstanding
500 +	%	= incredible

A 25% DGR is minimal because most churches should gain this by biological growth over the ten years.[17] A goal for good growth is 100% DGR, or to double in a decade. In the survey, I took the 25% DGR and added 5% for some converts, making a base of 30% as a reasonable standard for growth. What did we discover? 65% of the churches grew by 30% or more over the last ten years; 35% did not. However, what is even more significant and heartening, is that 40% of the churches achieved 100% DGR or more, which is excellent. Some results were even more dramatic. Growth was not limited to one brand of church. There is a Presbyterian church with 215% DGR, a Methodist church with 109%, a New Life church with 400%, an Elim church with 314%, a Baptist church with 286%, an Assembly of God with 382%, an Apostolic church with 816%, a Brethren Assembly with 150%, an Anglican church with 208%, a Salvation Army Citadel with 163%. The most dramatic growth is in new churches planted over the decade. Not all the growth though came from conversion growth. A high percentage was transfer growth of Christians from other churches.[18]

How effective are churches in terms of reaching new people for Christ? This is a difficult question, for every church has a different perception and their own way of evaluating this. However, in the total survey the number of converts estimated over the last five years averaged at 126 per church or 25 per year. For those churches who experienced 100% DGR or higher, the average was 172 converts or 34 per year. This does not seem very great until one realises that 50% of the estimated converts come from only 13% of the churches! In other words, some estimate they are doing well in effective evangelism while others are not. A few of the churches with high numbers of estimated converts had an average DGR, which suggests that few stayed and became members of that church. What happened to them? That is the challenge of effective incorporation. The back doors of some churches are wide open.

In effective evangelism we do need to respect the spiritual decision process[19] and focus on making disciples and not just gaining decisions.

Growth Contributing Factors

The churches were asked: what factors contributed to your growth as a church? Some clear agreement was expressed and this provides a useful checklist to ponder and perhaps to implement. As these factors mostly reinforce what we have already discovered from the survey, I commend them without particular comment.

The top ten in descending order are: culturally relevant and lively worship, friendship, prayer, vision and purpose, small groups, Bible teaching, community involvement, lay ministry, love of Christ, pastoral care. These are all significant factors for church growth. I would personally consider vision and purpose as number one, but I have no argument with the list, except that the role of the pastor/minister is of critical importance and certainly should be included in this top list and not as it was rated by the respondents. Friendship, remember, is an essential basis for effective evangelism.

For the sake of completeness the other factors listed are included, in descending order of importance. It is interesting to see again where crusades come! The second group of factors, are: responsive preaching, social events, open worship, variety, youth ministry, children's programme, evangelism training, obedience.

A third group of factors which rated quite low, are: media evangelism, personal explanation, planting churches, pastor/minister, special services, signs and wonders. Those with virtually a zero rating were: crusades, spiritual hunger, religious background, reality of God.

Conclusion

The intent of this chapter is not to highlight one particular strategy but to indicate the encouraging signs of hope that are occurring throughout our land. We can learn much from each other in order to increase our effectiveness for the sake of the gospel. But God forbid that we should just blindly duplicate what others are doing. Each church is unique and is placed in a particular community by God for a special purpose. Every church must therefore seek God's will and the Holy Spirit's guidance for the specific ministry and witness that will meet the needs of that community. I pray that as we do so, Jesus Christ will be known to the peoples of our nation.

FOOTNOTES

[1] In growing churches the norm for biological growth is 1-2%, transfer growth 3-6% and conversion growth 10-12% per year. The percentages for plateaued or declining churches are obviously much lower.

[2] Anglican, Apostolic, Assembly of God, Associated Churches of Christ, Baptist,

Elim, Methodist, New Life Churches, Open Brethren, Presbyterian, Salvation Army.

[3] C. Peter Wagner is Professor of Church Growth at Fuller Seminary's School of World Mission. His book *Leading Your Church to Growth* (Ventura: Regal, 1984) is important reading in this area.

[4] *The Logic of Evangelism*, by William J. Abraham, page 171 (Grand Rapids: Eerdmans, 1989).

[5] Some churches find the kit *Celebration of Friendship* is a helpful resource.

[6] See the place of crusades in the research discussed in the previous chapter.

[7] An outstanding example of a church with a plan for evangelism is Willow Creek Community Church in Chicago. Their impressive seven-step plan is discussed in *How To Reach Secular People* by George G. Hunter, page 158 (Nashville: Abingdon, 1992).

[8] As previously noted, 75 - 90% of people come to Christ because of these relationships.

[9] *The Master's Plan for Making Disciples* (Monrovia: Church Growth Press, 1982) is the key resource book and Church Action Kit for Oikos evangelism which churches are using.

[10] Called the Meta church model, the key resource book is *Prepare Your Church for the Future* by Carl George (Old Tappan:Revell,1992)

[11] See also Chapter 11.

[12] A helpful video resource on worship is *Worship That Attracts and Holds the Unchurched*, by Robert Orr and Ray Muller. Available from: Church Growth Resources (NZ), Box 26.119, Wellington 4.

[13] Many Catholic churches have their largest attendance at Saturday evening services.

[14] For the difference between seeker-sensitive and seeker-driven worship, see George Hunter's book *How to Reach Secular People* ,and also consider the philosophy of ministry of Bill Hybels and the example of the Willow Creek Community Church.

[15] Robert Bast in *Attracting New Members*, page 67. (Monrovia: Church Growth Press, 1988).

[16] For excellent resources on Incorporation see *The Shepherd's Guide for Caring and Keeping - a Church Action Kit*; also my one day seminar - How To be A Welcoming and Friendly Church.

[17] ie. children born to members of the fellowship.

[18] eg. one church increased attendance from 100 to 300 per Sunday over 5 years, and in that time an estimated 70 conversions. Assuming they all stayed in that church, the other 130 must have come by transfer growth.

[19] This process is well illustrated by the Engel Scale. An example of this is in Chapter 10.

14

Research for the Local Church

by Jill Richards

The value of research for church growth and setting strategies for evangelism should now be clear. A knowledge of our community can help us set more effective goals and give us insights to improve our communication of the gospel. Without research we have an inadequate understanding of the issues confronting us, the environment in which we are working, and possibilities for future directions. Most of the research in this book is in the 'macro': broad strokes painting a picture of the nation and the Church. What about the 'micro', the small units that affect a local church? It is necessary to find ways of looking at the neighbourhood. Local churches need to conduct their own research in order to plan appropriate local ministries.

We should distinguish between our church's catchment area (the area from which committed Christians commute to attend our church out of preference, which can be a large area) and our church's target community (the community or communities for which we believe we have a special God-given evangelistic responsibility). A careful distinction made here can help immeasurably to focus our efforts. We may define our catchment area simply by marking on a map with pins the homes of those who attend our church. On the other hand defining our target community or communities may take time in research and prayer. Being realistic, who, and how many, could we claim to reach and serve for the Gospel?

Research is Listening

An example of 'listening' research that made a difference comes from a small congregation in a New Zealand suburb. The congregation was an aging one in an older part of the city, with a number of small businesses and shops occupying what had been residential streets. Many of the members lived outside the immediate area. Most of the houses remaining in the neighbourhood were rented and not very well kept.

What kind of evangelism would touch the lives of people living and working here? Careful listening to shopkeepers, shoppers, public health workers and doctors, teachers and parents at the primary school and kindergarten, police and community workers, as well as members of the church, and gathering of statistics, led to the writing of a report. The report was in demand by local council and health workers and raised the profile of the church in the community. It showed evidence of a great turnover of population. For example in one school, in a class of 31 pupils, 23 entered and 19 moved on to other places during the year. More than half the families in the school had English as a second language. Because many of the homes were privately rented, as soon as families gained a Housing Corporation home they left the district. Nearly 80% of children were non-European.

Armed with this new information the church, already attracting some Samoan and Tongan families, resolved to plan outreach to meet the needs of the transient and newly arrived families. Family socials, funding for a Samoan pre-school worker in the school setting, and an opportunity shop with a social component, are helping the church to come to grips with the realities of people's lives. As increasing numbers attend worship, the shape of the Sunday service will need to change with more multicultural participation.

The research method used to survey the area immediately around the church is detailed later in this chapter. It did not ask direct questions about the role or place of the church. (If desired, this can be done quite simply.) Open-ended questions allow people to express their opinions about the church, which can be helpful in the planning of new programmes. The important thing is to listen carefully to what people are saying about their needs, about their lives, about the church and the good news as they see it, and then to prayerfully consider the results.

To help local churches with research in their communities, the following has been prepared as a first step. Using it to get church people to listen to the community, as well as to other members of the community of faith, is worth the effort. It will supply information on what the community senses are its needs and will point the way to some possible ministries. Adapt the questions to suit your situation and use the method to crystallize the congregation's vision for its community.

Preparing a Community Profile

In all communities individuals and families have basic needs which must be met to ensure health and vitality. Established areas often have a settled population, good housing, access to employment, adequate transport, education, health and welfare services, along with community facilities such as a recreation centre, social clubs and neighbourhood support services (formal and informal). People living in new communities often need more support than those in established areas because they have a minimum of community services. They may lack pre-schools, transport, local meeting places, recreation facilities, etc.

At different stages of life people's needs change. Mothers and young children generate a demand for health facilities, local doctors, pre-schools, child care, etc. Younger children need educational and recreational facilities that provide supervision and assistance, while older children need less supervision but more entertainment and excitement along with vocational training and work opportunities. Families create demand for local housing, open spaces, work and support services, while the aged may require specialized housing, health and social services. It is important therefore to understand your community before planning outreach or services. Compiling a community profile is a useful way to begin to analyse opportunities so that appropriate ministry programmes can be planned.

How to Go About It

A parish or congregational group may compile this information as a group exercise. This provides a wide base of understanding within the group and makes any further plan of action easier to instigate. People are more likely to be motivated and supportive if they have been involved in the analysis. Research is not only a science (there is methodology, how to do it) but also an art (knowing how to adapt it to your situation and need). Every church's context is different. A rural church will not have the same need for demographics on ethnic origin or new housing developments as will the urban or suburban church, but attitudes and social needs in the community could be more important.

The steps on how to do it should be followed. The kind of information you look for can be adapted to your needs. The contents of this study will include:

> purpose and objectives of the community profile
> mapping the community
> community demographics
> social needs of the community
> attitudes survey.

Purpose and Objectives

A clear understanding is needed of why you are doing this and what you hope to gain as outcomes. Stating your purpose and objectives will help you to evaluate which are the most important issues for you, and to decide how and when to adapt. For example, the purposes of the study for one of the Presbyterian churches in New Plymouth might be:

1   To determine one target group for ministry the church is not presently reaching

2   To determine other factors in the community that could affect how existing programmes are presented.

Objectives could be:

1   Locate significant people groups or socio-cultural groups[1] within the church's target community (or communities)

2   Determine which of these is likely to respond to approaches and programmes of the church

3   Identify felt needs in the community the church can meet, noting the skills of the people in the church and other groups that may already be involved.

Mapping the Community

Acquire maps of the target community from the local Council, the AA, or other sources. What are the boundaries? These may be paper boundaries such as census or council areas, or natural barriers like rivers, hillsides, motorways or industrial developments. On a large map mark the location of the church centre and draw a circle to mark ten minutes walking distance and another to mark the edge of the target community (which may be the parish area). It may be helpful to mark the homes of members of the congregation with coloured pins, etc.

Community Demographics

Acquire this information from the census figures. Note trends by comparing the latest census figures with the previous census. Demographics describe what the community is like in terms of: age, sex, ethnic origin, marital status, household types and housing, employment, income, education, etc. First note population. Is it stable, increasing or decreasing?

Age groupings. What is the largest age group represented in your area? Compare this with other areas. This may explain the preponderance of older folk or young singles in your congregation. Has the area changed greatly in recent times? If it is some time since the last census and the area has dramatically changed, e.g. large scale housing or motorway development etc, then gather information from school enrolments and pre-school health workers which will provide clues as to family movements in, or out, of the area.

Sex. Note any marked differences in numbers of male and female in the age groups in census figures. For example in one suburb there were many more males than females in the 12 to 15 age group (due, it turned out, to a boys' boarding school in the census area).

Ethnic groups. A similar breakdown is required as for age groupings (see above) eg. what is the largest ethnic group? What changes have taken place since the last census? What does this mean for the local church? In one example a dwindling, aging congregation, with a part-time minister, was set in a state housing area where increasing numbers of homes were being allocated to Samoan and other recent arrivals from the Pacific. Initially these new families travelled to inner city churches for worship in their own language. The appointment of a full-time Samoan minister led very quickly to many families choosing to worship locally, and soon several services were held every Sunday, some in other Pacific languages. A large hall was soon required and then a bigger church.

Housing and household types. How many privately owned and rented dwellings are there? This gives clues as to socio-economic status, and stability or transience of the population. Note any special needs, eg. rest homes and hospitals, hostels or institutions. Note household types; one family, one family plus others, two or more families, persons living alone, solo parent families, de factos, etc.

Employment and income. These figures will give an idea of the socio-economic range in the area and where the church might offer ministries. For example, many young unemployed men might respond to a drop-in facility for games, a social club. In a more generally affluent area there may be hidden needs, eg. for those made redundant in mid life. The church might set up a support and discussion group to plan new careers, and to offer retraining in new skills.

Community Social Needs

It is important to hear what community people believe are their social needs. This can be done using a community survey in which amenities and programmes are identified and the community response assessed. For example, a local body runs a school holiday programme in its recreation centre. Large numbers of children do not attend. They are clearly at a loose end. Programme content and leadership are good but the cost is found to be prohibitive for low income parents. A group of church and community helpers plan and run a programme at 20c per child per day and have follow-up contact with the families.

Follow the chart below as a guide. Go in twos and interview professional people, eg. police, health workers, shopkeepers, schoolteachers, as well as consumers, parents, young people and senior citizens. What is the amenity? For whom does it cater? Is it physically accessible? How much does it cost? Is it user friendly? What about transport?

AMENITY	Felt needs met	Gaps in Services

Health Services
doctors/clinics
disabled/psychiatric
plunket
public health staff

Education Services
pre-school centres
support for parents
day, after-school care
school holiday programmes
extra help for reading etc.
truancy
counselling
health education
community education
retraining
workskills
education for parenthood

Recreational
leisure facilities
meeting places
outdoor sports
indoor sports
community centres/houses
clubs

Business Centre
shopping centres
transport
information services

Do not overlook the expertize of church people when gathering this information. People who live, work or worship in an area know an enormous amount about local patterns of behaviour, trends, difficulties experienced by people, increase in numbers of babies, numbers of homes on the market, etc. They may not be aware that others do not know what they have noticed. Again, you need to be good listeners.

Attitudes Survey

It is not enough just to know facts about the community. You need to know how the community thinks and feels. Is there something that has caused a negative attitude toward the church that you should know about? A campaign to invite people to the church may be hindered if you are oblivious to these attitudes.

The following survey tests receptivity to the gospel and attitudes to the church. It may suggest openings for direct ministries. Adapt it for use in your church neighbourhood for researching responsiveness to your particular ministries or proposed outreach.

Survey Questionnaire : Attitudes Towards the Church

1   Are you an active member of a local church?
    Yes/ No   Church:
2   What do you think is the greatest need people have in our area?
3   Why do you think some people don't belong to a church?
4   What should the church be doing to help make this a better community?
5   Would you consider sending your children to Sunday school or a children's group or programme at the church?
    No/ maybe/ interested/ yes/ not applicable
6   Would you/ your partner/ your friends/ family members, be interested in attending worship at our church?

7　　What would best express your reasons for wanting to know more about God and the Bible? Please indicate first and second choices.

... need guidelines for living a good life
... find answers for happy home life
... help find a purpose for living
... know God in a personal way
... find forgiveness of sin and removal of guilt
... answer questions about life after death
... fill a loneliness I feel inside

8　　Would you be interested in studying the Bible with others in your area?

Selecting and Supporting Researchers

Interested people might be invited to a meeting where you explain the process and answer questions. It is generally best to go in pairs to see professionals such as police, doctor, etc. Then reflect together on the conversation. Write up findings as soon after interviews as possible. Arrange to meet within an agreed period, say four weeks, and collate findings. Draw out significant points, do any additional fact-finding, and take your results to church leaders or a parish meeting for priorities to be set. Remember, it takes courage to go out and ask questions, so be sure to engage the whole church in a supportive prayer ministry for researchers. Decide how people are to introduce themselves, always be courteous, respect privacy and other viewpoints. Remember you represent your church.

It is also helpful to look carefully at your congregational life and mission. There are methods to do this through the Development Divisions of some of the New Zealand churches.

HELPFUL BOOKS AND MATERIALS

Kennon L. Callahan, *Twelve Keys to an Effective Church*, (San Francisco: Harper and Row, 1983).

Ralph Neighbour, *Auckland, Resistant or Neglected?* (Auckland: Touch International Ministries, 1988).

Bruce Patrick, *Sample Community Surveys* (Auckland: MISSIO**NZ**, 1991).

Roy Pointer, *How Do Churches Grow?* (London: Marshalls, 1984).

Roy Pointer, *The Growth Book*, (London: MARC, 1987).

Bob Waymire and C Peter Wagner, *The Church Growth Survey Handbook*, (Milpitas, CA: Global Church Growth, 1984).

FOOTNOTE

[1] See definitions of these terms in Chapter 18.

Multiplication :
The Key to Growth

by Bruce Patrick

"We don't need more churches! We need to disciple people." Typical talk from John, who is committed to Christ and to the growth of the kingdom of God but unsure about the role of the church. "New Zealand has enough churches, and anyway, we can do without more struggling causes," he says. Others have similar concerns. "Church planting is too expensive; the money would be better spent on people. Anyway, what we need is revitalized churches; why start more churches until those we have are in better health?"

John's heartfelt concerns are common to many sincere Christians. Their commitment to reach out to the unchurched with God's love is not in doubt. Fears about church planting are shared by some who have had good church experiences, and more commonly by those who have not. John has never considered the reasons for church planting, nor the range of models in use.[1] He is probably unaware of the rapid growth God is giving in New Zealand to parts of the body of Christ committed to the multiplication of disciples, leaders, and congregations. He needs to balance the emphasis between revitalizing old churches and growing new churches.

The Hamilton Apostolic Church consisted of 16 people in 1984, led by Pastor Philip Underwood. In 1987 they had only 50 members but agreed in faith to simultaneously plant a daughter congregation in West Hamilton while growing the mother church. In 1988 they assisted Cambridge Apostolic church. When Philip Underwood became Principal of Te Nikau Training Centre in 1989, Nick Klinkenberg became pastor in Hamilton. (He had pastored Waikanae Faith Church for seven years during which time they had planted four churches, in Paraparaumu, Titahi Bay, Upper Hutt, and Plimmerton; and had indirectly assisted the planting of Whangarei Apostolic Church.) In that year Hamilton Apostolic released an elder, Noel Bowker, as church planter for North City. In 1991 they planted South City. From only 50 attending one Apostolic church in Hamilton in 1987, the cumulative attendance of these churches by August 1992 was over 1000 people. Their denominational surveys show that at least one third of the new people had no prior church commitment. By planting new congregations they have reached new pockets of unreached people, not only to evangelize but also to nurture new believers.

There are impressive theological, historical, contextual, and strategic reasons for multiplying congregations. This chapter discusses these reasons, then lists and illustrates 13 models of multiplication currently in use in New Zealand. Most are recent examples from a cross-section of the body of Christ; many reflect my own background.

Theological Reasons for Multiplying Congregations

Christ is incarnate in his people. He dwells in every local body of Christ through whom he expresses his life and love.[2] "Christ could be alive and well and present in all his power and glory and compassion while communicating His wonderful message of the kingdom in a totally contextualized way in every small community of people if only there were some truly born again believers exercising the gifts of the Spirit and functioning there as the body of Christ." (Jim Montgomery)

Second, Jesus said, "I will build my church."[3] The Church, the ecclesia or called out ones, remains central in God's plan for the ages. It has universal existence throughout the world, across the centuries, on earth and with Christ. It also has local expression. New Zealanders planting churches today are his agents as they bring people to Christ, nurture and disciple them, release them into their gifts and ministries, and grow new and varied expressions of the body of Christ. Third, the Great Commission is found in five complementary forms in the New Testament.[4] The Matthew commission includes strategy. There are two aspects. The first is to evangelize, ie. to disciple people so that they in turn can disciple others. The second is clearly implied: to establish congregations where responsive persons can be baptized and then taught continuously in the context of supportive relationships in a local fellowship that is itself starting other congregations. Specialist ministry and missionary organizations are recognizing that though they have significant roles in their various distinct callings, they must equip the body of Christ and serve local churches as they make disciples, baptize and teach. By working together the whole Church will most effectively fulfil the Great Commission.

Fourth, in Acts the early Church's obedience to the Great Commission is described. After Peter preached on the day of Pentecost, the church in Jerusalem was planted, and more people became disciples, were baptized and taught.[5] A mission thrust from the Antioch church initiated by the Holy Spirit naturally became a church planting enterprise.[6] Paul's Macedonian call resulted in a rash of new churches.[7] Fifth, the New Testament letters, including the letters to the churches of Asia in Revelation, are almost all addressed to local churches or pastors of local churches. Besides doctrinal issues these letters contain much instruction about local church life. Local churches were planted to then have a crucial place in the world mission plans of God.

Historical Reasons for Multiplying Congregations

Many stories could be told to illustrate the outworking of these theological truths, throughout history and throughout the world. Wherever the Holy Spirit has moved powerfully to bring lasting social change, effective congregations have been established. The ministries of John Wesley and William Booth are prime examples. In Aotearoa New Zealand during the first half of the 19th century Maori evangelists established churches in a people movement described at that time as without equal in the annals of missionary history. As many thousands of Maori became followers of Jesus Christ, their communities became centred on congregational life. During our brief history since then there have been periods of vigorous growth through the starting of new congregations. New Zealand Christians need to seriously consider again what the effect would be of saturating our modern nation with live cells and congregations of believers.

Contextual Reasons for Multiplying Congregations

Are new congregations needed here and now, in New Zealand? Most researchers agree that at least 85% of New Zealanders rarely or never attend a church. To put that another way, up to three million New Zealanders are not being reached by existing churches. We are predominantly a secular or pagan nation heavily camouflaged by overlays of Christian tradition, and 4,000 church buildings. Every existing church needs to be revived, renewed, and strengthened to be effective in its community. But many more new congregations are also needed; they have greater potential than existing older congregations to reach new people, sooner.

Second, the unevangelized population is in fact increasing: by birthrate, secularization, and immigration. Few would argue that a population increasing biologically needs no new churches. Add to this the rising tide of secularization. Every year there is an increase in the number of people not being reached by existing churches. Those who declared themselves of "No Religion" and "Object to State" rose from 24% of the population in 1986 to 27% in the 1991 census. For comparison, "Belief in a personal God is significantly lower in New Zealand than in Australia."[8] We must note that the "No Religion" people are younger rather than older, 81% being under the age of 40.

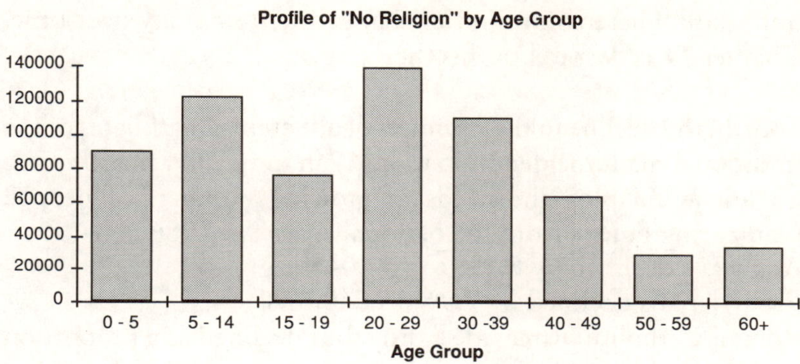

"Older people who believed in God were more likely to believe in a personal God, while younger people who professed a belief tended more to thinking of God as some sort of spirit or life-force... This New Zealand pattern is more like that of Northern Europeans than either Australia or the USA. In international terms New Zealand has a low level of religiosity... By age level, those in their 20s are much the lowest church attenders, but youth and young adults in general fall well below the post-parental generation."[9] This younger generation has not related well to the traditional forms, structures and worship styles of many churches. New congregations are more able to begin with contemporary patterns that fit the new generation. Roger Forster of Ichthus Fellowship in London notes five essentials for church planting to reach contemporary people. New churches must have greater informality in structure and style. They should be less institutional, less hierarchical, and more relational. They must be culturally relevant, for instance in language and music. They should set about their mission with urgency.[10] And they ought to be reproducing rather than sterile.[11]

Our population is increasing, and becoming more secularized. It is also growing through immigration. Different ethno-linguistic, socio-economic, and culture groups are usually not attracted to existing congregations of another cultural type. They must be reached by developing new congregations. This is especially important where communities change their ethnicity over time. Chapter 17 is devoted to this theme.

Fourth, the decline in the numbers of adherents or affiliates of the traditional mainline denominations is an indication that they are no longer meeting the needs of growing numbers of people. Comparing figures from the national census in 1986 and 1991:
Anglicans declined by 8.7% to 732,045
Presbyterians declined by 7.9% to 540,678
Roman Catholics increased slightly, but declined as a proportion of the population by 0.5%, with 498,612
Methodists declined by 9.5% to 138,708
Baptists increased by 3.2%, but declined as a proportion of the population by 0.1%, with 70,155.

"The mainline churches represent 58.6% of the New Zealand population. That Anglicans declined by 59,802 people, thus reducing our percentage of the population to 21.7%, is not the only fact that the census reveals. What is even more disturbing is that of all the churches we are the most aged. Almost a quarter of our constituents are aged 60 years or more, 23.5% to be exact, whereas in the population as a whole only 15.3% are aged 60 or over. It is no consolation to note that the Presbyterians and Methodists are almost as aged as we are."[12]

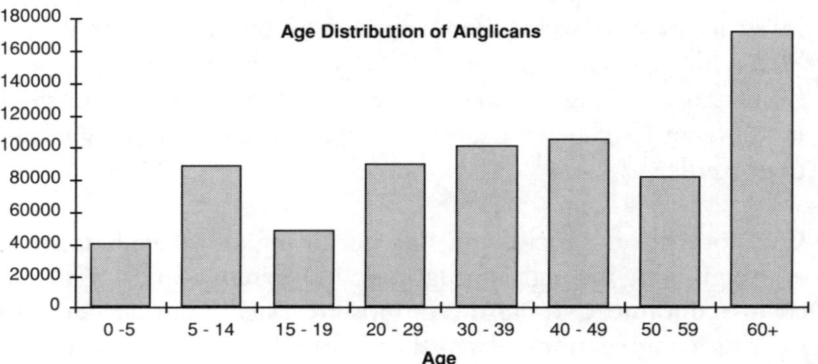

While traditional forms of church life are still needed to minister to older people, (and some churches are starting new traditional-style congregations to reach them) renewed congregations and new cultural forms of the church are needed to reach those whose needs are no longer being met by traditional churches, and who are voting with their feet by leaving in tens of thousands. They want more than a philosophical, intellectual, doctrinal, ethical, or ecological Sunday lecture. People do want to discover meaning and purpose in life. They do want to be informed from a Christian perspective. But more, they want to meet with God, they want to experience God in their daily lives. Do they, in our churches? "To put it rather more bluntly, only about half of those who worship reasonably regularly and pray frequently to a God whom they regard as highly important to them report a commensurate experience of spiritual presence or influence."[13] New churches have to be alive to survive, let alone to thrive.

Fifth, there are specific local communities that are growing rapidly as New Zealand's population shifts. Too often, Christians and churches near growth areas are desperately slow or unresponsive to these patterns. This has been true in one of New Zealand's fastest suburban growth areas, the East Tamaki corridor between Howick and Otara. One bright exception is church planter Luke Brough of the East City Elim Church in Botany Downs who says, "We looked for high profile land on the doorstep of the old suburbs but next to the developing areas. Our vision was for a 1000 member church, a community church large enough to have an impact on its community. The congregation began in 1985. A year later we bought four acres in Botany Road for $160,000. The church met in the Howick Intermediate School hall until the end of 1991, when we moved into our new building with about 450 people. Most new people are won through friendship; adults and families are responsive. Many of these have just felt the need to come back to church." Just felt the need to come back to church! The pastoral team is increasing to meet the demands of growth. Lively and caring evangelistic churches planted early in new suburbs have great growth potential. And this church has already planted two further new churches.

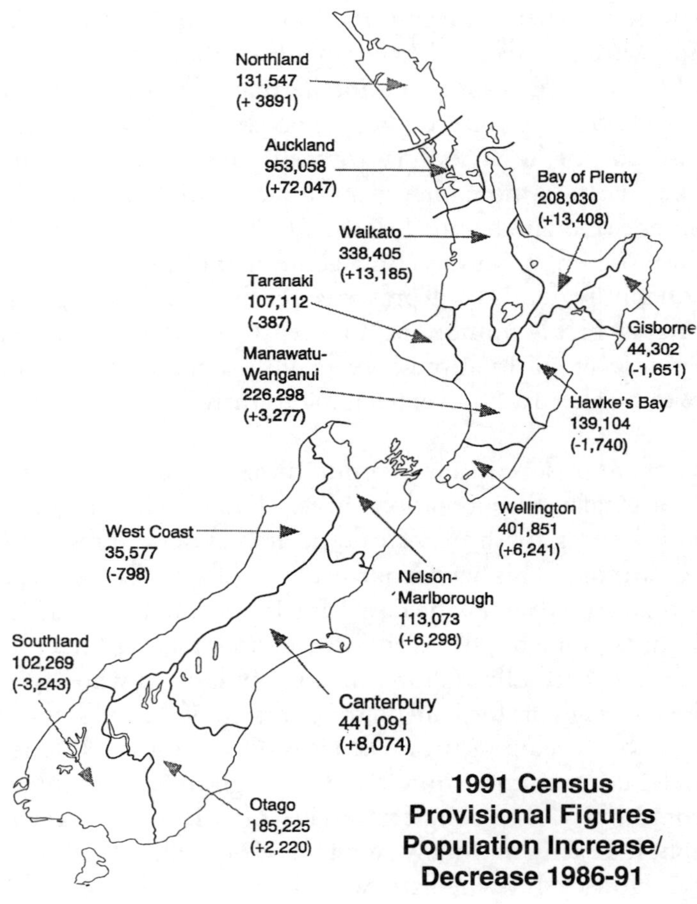

In 1988 a struggling Pakeha church in Porirua, the Titahi Bay Anglican Parish, made a generous gift of one of their halls to a small local community of the Maori Pastorate.[14] The name of the building was changed from St Edmunds to Rota Waitoa. Non-stipendiary priests John Tamahori and Bill Tangahou pastored the new congregation. Has this approach been effective? The new congregation is now well-established and thinking of expanding its building. New people come through the congregation's own network of family and friends. Their ministry now includes responsibility for two other congregations in the area. Where a suburb has an in-migrating population from different cultural backgrounds, new congregations will be needed to serve their needs. As demonstrated here in Porirua, a generous, servant attitude to the re-allocation of church properties can help to advance the kingdom of God.

Strategic Reasons for Multiplying Congregations

There are also important strategic reasons for the starting of more and more caring, lively, gospel-sharing churches and congregations. Mission agencies and denominations world-wide are now recognizing this. Though this strategy is prominent in Acts, it is as if many are seeing it for the first time. Generations of writers on evangelism and church growth have omitted to discuss church planting, a fact which has contributed to its widespread neglect in the West.

First, all over the world the vast majority of churches eventually plateau (at a higher or lower level). Logically, the only way to increase the kingdom of God is to start more and more new churches to reach every segment of society. Second, from the day God said to Adam and Eve, "Be fruitful, multiply, replenish the earth," multiplication has been the secret of the growth of the human race. Christians will lose the race to tell the world of Christ unless we are converted from our dedication to mere addition. But multiplication of what? There are three levels at which local churches must multiply: we must multiply disciples who can multiply disciples; we must multiply leaders who can multiply leaders; and we must multiply churches that can multiply churches.

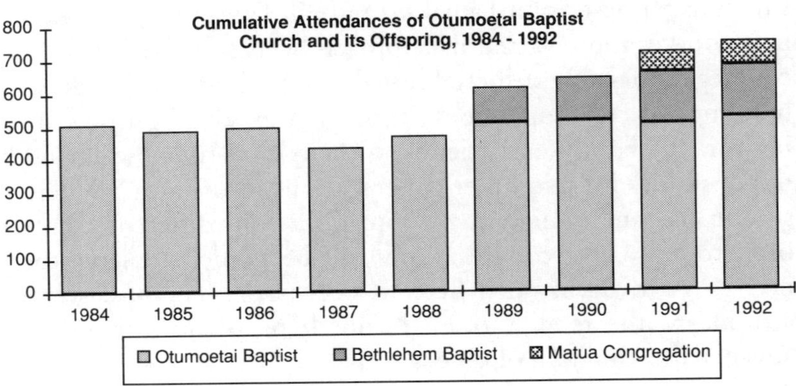

Third, just as it is being recognized that the so-called parachurch, or specialist mission agencies do not exist for themselves, it is being recognized increasingly today that denominations do not exist for themselves. They exist for their churches. They are at best mission facilitators. They are church planting agencies. Many began in reformation or revival movements, coming into existence as they spawned hundreds or even thousands of churches. Denominations are stewards of immense resources of prayer, personnel, property and finance. When all of the denominations in New Zealand, assisted by every specialist mission agency, share in a mission thrust to reach New Zealand through church strengthening and church planting, their huge potential will be released.

Denominations that plant churches have increasing memberships, according to Lyle Schaller. The contrary is also true. Denominations that do not plant have decreasing memberships. He concludes, "The first step in developing a denominational strategy for church growth should be to organize new congregations."[15]

When Lieutenant Fiona Kirk graduated from the Salvation Army Training College in Trentham she was sent with only a few days notice to the St Albans Corps in Christchurch. The Corps officer Captain Terry Heese had a vision for a new Corps in Belfast just north of the city. He assigned Fiona to this task when she arrived in 1987. She was single, and in her late twenties. A Sunday school in Belfast had fruited into a monthly family worship service, which had then become a weekly service led by St Albans people. Fiona developed the service. It was relaxed and relevant in style, with a high level of all-age participation. People felt they belonged. There were opportunities to build relationships over a cup of tea.

"People suddenly found they were meeting others. The church was built on fellowship and visitation," she says. "Being focussed on the Belfast community helped me to build realtionships with those who started to attend." The visibility of the Salvation Army uniform, and activities such as teaching Bible-in-schools at the local primary school added to her impact in the community. Terry and Glenys Heese provided her encouragement and support. Salvation Army central funds bought a disused Methodist property, built ten pensioner units, and renovated the old church building for multi-purpose use. A thrift shop was staffed by the pensioner community. The Corps grew. Fiona left three years after she arrived, handing over a viable church to a Salvation Army couple who are continuing to develop the work.

Ethical Issues

Should we start a new church where one already exists? Does that not reek of competition? Could it be that starting a new church where one exists already, as one pastor claimed vehemently, "is not honouring to God!" A high-sounding and plausibly spiritual opinion, but taken to its logical conclusion this would not only halt the growth of the Church in New Zealand, we should also close thousands of churches to leave only one in every community. No, the real question is this: how many people can one congregation claim to evangelize? An English study estimated about 1,800 as an average maximum.[16]

Christian ethics demand that intending church planters establish valid empirical reasons for commencing in any community; they target clearly an unreached group or groups; they initiate open relationships with other church leaders when they commence; they minister with Christian integrity; they evangelize and refuse to proselytize; and they actively promote good relationships and cooperation among leaders and congregations in the same community. Where congregations are being multiplied in a community, (and where they are not) well-publicized combined services twice a year are recommended as a demonstration to the watching world that diversity is no denial of unity. Other combined activity may also be possible.

Should we resist the starting of new congregations? Ethics cannot be mis-used to stake out exclusive territorial claims that prevent further effective evangelism. Ironically, where turfism is a problem it prevents church planting only by groups from the same denomination over whom some form of control can be wielded. The problem of the parish boundary produced headlines and a memorable exchange reported in *The Independent* newspaper in London in 1991.[17] Bishop David Pytches, a former Anglican Bishop in Chile, planted a congregation of 180 people from his church, St Andrews Chorleywood, in the neighbouring parish of Watford where most of these people lived (along with many thousands of unreached people). The local vicar, Rev John Woodger was rather upset. The Bishop of St Albans, the Right Rev John Taylor, said the new congregation would have to go. "Church planting is a splendid idea," he said, "but as far as the Church of England is concerned it has to be done either within one's own parish, or in another parish with the consent of the parish priest and the diocesan bishop." David Pytches saw it differently: "Parish boundaries are the condom of the Anglican church!" he said. "They are a necessary safeguard but they inhibit natural growth." One might assume the Archbishop of Canterbury has some sympathy with David Pytches' dilemma. A missionary leader with a clear commitment to church planting, Archbishop George Carey has said, "Church planting is a tool for mission. It is not a replacement for the parish church but an extension of its life. That is why I strongly encourage all churches of moderate size to consider church planting in their area."

Models of Church Planting [18]

A: Modality Models and Examples

'Modality' refers to congregational structures, usually involving one local church giving birth to another. For good reasons, many believe the ideal process is for churches to plant churches.

Planting Autonomous Churches

1 Hiving off

This used to be a common method of planting new churches, and in some denominations is still common. A congregation is challenged to start a new church, a nucleus forms, and moves out usually with a church planter to start a new congregation. The new church is close enough to the sponsoring church so that people in the nucleus will not need to move house. The size of the nucleus varies. The hiving off model has some distinct advantages. It is the more committed people who respond to a challenge to go and start a new church. Experienced people will usually be involved. The combination of commitment and experience lays a good foundation for a new congregation. They will normally take with them a common philosophy of ministry, which contributes to harmony. The sponsoring church can nurture the new work while it grows and is progressively released.

The major disadvantage is that the leaders of the sponsoring church may not welcome the loss of too many members, and some of their best, as they see it. It seems to them that the massive haemorrhage which is to accompany the birth will so debilitate mother, she is unlikely to recover. Often this fear is expressed, or left unexpressed, in dollar terms: we will lose too many givers. For this reason alone many pastors resist planting a new church. Typically, those who do step out in faith and plant a new church using this method report that the empty seats were filled within a few months, and that their giving suffered only a slight hiccup. They see the promise, "Give and it shall be given to you,"[19] as applying not only to finance but also to church members.

2 Colonization

Colonization is a more radical form of hiving off, in which the members of the nucleus shift house and may move jobs and schools to locate in the target community. The recently planted Gonville Baptist Church in Wanganui had its genesis when optometrist John and Judy Mellsop returned from the Bible College of New Zealand in 1985. Encouraged by leaders at Wanganui Central Baptist they chose to buy a house in a suburb of 14,000 people served only by several small churches. The local Anglican vicar urged them to start a new church in his area, such was his spiritual concern for the thousands of people he was unable to reach. During the next three or four years another couple with children bought in the area and moved, relocating their children into new schools. Then two single women bought homes in Gonville. All of these adults had been trained at the Bible College of New Zealand. Next, two young couples without children bought homes in the community. When MISSIONZ church planters Stephen and Beth Tyrrell were called they also bought in the area. A total of 12 adults had relocated into seven homes to become the foundation of this new evangelistic church which is now touching increasing numbers of people.

3 Spontaneous

In New Zealand's earlier years when the pioneering spirit was more evident, this method was common among baptistic churches where local church independence was the pattern. Brethren Assemblies multiplied rapidly in this way. A few like-minded families living in an area would meet and spontaneously decide together that God was leading them to start a new church for their community. They would pray, prepare, and launch the new work, possibly without reference to outside agencies or authorities.

On Resurrection Sunday 1992 such a church began in Swanson, West Auckland, based on a nucleus of four couples from three different denominational backgrounds. They shared a spiritual concern for their community, and began to meet for prayer. They were well down the track before they linked up with MISSIONZ, the Baptist church planting agency, for help in their planning process and a degree of financial sponsorship. One of the founding couples, Michael and Trudy Hall, emerged as leaders of the new church. Through a children's after-school programme they are reaching 30% of the local primary school children, and making positive contacts with non-Christian parents who greatly appreciate their ministry. About 70 adults are now attending on Sundays.

4 Adoption

There are churches around New Zealand in the last stages of decline. All they hope for is death with dignity. In many cases they could be adopted by another more vital church (usually of the same denomination), and resurrected. This was the experience of the Naenae Baptist Church. When the last few faithful members finally raised the white flag, the Avalon Baptist Church prayerfully and diplomatically responded to their request for help with a total takeover. They released a dozen of their members with the pioneering spirit, and called Roger and Sue Everson from the Baptist MISSIONZ Training School[20] to replant the church. It grew. As Roger Everson noted, "There are 9,000 unchurched people around us in Naenae. Why should a church die here?"

Why indeed? To answer in a round about way: the secret of growth is the spiritual gifting (vision, faith, leadership, evangelism, communication, with openness to the Holy Spirit), and the training and maturity of leaders. A team of church planters were on a retreat together when they read in a church newspaper of the closure of a church. It had 20 members at the time. They hooted, shouted, laughed, and almost cried: "We start churches with fewer people than that!" The secret is spiritual gifts, openness to the Spirit, training and maturity. New Zealand has many churches that need reviving. For many, their best hope could be adoption by another church that has the vision and vigour to bring it to life. Inevitably this necessitates a surrender of proprietary rights. The Papakura First Presbyterian Church has adopted two ailing parishes with excellent results.

5 Church splits

This method is not advocated. Sometimes a theological shootout, personality conflict, leadership struggle, disagreement on priorities, or cultural difference, brings such tensions that a congregation splits. Commonly, after one faction pulls out and starts another congregation, both congregations prosper more than the former church did. Facing such a situation realistically, it might be possible to handle it positively. A recent example comes to mind. After fruitless local efforts to resolve a deep division, national leaders intervened. An honourable separation was suggested. This potentially traumatic experience was managed positively with the help and wisdom of national leaders. Church B commenced, new and vigorous, careful to avoid the dangers of reaction and negativity by cultivating a vision for mission in their new location. A building was purchased promptly. This greatly assisted the rapid formation of their new identity and provided a base for worship and community ministries. Church B immediately began to grow. Meanwhile Church A enjoyed the interim ministry of a very experienced and gracious newly retired couple, to good effect. Healing has been facilitated, hope restored, and promising couples called to pastor and grow both churches.

Planting Semi-autonomous Congregations

6 Radial model

By intention, the radial model results in congregations that radiate out from the parent church, and like satellites they remain only semi-autonomous. The bond that holds them together is the spiritual leadership of the senior pastor and the loyalty of the satellite pastors to the vision of the church. New Zealand's best known example is the Spreydon Baptist Church, led by senior pastor Murray Robertson since 1968. The church has eight congregations meeting at six locations around Christchurch city. The number of people attending on any Sunday totals about 1575, making this one of New Zealand's largest churches. A large low-cost multi-purpose facility is being built both for community ministries and for Sunday celebrations. In Murray Robertson's view, "This model of the church has the benefit of planting small mission-related congregations that can focus on evangelism, either in their neighbourhoods or among the groups of people to whom they minister. The congregations together as one church provide the resources that enable the development of a large number of community ministries, and the base for a movement outwards in world mission."

The powerful impact of the radial model for the gospel is being reported world-wide. John Vaughan has researched it extensively. He reports, "Large churches with satellite groups combine the best of two growth strategies... Although many of these churches are committed to building a large central church, most are just as committed to penetrating and reaching the city through the use of small groups coordinated fully, in most instances by the parent congregation."[21]

Faced with the immense challenge of reaching burgeoning populations in the world's cities, and the inability of traditional models of the church (eg. churches with the parish mentality) to grow rapidly enough to penetrate dense populations, Ralph Neighbour is promoting the cell church concept. The cell church is ideally adapted to penetrate the cultural and ethnic mosaics of the city. It is a highly developed variant of the radial model. Some New Zealand churches are moving into the cell church pattern.[22]

7 Multi-congregational churches

The multi-congregational church was originally defined as ministering to different ethnic groups, with more than one congregation meeting in the same facilities. Where differences are based on ethnicity, congregations may share only the facilities while retaining their autonomy. This is the case at the Baptist Tabernacle in Queen Street Auckland, which also accommodates a Chinese congregation and a Korean congregation, each autonomous, each with its own pastor.

Others go as far as to share administration. This is usually the case where a multi-congregational church's different congregations vary not ethnically but only in socio-economic levels or in worship style. Senior pastor Maurice Milmine at Glenfield Baptist Church in Auckland initiated a new congregation in the same church building under the leadership of pastors Stuart and Christine Hight, based largely on their different personalities which are reflected in the worship style. Both congregations are growing. At the same time they have planted an autonomous church in Albany led by ministry students Eddie and Michelle Houghton.

St Andrews Uniting Church in Whangarei is pastored by Presbyterians Grahame and Maureen Drummond. When a less formal service was requested they started 'Worship in the Round' at 8.30 am, and found that it attracted a steady stream of new worshipers. People commented, "I feel at home. It's more personal. I like being able to see people's faces. I like to hear what others think. Our family was going through a crisis, and it's been a healing experience." It has remained small at about 25, but new people come then move through it into other services.

The Sunday evening services are held on alternate Sundays, one being a monthly youth service. Another service held on Friday mornings started years ago for farmers who came to town once a week. This is now attracting the elderly. Lunch is provided. Then people expressed their need for a larger, more contemporary service on a Sunday morning. After much preparatory discussion and prayer, the 8.30 moved to an 8.15 start, the traditional service with organ accompaniment moved from 10.00 to 9.15, and a new (fifth) service began at 10.30 am. This is now a popular all-age service, with a simultaneous children's programme that interlocks with the adults' worship. Singing is accompanied by a varied group of instruments.

8 Network model

The best known example of this model world-wide is the Ichthus Fellowship in London, led by Roger Forster.[23] One of New Zealand's largest Presbyterian churches is a multi-congregational, multi-campus network of congregations spreading through South and rural South Auckland. Now attracting over 900 people to worship, it has grown under the long-term leadership of senior pastor John Balchin, who commenced his ministry at First Presbyterian Papakura in 1966. "My predecessor Graham Miller had a policy of church planting, which I inherited," John says. "They had started Takanini and Papakura East as independent parishes. Land had been purchased in Rosehill, South Papakura. We thought this was too close to the mother church. It was sold, and another property purchased. Meanwhile a Sunday school was started in a South Papakura school building, then a monthly service. A multipurpose building was constructed for weekly services and community use." John Balchin pastored both churches. "But the South church became white middle class, which was not reflective of its community, and it plateaued. There was no conversion growth. We needed a new worker with cross-cultural gifts who could reach Maori and Polynesian as well."

In 1985 John Balchin recruited Bible College graduate Steve Millward, a young man with apostolic gifts: a pioneer evangelist, a visionary and an initiator. The son of a Presbyterian minister and Maori missioner, he married John Balchin's daughter Ruth, who was a trained social worker. Steve's comment: "In our ministry we married evangelism and good works." A medical centre operates from their building on an honesty box basis, reaching 500 families. They run a drivers' licence class (every lesson opens with prayer!), seeker classes, and various other community services. The Rosehill congregation has grown from about 70 to over 200 including children, with a high proportion of Maori and Polynesian.

First Presbyterian added more home-grown staff, and multiplied their services to provide a smorgasbord of options: 8.30 am communion, a 9.30 am traditional service, and an 10.30 am non-traditional service. When the 10.30 am service outgrew the building in 1992 they shifted to the High School hall. Two country parishes approached First Presbyterian for help, and were adopted. New staff were appointed and placed, initially underwritten by First. This network of parishes has many unique features among Presbyterian churches in New Zealand. There are seven preaching places, with up to 13 services on any Sunday. John Balchin is the only ordained minister. His ministry team meets with him every week, and the combined Session for the whole parish meets quarterly. Each congregation has its own eldership and is financially independent.

B: Sodality Models and Examples
'Sodality' refers to denominational or parachurch structures, usually not based in the local congregation. Some of these models may be adapted for use by local churches.

9 Mission team
A church planting agency can recruit, finance, and support a team of workers to plant a new church. Generally these mission agencies are so-called parachurch, coming from outside the denominational structures, but these agencies do not generally plant churches in New Zealand. New Zealand Baptists have taken an innovative approach by forming such an agency within their denominational structure, known as MISSIONZ (pronounced mission en zed).[24] While remaining committed to the philosophy that churches plant churches, they recognize that church planters are the key to effective church planting. Planters are therefore recruited, trained at the MISSIONZ Training School, and made available to a church to help accomplish that church's church planting vision.

Some funding is available from denominational sources to support MISSIONZ church planters. To date these workers have planted 13 congregations, from Doubtless Bay to Christchurch. Various other denominations are also training church planters and pastors at this school.

The mission team referred to in regard to church planting is usually the local team. David Shenk and Ervin Stutzman argue that "a team is essential for church planting".[25] Team members contribute the range of gifts needed in starting a new church, and model unity, community, and ministry from the outset, enhancing the process. Though the mission team model may generally be a sodality approach, local churches can use it to good effect. Wanganui Apostolic Church had closed, but was revived by pastor Bruce Monk in 1978. His vision for church planting has resulted in the amazing record of a new church every second year despite the relatively small size of the mother church (an average of about 100 members through this period). They have accomplished this by utilizing the mission team model. In 1983 a team of two, Graham and Tricia Lee, was sent to plant the Masterton Apostolic Church, which in its turn planted Carterton in 1988. Te Nikau graduate Kevin Martin was sent to start a church in Ohakune in 1985.

Through 1987 pastor Graham Lee, now back in Wanganui, had Te Nikau Training School graduate Owen Raleigh on his pastoral team for further on-the-job training. In mid 1987 they selected a team of 12 adults to start a new church in Wanganui East under Owen Raleigh's leadership. Three others on the team had been trained through the Ministry Development Course, two of them at Faith Bible College. Team members were asked to make a two year commitment. They built their relationships, and prepared through study and community contact. Sunday evening services commenced in a public building, and a year later Sunday morning services began. Attendance peaked at 125 in 1989. They then commissioned a group to start another church in the country area of Turakina. This daughter church now has a two-weekly service attended by 30 people.

A two or three year venture in Wanganui West with a team of seven key leaders, 32 people (including 18 children) in all, has recently been pulled back. Not all churches that are planted survive. Despite the closure of both Wanganui West and Carterton the cumulative attendance of this young family of six churches has continued to grow each year. Attendance is currently over 600.

10 Catalytic church planter

God gifts and calls some special people as catalytic church planters. They go into a new area and develop the nucleus of the new church from zero. The Apostle Paul was such a church planter. He went into new areas and started new churches. He usually did not stay very long. Such church planters may be deployed by denominational agencies, or sent out by local churches. There seem to be few examples in New Zealand, where church planting in this manner is very demanding. One catalytic church planter with the New Life movement is Ray Bloomfield. When asked, "Where is your next church plant, Ray?" he replied, "God would have to scream!" and cited the stresses of repeated church planting on his co-worker and wife Pat and their five children, plus the struggle to raise finance. He is now moving into the apostolic church planter model where his passion for extending the kingdom of God, and his experience, can motivate and mobilize others.

11 Founding pastor

The founding pastor is called by the agency to plant and grow a new church for an indefinite period of time. One of the most exciting recent examples of church growth in New Zealand is the story of founding pastor Ian and Margaret Bilby, who were called from a lengthy and effective ministry in Blenheim to found Auckland City Elim Church. Bilby, a gifted and practical communicator, draws people to his vision for training and growth. He became President of the Elim Churches of New Zealand at the age of 30, a position he has held for over 17 years. The Bilbys arrived in Auckland in January 1985, with worship leaders Bruce and Christine McGrail. Initial meetings in a home led to services in the Freemans Bay Community Centre, now superceded by three services each Sunday in the Auckland Girls Grammar School auditorium, with approximately 1,500 people in the church. A multi-gifted team, which includes seven pastors, serves the church. They have no plans to build a worship centre but have recently bought an ideal facility as an administrative and training centre. Their vision includes a new International Ministry Development School to train pastors, church planting teams, and lay leaders. They are a mission sending church, desiring to impact Auckland city. Ethnic home groups reach Persian, Spanish, Chinese, Indian, Vietnamese, African, Philippino and Pacific Island peoples. The Elim Church of New Zealand has specific goals for church planting in the 1990s.

12 Independent church planter

Independent church planters who go out on their own to start new churches are not common in New Zealand. They serve neither a denominational nor a parachurch agency. They are not strictly a sodality operation except that in themselves they consititute a kind of sodality. Their church planting procedures are not much different from others apart from their lack of initial outside financial or structural support.

Geoff Smith planted an independent church in Auckland in mid 1990 at the invitation of a small group of Navigator and Campus Crusade national leaders. They were concerned to provide a church for the people they were winning to Christ, a theologically conservative evangelical church with an emphasis on life-related expositional preaching of Scripture. Their vision was for worship and lifestyle that was non-charismatic but adventurous. When they outgrew their small beginnings in a community centre in Greenlane, they moved to a school hall in Epsom. After two years Geoff Smith reports an attendance of 300 coming to the Auckland

Bible Church from all over the city. Their members tend to be from the middle class, professional, business, and student populations. The church is baptistic in its constitution and its understanding of leadership, with two full-time pastors.

13 Apostolic church planter

World-wide the charismatic and pentecostal movements are developing new and effective models for planting churches. Many believe that all the New Testament gifts including that of apostle are operative today. Those who are recognized as apostles function with spiritual authority. Often they found their own church themselves, which then becomes the base church for a church planting movement. Usually church planters emerge from the base church: the apostle recognizes them, oversees their training, and commissions them to plant new churches. These new churches are typically not satellites but autonomous churches with their own property. They may or may not be part of a denomination, but do relate to and accept the oversight of the apostle. Where these develop outside a denominational framework, they might be described as a fellowship of churches, a movement, or network.

New Zealand's Christian City Churches are not everybody's scene. They are not intended to be. "Our target audience is the baby-boomers and their children; our culture is casual, our music loud, upbeat and contemporary rock and roll." Hamish Divett's vision is to pastor pastors, to plant churches that plant churches, and to build a large prototype church in Auckland as a model of an alternative church. Currently 500 attend. Divett's background includes an early age conversion in a Baptist church in Hamilton, a slide into alternative living in his late teens, followed by a period of acculturation into the contemporary pentecostal scene. During this time he bought a tie, married and settled down. He planted an Assembly of God church in Raglan in 1986, and spent a short time on the staff of a growing independent pentecostal church in Auckland. He investigated new churches on Australia's East coast, and was blown away by Phil Pringle's Christian City Church in

Sydney. He began to study baby-boomer and contemporary culture seriously. Then through a model 5 experience (see above) he was thrust out to start the CCC in Mt Eden in 1987. The eight New Zealand CCC churches now reach over 1,600 people. "Our goals for this decade are to plant 50 churches in New Zealand."

Conclusion

Multiplication of congregations is the essential strategy for the discipling of whole nations. As New Zealand's traditional denominations recover apostolic confidence, and as new denominations gain momentum, pioneering church planting will increase. Jesus said, "I will build my church."[26] As illustrated in Acts, the gospel spreads by the evangelistic planting of churches and congregations[27] that then vigorously multiply disciples, leaders, and churches, to reach and bless their communities.[28] Renewal of existing churches will lead to many mission strategies. The primary strategy for the growth of the kingdom of God is the planting of more and more lively, caring congregations of Christians who reach target groups in their communities for Christ.

BIBLIOGRAPHY

Charles Brock, *Indigenous Church Planting* (Nashville, TN: Broadman, 1981).

Charles Chaney, *Church Planting at the End of the Twentieth Century*, (Wheaton, Il: Tyndale, 1989).

David J. Hesselgrave, *Planting Churches Cross-Culturally*, (Grand Rapids, MI: Baker 1980).

Johan Lukasse, *Churches With Roots*, (Bromley, UK: STL, (Monarch, 1990).

Jim Montgomery, *DAWN 2000*, (Pasadena, CA: William Carey Library, 1989).

Bruce Patrick, *The Life Cycle of Reproducing Churches, Guidelines for Establishing Daughter Congregations, Problems in Starting a Daughter Church, Evangelism in the 1990s, The Church Planter and Church Planting Team, Community Survey Samples*, (Auckland: MISSIONZ, 1989 - 1991).

Martin Robinson and Stuart Christine, *Planting Tomorrrow's Churches Today*, (Tunbridge Wells, UK: Monarch, 1992).

Lyle E. Schaller, *Growing Plans*, (Nashville, TN: Abingdon, 1983), chapters 4 and 5.

David W. Shenk and Ervin R. Stutzman, *Creating Communities of the Kingdom: New*

Testament Models of Church Planting, (Scottdale, PA: Herald, 1988).

William C. Tinsley, *Upon This Rock*, (Atlanta, GA: Home Mission Board SBC, 1985).

C. Peter Wagner, *Church Planting for a Greater Harvest*, (Ventura, CA: Regal Books, 1990).

FOOTNOTES

[1] 'Multiplying congregations' is a more general term than 'church planting'. By 'church' we mean ecclesia (New Testament Greek = called out ones), the people, the congregation. No one model is implied. Words like cell, congregation and church are often used interchangeably in this chapter.

[2] Matthew 18:20, Colossians 1:27, 1 John 4:4.

[3] Matthew 16:18.

[4] The strategy of multiplication is foremost in Matthew 28:18-20, the recipients in Mark 16:15, the content of the gospel in Luke 24:46-49, the wonderful mystery of the commission in John 20:21, and the source of power, and geographic priorities, in Acts 1:8.

[5] Acts chapters 2, and 3, and see 8:25, 40, 9:31, and 11:19.

[6] See Acts 13:1-3, 14:1-23, and especially 14:23.

[7] See Acts chapters 16 - 18.

[8] Michael Hill in Webster and Perry, *The Religious Factor in New Zealand Society*, (Palmerston North: Alpha, 1989), Foreword.

[9] Webster and Perry, Ibid., pages 48 - 49.

[10] "God is not slow," (2 Peter 3:9).

[11] Roger T. Forster, *Models of Church Planting*, (London: Ichthus Media Services).

[12] Ray Muller, Church Growth Consultant with the Wellington Anglican Diocese, in *From the Parish Consultant*, (Wellington, April 1992).

[13] Webster and Perry, Ibid., pages 48 - 49.

[14] This example is taken from an article by Peter Stuart in *Crosslink*, Wellington, June 1992.

[15] Lyle E. Schaller, *Understanding Church Growth and Decline, 1950 - 1978*, (New York: Pilgrim Press, 1979), page 351.

[16] Source: Bob Hopkins, a national church planting leader with the Anglican Church in the UK.

[17] *The Independent*, Monday 4 March 1991.

[18] For the benefit of international standardization the outline of this section is adapted from C. Peter Wagner, *Church Planting for a Greater Harvest*, (Ventura, CA: Regal Books, 1990), chapter 4. Some descriptive material is derived from this source.

[19] Luke 6:38.

[20] The MISSIONZ Training School was founded in 1984 to train church planters and growth leaders. It was initially known as the Church Growth School.

[21] John N. Vaughan, *The Large Church*, (Grand Rapids, MI: Baker, 1985), page 23.

[22] Ralph Neighbour, *Where Do We Go From Here? A Guidebook For The Cell Group Church*, (Houston, TX: Touch, 1990).

[23] Roger T. Forster (Ibid.) writes of 8 models, found in embryonic form in the Gospels, and in Acts in practice : 1 Mass evangelism church plant (Acts 2:41); 2 Mega church plant (8:1); 3 Maybe church plant (10:24, 16:13-15, 19:1-2); 4 Mushroom church plant (11:21); 5 Mobile church plant (13:3, 20:4); 6 Mini-mission church plant (18:1-4); 7 Mother church plant (19:10, see also Colossians 1:7-8, 4:12-13); 8 Multi-cell church plant (2:46, 28:30-31, see also Romans 16:3-16).

[24] See Ralph Winter, "Two Structures of God's Redemptive Mission", All-Asia Mission Conference, Seoul, 1973, printed in Ralph D. Winter and Stephen C. Hawthorne, *Perspectives on the World Christian Movement*, (Pasadena, CA: William Carey Library, 1981) pages 178 - 190. Mission teams and local church structures are both found in the New Testament. Many mission teams world-wide are now focussing on planting churches.

[25] W. Shenk and Ervin R. Stutzman, *Creating Communities of the Kingdom: New Testament Models of Church Planting*, (Scottdale, PA: Herald, 1988), page 44.

[26] Matthew 16:18.

[27] Acts 14:23, 15:41, 16:5.

[28] Acts 19:10.

Haere, Meinga Hei Akonga Nga Iwi Katoa

(Go Make Disciples of All The People Groups)

Matthew 28 :19

by Lionel Stewart

The Great Commission in Matthew 28:19-20 stands for all peoples and for all time, until the return of Jesus Christ. It stands now for the Maori. On the face of it the task of fulfilling the Great Commission seems relatively straightforward. "Go, make disciples... teach them to obey everything I have commanded you." It probably would be straightforward but for cultural differences. Because of these differences the communication of the gospel message must be adapted to fit the world-view of the hearers in specific cultural situations. The essential truths of the message remain constant but the style of communication will vary enormously from culture to culture. Jesus Christ is our supreme example. He did not communicate with the rich young ruler in terms of the new birth, or with the woman of Samaria in terms of selling what she had and following him, or with Nicodemus in terms of the water of life. Cultural sensitivity by messengers is paramount. It is paramount for effective evangelism among Maori. What is the essential unchanging message? This is a prior question before discussing cultural differences between Maori and Pakeha. Second, what does the conversion of Maori mean, or for that matter what does conversion mean for any cultural group, including those in the various sub-cultures of Pakehatanga[1] in Aotearoa[2] New Zealand?

The Message

It has been stated that the gospel "is like a multifaceted diamond, with different aspects that appeal to different people in different cultures. It has depths we have not fathomed. It defies every attempt to reduce it to a neat formulation."[3] Nevertheless there are central themes at the very heart of the message: God is the Creator; sin is universal; Jesus Christ is the Son of God and Lord of all, the Saviour through his death on the cross and his resurrection from the dead; conversion is through the power of the Holy Spirit and the new birth experience; the Church of God is the body of Christ and has his mission; Jesus Christ is coming again in glory as judge. The great challenge to the Church is to present this message without resorting to cultural imperialism, ie. by imposing the missionaries' own cultural customs and way of life along with their message. A friend of the writer visited Indonesia several years ago. He observed in one part of the country that the Indonesian men wore black jackets when preaching the Scriptures. Black is not the ideal colour for the tropics. Why did they wear black jackets? Decades earlier, Dutch missionaries to Indonesia had worn black jackets when preaching the gospel. The central message had been delivered by these missionaries but there was an addition to the message. The Indonesians came to believe that wearing black jackets for preaching was essential. Examples like this are found everywhere in the history of missions, especially from the 19th century. The tendency was to produce cultural replicas from missionaries' home countries, eg. in church architecture, musical forms, musical instruments, ministerial dress and so on, all based on a false assumption that the New Testament Scriptures had spoken on these particulars. Theology was trapped in a monocultural straitjacket.

Leaders of modern missions have come to a much clearer perception of what constitutes the Great Commission message. The concept of a church expressing itself in the indigenous culture is now a widely accepted principle of church formation and development. In New Zealand churches there is renewed recognition of the rightful place of Maoritanga[4], but some Maori still perceive the gospel as Pakeha, involving a Pakeha God. Even if the message could be delivered relatively culture-free in order to prevent this thinking, the charge undoubtedly would still be laid by some, since the gospel speaks about the Lordship of Christ and he will challenge the very core of Maori culture or any culture. This accusation may even be levelled at a messenger of the gospel whose cultural background is the same as the hearers. The Apostle Paul had this experience: "This is the man who goes everywhere teaching everyone against the people of Israel, the Law of Moses and this Temple."[5] Yet it is quite clear he respected Jewish culture. Paul did not throw away all of his Jewish cultural background when he became a Christian.

Conversion

The Willowbank Report was the result of a "Gospel and Culture" consultation in 1978 sponsored by the Lausanne Committee on World Evangelization. The 33 theologians, anthropologists, linguists, missionaries and pastors who produced the report considered the fundamental meaning of conversion for all cultures to be "a change of allegiance". "Other gods and lords - idolatries, every one - previously ruled over us, but now Jesus Christ is Lord. His authority over us is total."[6] Their definition has behind it the authority of Scripture. Christ is "the source of eternal salvation for all those who obey Him."[7] This being the case, the cultural inheritance of Maori is bound to come under the examination of the Lordship of Christ as does the inheritance of all cultural groups in whatever country. The materialistic gods of Western culture as much as the departmental gods of Maoritanga must yield to the Lordship of Christ. Further, Jesus is not only Lord but he is and has supreme authority and power in the spiritual realm. So, for example, the binding fear of some tapu[8] is to be broken by the power of the Holy Spirit. A Maori pastor relates how, on becoming a Christian, he made a pilgrimage back to a certain tapu tree fenced off on the marae.[9] In historical times the tree had been used to string up dead bodies in transit. Traditionally, Maori regard a dead body as highly tapu, hence the symbolic cleansing by the washing of hands on leaving an urupa.[10] He stood in front of the tree and prayed that God would help him in his thinking with respect to the tree. He said God spoke to him: the only tree that was to have power over his life was the tree of Calvary. At that point he knew he was free from fear associated with the tree. He broke off a small branch, not to desecrate the culture but to prove to himself the supreme power of the Lord Jesus Christ.

The Way Ahead

For evangelism to be effective among Maori it is imperative we have clarity on the two issues discussed above: the essential theme of the gospel message, and the essential nature of true conversion. Some of our evangelistic methods appear to have been counter productive in their attempt to touch Maori people. Maori tend to be both group-oriented and feelings-oriented. Certain evangelistic methods rely on an emotionally charged group atmosphere, but when the emotion disappears people are not so easily affected a second time. True conversion requires an act of will, radical counting of the cost, repentance towards God and turning away from the life of habitual sin. Response solely on the grounds of emotion will inevitably produce a spurious conversion which will fail the test of time. Given that we are clear in our minds about the gospel message and what it means to believe that message, what are some other considerations for the way ahead?

The Issue of Contextualization

It has been already stated that there is renewed recognition of Maoritanga having a rightful place in the life of the kingdom of God. Maori are identifying more with their cultural inheritance. From the 1986 to the 1991 census the Ratana church[11] recorded a 21% increase. Over this five year period 7,866 members were added, making a total of 47,595 (cf. the Ringatu church's 1991 total of 8,052). According to Roger Maaka,[12] head of the Maori Department at Canterbury University, the Ratana church has a particular appeal to younger Maori who are embracing a resurgent Maori identity. He said the Ratana church is seen by many, especially younger Maori, to be an expression of organized Christianity not imported by missionaries. It is not colonial. In missions worldwide it is being recognized more and more that the gospel does not presuppose the superiority of any culture. Western culture is no longer seen to hold all the answers with respect to organizing and running a church. The recent publication by Lloyd Martin, *One Faith, Two Peoples*,[13] is aiding the process. We ought not however adopt a stereotyped view of Maori and how they relate to their cultural background. In the 1991 census 511,000 people declared themselves as Maori, ie. as having Maori ancestry.[14] The degree to which 'Maoriness' is possessed by this number varies greatly, from locality to locality, tribal area to tribal area, age group to age group. For example consider the language of the Tuhoe people of inland Bay of Plenty which is still relatively intact by comparison with other tribal groups. The old waiata[15] are still a living musical expression, certainly with their old people. By contrast a Maori iwi[16] radio station in Auckland has recently commenced operations. Initially they are playing American rap music to reach the youthful Maori population in the greater Auckland City region. The station has clashed with official broadcasting policy which states that iwi stations are to promote Maori language and culture. The station however declares rap music to be Maori music to these young listeners, an interesting commentary on the fact that culture is constantly changing. There is a lesson here for Maori evangelism. The basic message remains unchanged, but there must be flexibility in the cultural approach. What works in inland Bay of Plenty will not necessarily be appropriate for downtown Auckland. In the former situation, use of Maori is imperative. In the latter, contemporary English is the medium.

The Issue of Syncretism

All churches in all cultures face the danger of syncretism. Syncretism occurs where a church fails to distinguish clearly between what is consistent with life in the kingdom of God as distinct from life in the kingdom of darkness. False and evil elements of the culture are allowed to persist in the life of the church. All cultures have had elements of the demonic in them since sin entered the world. In the past, so-called 'third world' churches have been singled out for attention but Western churches have fallen into the same sin. According to the Willowbank authors the most insidious form of syncretism in the world today is the attempt to mix a privatized gospel of personal forgiveness with a worldly (even demonic) attitude to wealth and power. With the current resurgence of traditional Maori values, customs and beliefs, churches with a strong Maori character will need clear guidelines for accepting or rejecting compatible or incompatible customs and beliefs if they are to be effective witnesses for the gospel and live in the power of the Spirit.

How can a church detect and eliminate wrong teaching, and prevent the carry-over of cultural forms and beliefs inconsistent with the gospel? First, by keeping Christ and the cross central to its thinking and action. He is to have first place, not culture. One does not put culture first and then ask where does Christianity fit. Jesus Christ is first; one then asks where do cultural customs, values and beliefs fit under his Lordship. Second, by seeing the Scripture as normative. That is, it is "without error in all that it affirms."[17] The task of discovering what it affirms is a serious one, requiring openness to the Spirit of God, the one who inspired the Scriptures. There are principles in Scripture which will give us answers to the specifics of cultural issues if we come with an attitude of readiness to obey where light is given. We can turn to principles such as "do it all for God's glory,"[18] and ask the question, "If we keep this cultural custom, value or belief, will it bring glory to God?" Again, there is the principle of love for the weaker brother or sister. The question becomes, "If we keep this cultural custom, value or belief, will it cause my Christian brother or sister to stumble?"[19] Love for our brother or sister may often limit our liberty in cultural issues. There are a number of such principles in Scripture that enable us to deal with cultural issues which we may be uncertain about accepting or rejecting. Undoubtedly there is much in Maoritanga that is entirely consistent with Scripture but which in the past has been condemned as inherently inferior or evil. Even te reo Maori[20] has been subject to such views. In this case the error was failure to distinguish between certain content and the structure used to convey that content. The structure of language is not itself inherently evil; some content clearly is. An early missionary to the Canadian Indians, acknowledged to be of apostle status, is quoted by his biographer as one who "never made any translation (of the Bible or any part of it) in their (Indian) language. He has such a pious veneration of Scripture that he can only think of an attempt to transfer it into their tongue as an absolute mutilation of the Holy Word."[21] Fortunately such cases are rare and in modern times probably no longer exist. But this is an example of an attitude which underpins the truth that we are all prisoners of our own cultural background, consciously or unconsciously. Third, we can test the consistency of cultural forms with the gospel by referring such issues to church leaders for their consideration and reflection. Leaders (elders, bishops, presbyters) have a special role in providing spiritual direction. Their qualifications include the ability to teach.[22]

The Issue of Provincialism

Undoubtedly one of the significant trends in modern Maoridom is reflected in the concept of mana motuhake, loosely translated as self determination. Whereas in the past it was principally the dominant Pakeha culture and leaders in that culture who gave direction on major policy matters affecting the development of New Zealand as a nation, there is now an increasing number of highly capable, educated, articulate and gifted Maori leaders in all strata of society. Their voice is shaping the destiny of Maoridom in ways not seen in earlier years. These leaders are pointing to the

Treaty of Waitangi[23] as the basis for a bicultural partnership between Maori and Pakeha. They are emphasizing equality between the two partners. The same trend can be seen in the life of the Church. Maoritanga is assuming a place in the life of the Church that extends beyond its historic place in the four mainline denominations: Anglican, Catholic, Presbyterian and Methodist. Newer churches are also seeking to indigenize their life to accommodate Maori perspectives.

World-wide, every church expresses its life in its own cultural medium, but there is a danger here. The Willowbank Report states, "Some churches... go beyond a joyful and thankful discovery of their local cultural heritage and either become boastful and assertive about it (a form of chauvinism) or even absolutize it (a form of idolatry)."[24] The paternalism of Western missions in the past is a reflection of this kind of attitude. Western culture was absolutized, often unwittingly, in mission policy. The same danger now presents itself in the current rediscovery of Maoritanga in the life of the kingdom. The Willowbank authors term this provincialism. Maori could retreat so far into their culture that they become cut off from the rest of the Church and the wider world. "It is to proclaim one's freedom only to enter another bondage."[25] At stake is the unity of the Church which may easily be sacrificed in the interests of diversity (though of course diversity does exist within the greater unity). The barriers which Jesus came to break down through his death on the cross may be erected again, whether they be barriers of social class, race, tribe, education, or socio-economics. We would then lose sight of the Church as God's new humanity where the two, the three, however many culture groups, have become one in Christ.[26] For the Maori Christian and for the Pakeha Christian, the primary identity is not in any one of their respective cultures but in the one Lord and the one body of Christ. The relationship is one of brothers and sisters in the family of God, a relationship that is to be rooted in love. "Despite the church's failures, this vision of a supra-ethnic community of love is not a romantic ideal but a command of the Lord."[27] [28]

Where the opportunity exists, and it does exist in Aotearoa New Zealand, we can enrich each other with the development of bicultural and multicultural churches. In the early 70s a church in Gisborne made such a commitment and developed its congregational life to a point where 60% of its membership was Pakeha and 40% Maori. One in three of Gisborne's population is Maori. The church gave practical expression to its bicultural character in a number of ways.

First, by seeking to educate each group, encouraging one culture to learn about and understand the other through wananga,[29] forums, seminars, books, tapes and rap sessions. They recognized that ignorance is a breeding ground for prejudice and misunderstanding. Second, by ensuring reciprocal communication between the two cultural groups. Special liaison groups were set up when the need arose. Third, by interacting between the groups especially in the marae situation. Interestingly, when they came to interacting in each other's homes, they discovered it to be a very slow process. Fourth, by viewing the church buildings as a spiritual marae. Over a period of 18 months, five Maori families chose to hold their three-day tangihanga[30] in the church buildings. Fifth, by appointing both Maori and Pakeha as leaders of the church. Sixth, by adjusting worship patterns to incorporate unique aspects of both cultures. Where Maori led worship, the expectation was not that it should be done in the Pakeha way but for it to be a genuine expression of the Maori style. Seventh, by giving a place to te reo Maori in church services and church functions. Eighth, by investing money in those things necessary to meet the needs and aspirations of both cultural groups: cash for travel, vehicles for transport, mattresses for communal sleeping, crockery and cutlery for catering. Ninth, by incorporating Maori art forms in the architecture and decoration of church buildings.

A church needs to regard its bicultural partnership as a long term journey, often difficult, but worth the effort. If churches cannot model reconciliation and cross-cultural harmony, what other group in the community can do it? The natural bent of human nature in its fallen state is towards division and separateness of the wrong kind, splitting off into factions. It is a natural phenomenon. But the Church is not a natural phenomenon. It is a supernatural body born of the Spirit.[31] When New Zealand witnesses how Maori and Pakeha Christians love one another (practically and not in word only), not because of their common cultural heritage but in spite of their cultural differences, then we are indeed proclaiming the power of the gospel to break down natural barriers and walls of hostility.

More recently the Gisborne church decided on a church planting venture in the suburb of Kaiti where the majority of the Maori members lived. For several years a monthly outreach service had been held in Kaiti and it seemed a natural extension of this mission actively to plant a fully fledged church with its own constitution and leadership. Initially it proved a costly venture in the emotional sense, since practically all of the Maori members left from the central church to form the basis of the new congregation. Those left in the sending congregation felt a sense of grief, especially the pastor. The new congregation in Kaiti is substantially Maori but it also has a minority group of Pakeha who strongly identify with the new church as their spiritual home.

The Issue of Maori Church Leadership

Perhaps no other issue is as crucial as this one, if evangelism and discipling is to gather momentum among Maori. The issue has come into sharper focus with the recent deaths, within a relatively short space of time, of three prominent Maori evangelists, Norman Tawhiao, Muri Thompson and Bob Kingi, all of whom had national and international ministries.

Maori leadership in the past has not been without difficulties. The journey for Maori Anglicans, described in their Church's 1986 Report on Bicultural Development, *Te Kaupapa Tikanga Rua*, has been particularly painful. It took well over 100 years from the time the gospel was first preached here, by Samuel Marsden in 1814, before the first Maori bishop was recognized. Why this delay in recognition? It raises the question of the authoritative place of Scripture in the life of God's Church and second, the degree to which we are prepared to trust the work of God's Spirit in the lives of others, especially those who do not belong to our own cultural group. If we take Scripture as our reference point, it is clear that biblical leadership in the Church rests on at least two fundamentals. First, leadership is a gift from the Spirit of God. The Holy Spirit distributes this gift without favouring any one particular cultural group. Second, leadership has more to do with a person's character and life than with her or his formal academic standing or other cultural factors.[32] While it is true the ability to teach is required, formal academic qualifications do not necessarily guarantee the possession of the teaching gift. Given that these are two fundamentals for spiritual leadership, it is difficult to believe that for over 100 years no Maori was gifted to be a bishop. The Anglican journey towards Maori leadership has not been unique. Today there are healthy signs of growing numbers of Maori assuming leadership positions in the Church. There are 86 Apostolic churches for example, and at least 16 of these are led by Maori pastors. Currently two Maori serve on their National Executive of seven leaders. The Apostolics have adopted a vision for Maori leadership to rise to their full potential and responsibilities within the Church.

For some Maori to step out, constant and persistent encouragement is needed from others. Maori can defer to Pakeha leadership. They can be reluctant to respond to opportunities to take the lead in the presence of Pakeha leaders. Historical factors have contributed to this attitude. The worst scenario is for Maori to see themselves, or to be seen by others, as gifted solely in guitar playing and singing. Such a position cannot be sustained from the teaching on gifts found in 1 Corinthians 12:1-31. There is another aspect to this issue. Will we get to the point where Pakeha freely respond to and serve under senior Maori leaders in the same way that Maori have freely responded to Pakeha leadership in the past? As already stated, in some sections of the body of Christ we are seeing some encouraging signs. To move in that direction is to move towards maturity and a true understanding of what God desires for the Church.

However great the encouragement from others may be, the response to opportunities for leadership must finally come from Maori themselves. A pastor of a multicultural church in America, at a point in his church's journey, felt constrained to say to one section of the church, "It is up to you how long you want to ride in the back of the bus." Culturally they were retiring by nature and this, coupled with a more dominant approach by other sections of the church, led to them not accepting responsibility for leadership initiatives. Because accusations were being levelled by this particular group at those more dominant, the pastor responded with his bus comment. In a similar way this has happened in Aotearoa, both within and outside the Church. Accusations, especially where they are prolonged or bitter, can be spiritually destructive and lead to withdrawal from the life of the Church and the passing up of opportunities to assume leadership roles.

An encouraging sign for Maori Christians contemplating some form of leadership training is the way more of our training establishments are giving recognition to taha Maori[33] in their programmes and organizational structures. Recently the Bible College of New Zealand has appointed a Maori lecturer to teach courses in Maori customs, language and protocol. It has also set up an advisory board of Maori kaumatua[34] to advise on policy related to Maori studies and programmes within the college. Some denominational colleges had previously taken similar steps.

The Issue of Church-based Discipleship

We are not here referring to the church in the sense of a building or institution but in the the New Testament sense, ie. the 'ecclesia', the called-out ones. Each church is God's people, those joined to

Jesus Christ in a living relationship with him and with each other by the Spirit of God. It is clear from passages such as Ephesians 4:11-16 that maturity in Christ is a growing process and that this process takes place in the context of the body of Christ. We need each other. Moreover our commitment to each other is not an option but obligatory. We can go further and say that this commitment to one another is at the very heart of genuine conversion.[35] Maoridom has had its fair share of the hit and run type of evangelism. The message is preached, decisions are secured and the evangelist disappears. But it is one thing to start in the kingdom and another to keep going. At this point a true conception of the function and nature of the church is needed if we are to "no longer be children, carried by the waves and blown about by every shifting wind of the teaching of deceitful men..." The goal is to move from this immature state and come under the control of Jesus Christ, the head of the Church, for "Under his control all the different parts of the body fit together... When each separate part works as it should the whole body grows and builds itself up through love."[36]

This creates a special challenge for Maori, particularly in relationship to their church leaders, whether Maori or Pakeha. Maori tend to gather around a leader rather than the institution we have come to call the church. It is not difficult for an inspiring figure to gain a following in Maoridom particularly if ministering in the area of physical healing. Leaders must resist the temptation to control the church in a despotic way. They must strive to make space and create opportunities for all to exercise their spiritual gifts for the good of the whole church. It is the writer's opinion that those Maori who best stick to their profession of faith are those who have this perception of the church, and a deep commitment to the body, exercising their gifts not to gratify their own needs but in order to encourage and build up the whole church.

There is a phrase in Maori, 'tipi haere,' which means to wander aimlessly around. For many Maori believers in the past, this was the pattern. They made a good start in the kingdom but then tended to fall away. One factor contributing to this has been a disappointment with the established church. Its Western-type structures, management style and life have not recognized the relevance of Maori cultural background. It is on record that one church in the Waikato saw nearly 300 Maori enter its doors over a period of three years but lost virtually all of them in the same period of time. Maori culture was not acknowledged in the life of this church. Churches that want to be effective in winning Maori and seeing them grow towards maturity will need:

1   Strong but not autocratic leadership, role modelling 'hanging in' for the long term
2   Sound biblical teaching ministry
3   Structures to facilitate body life
4   Full recognition of aspects of Maoritanga that are consistent with the gospel. The degree to which this recognition is given will depend upon the kind of community in which the church is located
5   Structures to facilitate community ministries
6   Vision for mission beyond Aotearoa.

For Maori it is especially important that the teaching ministry be sound biblically. There is a certain spiritual dimension in Maoritanga that sets it apart from secular Western culture. Most Maori people acknowledge the spiritual world, but this has both positive and negative effects. On the positive side, Maori respond easily to spiritual influences and readily accept the supernatural. There are few if any Maori atheists. On the negative side, all spiritual or religious persuasions are culturally acceptable whether they be Ba'hai, Mormon, Jehovah's Witness, pentecostal, mainline church, etc. That there is one supreme God is freely acknowledged, but the belief that all roads lead to God is not uncommon. Jesus Christ may be seen only as a way to the Father. By invitation a Mormon minister may stand alongside a Christian minister at a typical marae service. It is not easy on a marae to "contend for the faith that was once for all entrusted to the saints"[37] and not slip into compromise. There is a constant temptation to edit the message of the gospel. We must note that the offense of the cross cannot be avoided, while every attempt must be made by the messenger to avoid unnecessary cultural offense.

The Issue of Maori and Overseas Mission

In 1989 a conference on world mission was held in Suva, Fiji. It drew Christian leaders from around the South Pacific. The theme was "The Deep Sea Canoe", an historical reference to the way in which indigenous peoples in the Pacific took the gospel to other indigenous groups. The question was asked, could it happen again? For Solomon Island representatives it was not a matter of could. It must. God in his grace brought revival to Solomon Islands in 1970 through the visit of Maori evangelist Muri Thompson and his team. More recently the leaders of the South Seas Evangelical Church in that country believed God was saying to them, "Launch out. If what you have is not shared, it will dry up." They are now taking ministry teams to minister in Australian churches, churches of the Western cultural tradition. Pastors from these churches have visited Solomon Islands to listen and learn from their brothers and sisters. Few Maori have gone beyond the shores of New Zealand in response to the Great Commission. Some have, but mainly to minister through missionary societies whose structures are essentially western in cultural style. There is a growing belief amongst some Maori leaders in New Zealand that Maori have a mission overseas, and that the ministry should flow from their own cultural background. Some tentative beginnings have been made. A concern to reach Maori in Australia in the context of their own cultural background is growing. There are more than 70,000 Maori living in Australia. Several years ago New Zealand Maori Anglicans established a mission centre in Sydney. Currently the Apostolic Church is seeking to establish a congregation in Sydney with the specific aim of reaching Maori people. Such initiatives can only help Maori gain a broader perspective on "Haere meinga hei akonga nga iwi katoa."

Postscript

The way ahead can be full of promise if we in the Church are determined to walk in love: Maori, Pakeha, and all other ethnic groups that make up New Zealand. What does love mean? It means to show respect for one another.[38] It means to serve one another.[39] It means to get rid of all bitterness; no more insults, no more hateful feelings of any sort. It means having a tender heart.[40] It means to be humble towards one another, always considering others better than yourselves.[41] It means to be tolerant with one another and to forgive one another when anyone has a complaint against anyone else.[42] It means not keeping a record of wrongs, and not being conceited or proud.[43] Love is the glue that will hold us together as we seek to express our diversity of cultural backgrounds within the unity of the Spirit.

Evangelism can be defined in a number of ways. One leader has defined it like this: "Evangelism is the overflow of reconciled relationships." If the body of Christ is not healthy in its internal relationships then whatever else we do in planned evangelistic activity will be correspondingly weaker. Is the Spirit of God waiting for us to take seriously what we readily affirm with our lips? "There is no longer any distinction between Gentile and Jew... (Maori, Pakeha, Polynesian, Asian) but Christ is all, Christ is in all".[44] Unity and love demonstrated by the restoration of relationships have characterized every true revival in the history of the Church.

No reira e te whanau, ma te Atua tatou e arahi. Family of God, may God lead us. Kia ora tatou katoa.

Te Arahou o te Hahi Mihinare[45]

(The New Way of the Missionary Church)

by Bruce Patrick

In May 1992 the Anglican Church in New Zealand constitutionalized its "new journey." Its 50th General Synod formally approved historic legislation recognizing three cultural streams with equal power and status. In his opening address Archbishop Brian Davis called the 100 member gathering the most momentous since the first constitution was laid down in 1858. The three tikangas[46] are: Te Pihopatanga o Aotearoa, responsible for ministry to Maori; the seven Pakeha dioceses within New Zealand; and Tikanga Pasifika, comprising the diocese of Polynesia, including Fiji, Samoa, and Tonga. To reflect the constitutional changes, the Anglican Church has also adopted a new name: the Anglican Church in Aotearoa, New Zealand and Polynesia. It was previously the Church of the Province of New Zealand, for 135 years.

The three tikangas will come together for voting on issues concerning the overall life of the Church, and must all agree for decisions to be made. Brian Davis said the Church had "modeled to the nation, and even to the wider world, a new form of cultural partnership and interdependence. It will offer the promise of partnership beyond paternalism and dependency to a relationship that respects and honours cultural diversity."

The general secretary John Patterson said the Church was no longer the same body. "We have reshaped ourselves. The three partners are equals and not one holds sway." Bishop Whakahuihui Vercoe, Te Pihopa o Aotearoa, said he was exhilarated and excited at the change, especially as the relationship was between a majority and minority groups. "We Maori are now responsible for the conduct of the Church's business in our own tradition and customs. The task is now to forge this new relationship so we don't go off on a tangent from the other tikanga."

Bishop Vercoe said, "In 1840 we signed a treaty in trust to form our partnership and a new nation. Today we have gone back to our roots to discover what we have missed in order to forge that trust and partnership." Bishop Vercoe denied suggestions that the new structure reflected separatism, saying it actually meant true unity in the Church. "This changes the whole democratic process that says that because one group is in the majority, it will always win. It is a new interpretation of democracy that recognizes each person has the sovereign right to be heard and listened to."

The Long Road to the Present

As Bishop Vercoe pointed out, these recent developments have a long history apart from which they will not be understood. In 1807 Samuel Marsden persuaded the fledgling Church Missionary Society to undertake a mission to the Maori people. One of the founders of the CMS was Henry Venn, whose enlightened philosophy of missionary activity contained three principles which have become known as the Three-Self Movement. These can be described as: Self-determination, the autonomy of the Church in its new environment; Self-propagation, the priority of self-development, indigenous ministry and indigenous evangelization; and Self-support, a structure of physical support governed by the forms of enterprise found in the local culture.

The 'Active' sailed from Sydney to the Bay of Islands in 1814, bearing Samuel Marsden and three lay missionaries, Kendall, Hall, and King, accompanied by ten Maori persons, led by Ruatara, Hongi and Korokoro. The lay missionaries were poorly equipped for the task, and seemed to have motives far removed from the noble principles formulated by Venn. They shared a determination to save the souls of the heathen and to replace their culture. The civilizing of the natives, it was thought, would eventually lead to their Christianization.

For at least 40 years the Anglican Church in New Zealand was a Maori Church. The earliest missionaries laboured for a decade without one positive act of commitment to the Christian faith by a Maori. In 1822 the tide turned with the arrival of Henry Williams. A number of Maori communities requested the presence and teaching of a missionary or took it upon themselves to spread the faith by their own means. A great deal of activity took place: teaching, the cultivation of crops, building, translation into Maori language of biblical and liturgical material, and printing. Eventually a number of Maori churches were built, and examples abound of Maori lay evangelists and catechists taking a lead in the propagation of the faith.

By 1842 when Bishop Selwyn arrived the Maori Church was well established. Before his departure from England, the Parent Committee of the CMS had reminded him that the missionaries were not at liberty to minister to European settlers. Their mission was to the Maori. Thus did a tension first become evident which remains 170 years later: how to provide for both Maori and settler in the one Church. Selwyn impressed with his ability to preach in the Maori language immediately upon his arrival, but he was never to enjoy the same trust and mutual respect in the Maori world as did Marsden and the Williams brothers, Henry and William. After ten years he acknowledged, "it was harder than he thought to plant the seeds of a new religion in the hearts of the Maori and harder still to unite settler and Maori in a single church." He turned his attention to matters of church governance, the division of his diocese, and the writing of the constitution. From this point on the division between the Maori Church and the Settler Church was to become even more evident.

Formulation and acceptance of a written constitution was hailed as evidence of growth and maturity in the New Zealand Church of

England, but it was by its very nature a document of the Settler Church. It was signed in 1857, yet without one Maori signature. In fact the missionary clergy felt the interests of the Maori Church were best safeguarded by the CMS, and so the provisions of the constitution were not at first intended to include the Maori Church. Bishop Selwyn addressed the first general synod in 1859, expressing "some doubts of the future stability of the Native Church," and asked Synod to consider "the best mode of drawing our Native brethren into closer bonds of Christian fellowship with ourselves." That same question, phrased in a variety of ways, was to reappear time and again in both diocesan and general synods. Selwyn also voiced his concern that it might "be found impossible to carry on a double government for the Colonial and Missionary Church."

The Land Wars of the 1860s placed immense strain on the faith and loyalty of the Maori people to a Church which "told us to close our eyes and bow our heads in prayer, and when we lifted up our heads and opened our eyes, our land had disappeared." There followed a long period of time in which the Settler Church took the ascendancy. Diocesan boundaries were established that bore no relation to tribal boundaries. Successive synods avoided calls for a Maori bishop to lead the Maori Church. Eventually in 1928 Frederick Augustus Bennett was consecrated as the first bishop of Aotearoa. As a suffragan bishop to the bishop of Waiapu he was without authority in another bishop's diocese where that was not granted. It took until 1978 for a general synod to inaugurate a Bishopric (Te Pihopatanga) of Aotearoa with its own structures. All Maori work came under its direct control. For the first time the Maori portion of the Church was represented on the general synod as of right. In 1980 the Council of the Bishopric was constituted as an Electoral Synod to nominate and elect the fourth Maori Bishop, the first time Maori had enjoyed this right. A new era was emerging. Indigenous peoples in other Anglican communions, eg. in USA including Alaska and Hawaii, Canada, Australia and Papua New Guinea, have been assisted to take similar steps towards self-determination following the example of Maori Anglicans.

The Treaty of Waitangi: Biculturalism, Partnership

In 1984 an important discussion paper led to the establishment of a Bicultural Commission and a lengthy study of the implications of the Treaty of Waitangi for principles of partnership and bicultural development that might apply to society and the Church. This paper quotes the Te Atiawa report of the Waitangi Tribunal:

"Governor Hobson's view of the broad implications is illustrated in his statement to each Maori signing the Treaty of Waitangi when he said, "He iwi kotahi tatou," which has been translated as "We are now one people". At Waitangi on 6 February 1981, however, the present Governor-General Sir David Beattie said, "I am of the view that we are not one people despite Hobson's oft-quoted words, nor should we try to be. We do not need to be. The Treaty was an acknowledgement of Maori existence, of their prior occupation of the land, and of an intent that the Maori presence would remain and be respected. It made us one country, but acknowledged that we were two peoples. It established the regime not for uniculturalism but for biculturalism. We do not consider that we need feel threatened by that but rather that we should be proud of it, and learn to capitalize on this diversity as a positive way of improving our individual and collective performance."

The Report of the Bicultural Commission of the Anglican Church on the Treaty of Waitangi confirmed that an overwhelming number of submissions held that the Treaty does contain principles of partnership and bicultural development.

The Treaty in Article One granted power to the British Crown to bring and maintain law and order. It also acknowledged both the prior existence of Maori people, and the right of new settlers to share the resources of New Zealand. The Treaty created one nation but acknowledged two peoples with two distinct cultures. It recognized and established the principle of partnership.

Article Two of the Treaty required the protection of the land, forests, fisheries and taonga (including cultural treasures) of the Maori. Article Three of the Treaty extended to "the natives of New Zealand all the rights and privileges of British subjects". A central feature of such rights was the freedom to take any action so long as the law did not prohibit it. That freedom included the right of Maori people to their own culture, including their language.

The Treaty guarantees Maori rights and interests and does not merely recognize them. This means the State is required to take positive action to protect cultural values and not merely refrain from interfering with the protective steps taken by Maori people themselves. The Treaty clearly implies the principle of bicultural development. Without denying the tension between the interests of the two main cultures, the Commission was convinced that partnership and bicultural development offered the way forward for a society ready to be enriched by its dual heritage. Partnership and bicultural development are essential parts of the foundation for a developing social contract.

What do these terms mean, bicultural development, and partnership? Bicultural development is the process whereby two cultures grow and develop within one nation in a spirit of mutual respect and responsibility. Partnership involves cooperation and interdependence between distinct cultural or ethnic groups within one nation.

Are the principles Christian? It was argued by some that the Treaty was exclusively a secular document and accordingly had no implications for the Church. Others submitted that because the Church had been so involved in the acceptance and promotion of the Treaty, the Church today has an obligation to implement the principles. Whatever the strength of these arguments, the

Commission noted that the Treaty is a fact and therefore is relevant for all the people of New Zealand, and more importantly, the Commission was convinced that the principles are consistent with the gospel of Jesus Christ. For these reasons the Church has an obligation to apply the principles of partnership and bicultural development to its own life and ministry to the people of New Zealand.

In studying the moral and spiritual implications of the Treaty, the Commission became aware of different perceptions of it by Maori and Pakeha people. Maori people generally have regarded life more wholistically. The spiritual permeates the whole of life. Pakeha on the other hand tend to think in terms of separate categories, Church and State, secular and sacred. This has resulted in Maori people having a higher sense of the moral and spiritual value of the Treaty than other New Zealanders. Different perceptions also arise from the communal values of Maoridom and the more individualistic values of Pakeha society. These differences need to be understood and accepted, and explored in the light of the gospel of Christ. The Commission appended 18 recommendations to its report.

Development of Te Pihopatanga o Aotearoa

In 1976 there were two Maori priests in the whole of the South Island. In the Diocese of Wellington there were seven, in Waiapu there were eight, Waikato three and Auckland nine. A self-supporting training scheme emerged in 1976 in the Diocese of Waiapu. This has led to dramatic and enthusiastic growth in the numbers of those trained for ministry, both ordained and lay, men and women, and has challenged and spread to other dioceses. Extraordinary growth and change led, in 1990, to agreement that four assistant and regional bishops be appointed to four new episcopal sub-regions. Church buildings are being restored and reopened, though the basic evangelistic strategy centres on the provision of a lay or ordained trained worker for every marae in the country (approximately 436).

The Maori population in New Zealand is 511,000 (see footnote). Current figures (1992) for Te Pihopatanga ministry personnel are:

	Men	Women	Total
Clergy	185	19	204
Kaikarakia (Lay Readers)	125	64	189
Total	310	83	393

The establishment of Te Whare Wananga o Te Rau Kahikatea on the St John's Theological College site is further evidence of the rapid thrust for education and training. Its primary purpose is to provide a tikanga Maori perspective within theological education and ministry training. At present the College offers full-time residential training for ten students each year, as well as distance education and regional training. It is anticipated that a full-time faculty of four will be led by Sir Paul Reeves from 1994, along with a network of 40 other trainers. The development of relevant and suitable courses is seen as a contribution to the Decade of Evangelism. A 'Diploma Social Services - Aotearoa' is now offered, part of a larger response to the needs of Maori who are numbered disproportionately among the suffering in Aotearoa.

The Mission Statement of the Sixth Anglican Consultative Council has been taken seriously and applied:

1 To proclaim the good news of the kingdom
2 To teach, baptize, and nurture new believers
3 To respond to human needs by loving service
4 To seek to transform unjust structures of society
5 To preserve the environment of the planet for future generations.

Every congregation, parish, regional diocese and Te Pihopatanga itself sets its mission goals and reviews each step as it proceeds. Worship, the gospel, and mission are kept central. Women and youth have appropriate and equal representation on all committees and structures.

FOOTNOTES

[1] Pakehatanga = Western culture.

[2] Aotearoa = most commonly-used Maori word for New Zealand, literally: "Land of the long white cloud".

[3] *The Willowbank Report - Gospel and Culture,* (Wheaton IL: Lausanne Committee for World Evangelization, 1978), page 12. This report appears as chapter 54 in Ralph D. Winter and Steven C. Hawthorne (eds.), *Perspectives on the World Christian Movement*, (Pasadena, CA: William Carey Library, 1981), page 515.

[4] Maoritanga = Maori culture.

[5] Acts 21:28 (TEV). Bible quotations in this chapter are mostly from *Today's English Version* (Good News Bible), used by permission of the Bible Society in New Zealand.

[6] Ibid., page 523.

[7] Hebrews 5:9 (TEV).

[8] Tapu = sacred, or a social or spiritual constraint.

[9] Marae = buildings and section of land which form the focus of Maori community and social life.

[10] Urupa = Maori cemetery.

[11] The Ratana and Ringatu movements are two indigenous Maori movements whose origins are in the New and Old Testaments.

[12] *The Press*, (Christchurch NZ, 29 August 1992).

[13] Lloyd Martin, *One Faith, Two Peoples*, (Paraparaumu Beach, NZ: Salt Company, 1991).

[14] The 1991 census contained two fundamentally different questions about ethnicity. The first asked with which ethnic group the respondent identified, the second whether he or she had any Maori ancestry, however remote. Further, in answering the first question, respondents could pick more than one box (eg. Maori, and Chinese). These questions gave three different totals for Maori numbers. Some 511,000 claimed Maori biological ancestry; 435,000 claimed to identify with Maori ethnicity; and of these 323,000 ticked only the Maori box, the remaining 111,000 ticking two or more boxes. The definition of Maori now standard in most statutes is: Maori means a person of the Maori race of New Zealand and includes any descendent of such a person. This definition is rightly ignored in practice. It is incompetent, racist, and completely at odds with the modern belief that individual preference should determine a person's ethnicity. (Summarized by the editor, from J.D. Gould, "How Many Maoris Are There Really?" *New Zealand Herald*, (Auckland, 16 November 1992).

[15] Waiata = chants.

[16] Iwi = tribe, tribal.

[17] *Willowbank,* ibid., page 9, and *Perspectives,* ibid., page 511, para 2.

[18] I Corinthians 10:31 (TEV).

[19] I Corinthians 8:13 .

[20] Te reo Maori = the Maori language.

[21] Dan Kelly, in an article "Undoing the Damage," in *The Enterprise* (Canadian Baptist Mission, Winter 1987 - 1988).

[22] I Timothy 3:2.

[23] The Treaty of Waitangi was signed in 1840 as a declaration of partnership between indigenous Maori chiefs and the British Crown. For a summary of its contents see on in this chapter.

[24] *Willowbank,* ibid., page 27, and *Perspectives*, ibid, page 531.

[25] Ibid., page 27, and ibid., page 531.

[26] Ephesians 2:14-16.

[27] Ibid., page 27, and ibid., page 531.

[28] Also see Chapter 18 which grapples with the effects of ethno-linguistic differences. The classification of ethnic subgroups in Chapter 18 applies as much to Maori in Western culture in New Zealand as it does Europeans in Maori culture or in any other unfamiliar culture (editor).

[29] Wananga = learning courses on Maori culture.

[30] Tangihanga = Maori funeral.

[31] John 3:6.

[32] I Timothy 3:1-7.

[33] Taha Maori = the Maori way.

[34] Kaumatua = elders.

[35] I John 3:14.

[36] Ephesians 4:14-16 (TEV).

[37] Jude 3 (NIV).

[38] Romans 12:10.

[39] Galatians 5:13.

[40] Ephesians 4:31-32.

[41] Philippians 2:3.

[42] Colossians 3:13.

[43] I Corinthians 13:4-5.

[44] Colossians 3:11(TEV).

[45] This section was written by the editor, based on conversations with Anglican Maori leaders Muru Walters and Frank Harrison, and drawing heavily on the following sources (in order): *Challenge Weekly* (Auckland, 21 May 1992), page 5; *Te Kaupapa Tikanga Rua, Bicultural Development,* Te Ripoata a te Komihana mo te Kaupapa Tikanga Rua mo to Tiriti o Waitangi, The Report of the Bicultural Commission of the Anglican Church on the Treaty of Waitangi, (July 1986); and *Te Whakapapa o te Pihopatanga o Aotearoa, A Mission Statement and Profile of the Bishopric of Aotearoa,* (Rotorua, 1992).

[46] Tikanga = stream

17

Emerging Ethnic Diversity : The World at our Doorstep

by Bob Hall

In the words of Lawson Lau, the world has come to our doorstep.[1] While New Zealand is still predominantly European and Maori, many other shades and hues are now being added to the spectrum. My concern in this chapter will not be with European, Maori and Pacific Island populations. In addressing the issue of emerging ethnic diversity in New Zealand, I want rather to identify where minority populations are located, consider what needs to be done to further consolidate our knowledge of these populations, and look at how the Church needs to respond to the missions challenge.

Ethnic Identification

An overview of the ethnic identification of the New Zealand resident population from 1976 to 1991 is provided in Table 1.[2] Allowing for differences in definition and response between censuses some trends are worth highlighting. First, the European segment of the population, while increasing slightly in numerical terms through this period, is nevertheless declining proportionally (83.0% to 78.8%). Second, the Maori segment (combining single and multiple ethnic identification) increased over the period (11.5% to 12.9%).[3] Third, while the Pacific Island component is still relatively small, it too has seen growth over the period since 1976 (1.5% to 3.9%). Fourth, ignoring the complications of multiple ethnic identification (All Other Combinations) and nil responses (Not Specified) the remaining segment (Chinese, Indian and Other) has also shown an increase over the period (0.8% to 2.7%). This last is the growing segment on which I want to focus for the rest of this chapter.

TABLE 1: USUALLY RESIDENT POPULATION BY ETHNIC IDENTIFICATION (1976-91)

	1976 Census	%	1981 Census	%	1986 Census	%	1991 Census	%
Single Ethnic Group:								
European	2577138	83.0%	2573007	81.9%	2651595	81.3%	2658738	78.8%
NZ Maori	164270	5.3%	154047	4.9%	295317	9.0%	323493	9.6%
Samoan	22330	0.7%	33585	1.1%	50199	1.5%	68565	2.0%
Cook Island Maori	15024	0.5%	19227	0.6%	23973	0.7%	26925	0.8%
Tongan	2932	0.1%	5172	0.2%	9225	0.3%	18264	0.5%
Niuean	4851	0.2%	6834	0.2%	8472	0.3%	9429	0.3%
Tokelauan	1575	0.1%	1947	0.1%	2316	0.1%	2802	0.1%
Fijian	619	0.0%	936	0.0%	1875	0.1%	2760	0.1%
Other Pacific	308	0.0%	495	0.0%	813	0.0%	1413	0.0%
Total Pacific	47639	1.5%	68196	2.2%	96873	3.0%	130158	3.9%
Chinese	12877	0.4%	16065	0.5%	19566	0.6%	37689	1.1%
Indian	7876	0.3%	9735	0.3%	12126	0.4%	26979	0.8%
Other	3305	0.1%	5637	0.2%	12078	0.4%	25926	0.8%
Combination Ethnic:								
NZ Maori plus other	192448	6.2%	178359	5.7%	109458	3.4%	111354	3.3%
All other combinations	29002	0.9%	106163	3.4%	29709	0.9%	31482	0.9%
Not specified:	68710	2.2%	32098	1.0%	36564	1.1%	28113	0.8%
TOTAL	3,103,265	100.0%	3,143,307	100.0%	3,263,283	100.0%	3,373,929	100.0%

Source: NZ Census Reports, 1981 and 1991.

Geographical Distribution of Population Segments

Before looking at the composition of the minority ethnic groups (Chinese, Indian and Other populations), we can sketch in how each of these composite population segments (European etc.) is distributed across the country. Table 2 presents the distribution by regional council (North and South Island), Table 3 by urban area (Main and Secondary), and Table 4 by area type (Urban and Rural).[4]

TABLE 2: DISTRIBUTION OF POPULATION SEGEMENTS BY REGIONAL COUNCIL (1991)

	European	NZ Maori	NZ Maori plus other	Pacific Island	Chinese, Indian and Other	TOTAL
NORTH ISLAND						
Northland	89,412	28,116	7,389	669	705	128,493
Auckland	667,375	71,637	31,578	94,110	48,894	936,438
Waikato	259,848	46,731	13,914	4,716	4,911	334,350
Bay of Plenty	145,977	42,237	10,254	1,728	1,629	204,144
Gisborne	25,110	15,129	2,427	261	339	44,040
Hawke's Bay	105,222	22,986	5,511	1,674	1,458	138,048
Taranaki	91,698	9,225	3,435	282	846	106,278
Manawatu/Wang	181,200	25,788	8,874	2,148	3,837	224,127
Wellington	307,755	30,072	11,859	21,138	18,408	397,788
Sub-Total	1,873,597	291,921	95,241	126,726	81,027	2,513,706
North Island %	70.5%	90.2%	85.6%	94.5%	88.6%	74.5%
SOUTH ISLAND						
Nelson/Marlbor	101,757	4,188	2,397	294	667	110,496
West Coast	30,708	1,389	678	60	132	33,408
Canterbury	397,062	14,637	7,086	4,278	6,378	434,262
Otago	166,230	4,851	3,015	1,605	2,925	180,774
Southland	88,944	6,294	2,817	1,068	417	100,431
Sub-Total	784,701	31,359	15,993	7,305	10,519	859,371
South Island %	29.5%	9.7%	14.4%	5.5%	11.5%	25.5%
TOTAL	2,658,738	323,490	111,231	134,031	91,458	3,373,929

Source:Columns 1-4, 1991 Census Report; Column 5, unpublished 1991 census data, Dept of Statistics

The data in Table 2 show that ethnic diversity is more pronounced in the North Island than in the South Island. The data in Table 3 show that ethnic diversity is more pronounced in the main urban centres than in the secondary urban centres. The data in Table 4 show that Europeans are reasonably evenly distributed throughout both urban and rural sectors as are Maori, although the latter are overly represented in minor urban and rural areas. What is of significance in Table 4 however, and this is substantiated by the data in Tables 2 and 3, is that the vast majority of Pacific Islanders and other ethnic minorities are to be found in the main urban centres. We shall note the significance of Auckland, Wellington, and to a lesser extent, Hamilton, Christchurch and Dunedin in this regard.

TABLE 3: DISTRIBUTION OF POPULATION SEGMENTS BY URBAN AREA (1991)

	European	NZ Maori	NZ Maori plus other	Pacific Island	Chinese, Indian and Other	TOTAL
MAIN URBAN						
Whangarei	32,514	7,782	2,250	216	342	43,713
Auckland	611,187	66,348	29,268	93,381	47,463	869,169
North Auckland	*153,108*	*5,835*	*3,555*	*2,616*	*5,358*	*173,160*
West Auckland	*103,782*	*9,834*	*5,694*	*11,283*	*4,992*	*138,978*
Central Auckland	*204,039*	*18,438*	*8,295*	*36,075*	*24,045*	*299,266*
South Auckland	*150,255*	*32,235*	*11,712*	*43,404*	*13,071*	*257,811*
Hamilton	117,066	17,703	5,682	1,431	3,333	147,066
Hamilton Zone	*95,952*	*15,120*	*4,740*	*1,371*	*3,162*	*121,972*
Cambridge Zone	*10,983*	*774*	*363*	*15*	*81*	*12,321*
Te Awamutu Zone	*10,137*	*1,812*	*582*	*45*	*84*	*12,777*
Tauranga	59,178	6,993	2,247	324	474	69,888
Rotorua	32,796	12,729	3,450	978	687	51,474
Gisborne	19,608	8,967	1,650	204	255	31,266
Napier-Hastings	85,296	15,852	4,095	1,572	1,293	109,122
Napier	42,966	5,745	1,692	366	690	51,942
Hastings	42,336	10,107	2,394	1,200	609	57,180
New Plymouth	42,462	3,021	1,386	177	504	47,991
Wanganui	33,087	5,097	1,617	369	351	40,920
Palmerston North	58,599	4,803	2,289	1,083	2,391	70,035
Wellington	241,812	24,177	9,522	20,592	17,739	321,468
Upper Hutt	*29,619*	*2,715*	*1,020*	*708*	*708*	*35,289*
Lower Hutt	*70,365*	*8,547*	*2,862*	*5,271*	*4,230*	*93,114*
Porirua	*25,971*	*6,285*	*2,502*	*8,856*	*1,068*	*46,113*
Wellington City	*115,863*	*6,630*	*3,138*	*5,757*	*11,736*	*146,955*
Nelson	43,383	1,245	789	147	342	46,284
Christchurch	271,656	11,049	5,250	3,978	5,664	301,455
Dunedin	98,538	2,436	1,863	1,410	2,352	107,979
Invercargill	45,027	3,423	1,683	801	282	51,720
Sub-Total	1,792,203	191,622	73,047	126,648	83,481	2,193,954
SECONDARY URBAN						
Pukekohe	10,494	2,580	639	171	750	14,907
Tokoroa	8,928	3,738	1,245	2,061	156	16,524
Taupo	13,371	2,784	843	360	84	17,586
Whakatane	11,655	3,678	891	87	126	16,581
Hawera	9,255	1,263	366	15	159	11,091
Feilding	11,652	1,014	399	51	84	13,281
Levin	15,282	2,091	720	252	354	18,861
Kapiti	24,639	1,089	588	105	165	26,976
Masterton	16,119	2,352	711	267	180	19,833
Blenheim	21,411	1,005	657	60	96	23,436
Greymouth	9,426	351	177	18	54	10,154
Ashburton	14,361	387	177	18	99	15,102
Timaru	25,755	714	342	96	225	27,366
Oamaru	13,008	300	177	57	111	13,734
Gore	9,774	774	210	30	45	10,896
Sub-Total	215,136	24,123	8,160	3,645	2,682	256,332

Source :Columns 1-4, 1991 Census Report; Column 5, unpublished 1991 census data, Dept of Statistics

TABLE 4: DISTRIBUTION OF POPULATION SEGMENTS BY AREA (1991)

	European	NZ Maori	NZ Maori plus other	Pacific Island	Chinese, Indian and Other	TOTAL
Main Urban	64.7%	59.2%	65.6%	94.5%	91.3%	65.0%
Secondary Urban	8.1%	7.5%	7.3%	2.7%	2.9%	7.6%
Minor Urban	8.7%	15.0%	11.6%	1.2%	2.9%	8.9%
Rural	15.8%	18.3%	15.5%	1.6%	2.9%	15.0%
TOTAL N.Z.	2,658,738	323,490	111,354	134,031	91,458	3,373,929

Source:Columns 1-4, 1991 Census; Column 5, unpublished 1991 census data, Dept of Statistics

Geographical Distribution of Minority Ethnic Groups

Ascertaining the geographical distribution of these minority ethnic groups (Chinese, Indian and Others) is not a straightforward matter. In its regional summary, the 1991 census report simply aggregates them together as Other and does not even distinguish Chinese and Indians.[5] To get a clearer picture of what these groups are and where they are to be found we need to go to unpublished census material. Using figures provided by the Department of Statistics we can initially divide the Other category into Chinese, Indian and All Other Ethnic Groups. See Table 5.[6]

The data in Table 5 show that sizeable concentrations of Chinese, Indians and Other Ethnic groups are to be found in Auckland and Wellington (particularly Central Auckland and Wellington City) and to a lesser extent in Christchurch, Hamilton, Dunedin and Palmerston North. Of the secondary urban centres only Pukekohe (with 201 Chinese and 504 Indians) and Levin (with 309 Chinese) merit mention.[7] We can therefore concentrate the rest of our attention on the main urban centres.

Table 6 shows the main urban centre breakdown of this Other ethnic category by Region (East Asia etc.) and also by Major Ethnic Group (Kampuchean etc.)[8] In addition to the major ethnic groups listed, a further 55 ethnic groups were identified in the census but in most of these cases the number of people involved was relatively small.[9]

Auckland and Wellington (particularly Central Auckland and Wellington City) again stand out as having significant concentrations of ethnic populations with the major numbers in this case coming from South East Asia. Ethnic groups with the largest concentrations in New Zealand (apart from Pacific Islanders, Chinese and Indians) are Kampuchean, Filipino, Japanese, Vietnamese, Sri Lankan, Laotian and Iranian. Previously identified patterns of concentration are replicated here.

TABLE 5: DISTRIBUTION OF MINORITY ETHNIC GROUPS BY URBAN AREA (1991)

	Chinese	Indian	Other Ethnic	TOTAL
MAIN URBAN				
Whangarei	99	90	153	342
Auckland	20,274	15,105	12,084	47,463
North Auckland	*2,724*	*978*	*1,656*	*5,358*
West Auckland	*1,923*	*1,632*	*1,437*	*4,992*
Central Auckland	*9,576*	*8,709*	*5,790*	*24,045*
South Auckland	*6,039*	*3,786*	*3,246*	*13,071*
Hamilton	1,017	1,182	1,134	3,333
Hamilton Zone	*966*	*1,137*	*1,059*	*3,162*
Cambridge Zone	*30*	*18*	*33*	*81*
Te Awamutu Zone	*27*	*30*	*27*	*84*
Tauranga	171	90	213	474
Rotorua	168	291	228	687
Gisborne	138	48	69	255
Napier-Hastings	693	279	321	1,293
Napier	*453*	*66*	*171*	*690*
Hastings	*240*	*210*	*159*	*609*
New Plymouth	189	159	156	504
Wanganui	150	123	78	351
Palmerston North	1,047	411	933	2,391
Wellington	6,588	5,415	5,736	17,739
Upper Hutt	*216*	*216*	*276*	*708*
Lower Hutt	*1,593*	*1,344*	*1,293*	*4,230*
Porirua	*195*	*300*	*573*	*1,068*
Wellington City	*4,587*	*3,552*	*3,597*	*11,736*
Nelson	129	36	177	342
Christchurch	2,835	756	2,073	5,664
Dunedin	1,053	240	1,059	2,352
Invercargill	87	90	105	282
Sub-Total	34,650	24,321	24,510	83,481

Source: Unpublished 1991 census data, Dept of Statistics.

TABLE 6: DISTRIBUTION OF MINORITY ETHNIC GROUPS IN MAIN URBAN CENTRES (1991)

	REGIONS							MAJOR ETHNIC GROUPS						
	East Asia	South Asia	SE Asia	Middle East	Africa	Latin America	Kam-puchean	Filipino	Japan-ese	Viet-namese	Sri Lankan	Laotian	Iranian
MAIN URBAN													
Whangarei	12	24	84	6	3	0	0	39	12	30	18	0	3
Auckland	1,623	1,284	6,483	1,146	207	480	1,461	1,821	1,086	1,284	726	654	531
North Auckland	*378*	*102*	*798*	*144*	*24*	*99*	*165*	*270*	*207*	*93*	*63*	*45*	*78*
West Auckland	*111*	*156*	*846*	*165*	*24*	*45*	*141*	*273*	*60*	*57*	*108*	*207*	*78*
Central Auckland	*1,017*	*822*	*2,640*	*579*	*117*	*228*	*405*	*975*	*738*	*345*	*438*	*189*	*303*
South Auckland	*114*	*204*	*2,196*	*249*	*42*	*108*	*750*	*303*	*81*	*789*	*120*	*210*	*72*
Hamilton	45	144	612	105	27	63	315	87	36	51	111	90	33
Hamilton Zone	*42*	*132*	*573*	*105*	*30*	*54*	*312*	*75*	*36*	*48*	*105*	*75*	*33*
Cambridge Zone	*3*	*3*	*18*	*0*	*0*	*3*	*0*	*3*	*0*	*6*	*3*	*6*	*0*
Te Awamutu Zone	*0*	*3*	*24*	*0*	*3*	*0*	*0*	*9*	*0*	*0*	*3*	*9*	*0*
Tauranga	42	12	126	15	6	12	0	54	27	39	9	0	9
Rotorua	39	27	96	21	15	12	0	60	36	9	24	0	15
Gisborne	12	18	12	9	6	6	0	9	12	0	18	0	3
Napier-Hastings	33	57	171	18	0	6	0	45	30	48	36	48	3
Napier	*27*	*24*	*96*	*6*	*0*	*0*	*0*	*15*	*27*	*21*	*15*	*48*	*3*
Hastings	*6*	*30*	*75*	*6*	*3*	*6*	*0*	*27*	*6*	*27*	*21*	*0*	*0*
New Plymouth	6	63	57	15	3	0	0	33	6	6	57	0	3
Wanganui	18	30	15	3	0	3	3	9	12	0	30	0	0
Palmerston North	111	117	480	72	30	78	318	60	102	24	75	0	48
Wellington	402	831	3,264	645	75	198	1,035	822	270	537	699	351	327
Upper Hutt	12	36	189	15	0	12	54	57	9	42	18	12	12
Lower Hutt	75	255	672	144	15	33	225	135	39	111	216	105	72
Porirua	18	36	459	15	3	27	180	36	15	6	27	213	12
Wellington City	300	522	1,950	471	57	126	579	597	210	384	441	18	237
Nelson	36	15	87	9	0	6	21	45	30	15	9	0	6
Christchurch	489	186	927	114	51	111	210	273	393	210	102	3	39
Dunedin	60	102	648	144	15	9	471	57	48	93	48	0	57
Invercargill	3	27	48	9	15	18	0	39	3	6	18	0	3
Sub-Total	2,934	2,931	13,137	2,316	660	1,003	3,840	3,459	2,109	2,349	1,977	1,143	1,083
TOTAL NZ	3,213	3,243	14,427	2,445	534	1,086	3,963	4,236	2,355	2,469	2,397	1,152	1,110

Source: Unpublished 1991 census data, Dept of Statistics.

A comment was made earlier on the significance of the major urban centres (Auckland, Wellington, Hamilton, Christchurch and Dunedin) in regard to concentrations of ethnic population. This is explored in more detail in Table 7.

The data in Table 7 confirm earlier comments. Centres with the highest ratio of ethnic concentration in the population (excluding Pacific Islanders) are Central Auckland (1 in 12) and Wellington City (1 in 13). Of the other major urban centres, Dunedin (1 in 46), Upper Hutt (1 in 50) and Christchurch (1 in 53) have the lowest ratios.

Worthy of note from this Table (apart from the ethnic diversity in Central Auckland and Wellington City and the spread of Chinese and Indians throughout most of these centres) are the numbers of Vietnamese and Kampucheans in South Auckland (789 and 750 respectively), Kampucheans in Dunedin (470) and Hamilton (312), Japanese in Christchurch (393), Sri Lankans in Lower Hutt (234), Laotians in Porirua (213), South Auckland (210) and West Auckland (207), Koreans in North Auckland (171) and Lebanese in South Auckland (102). These, along with the numbers in Central Auckland and Wellington City, represent major concentrations of these populations in New Zealand.

Finally, in confirming the ethnic diversity in these centres, Table 8 looks at the distribution of selected religious groups within these urban centres.

Again the strategic significance of Central Auckland and Wellington City stand out. With the exceptions, though, of Whangarei, Cambridge, Te Awamutu, Gisborne, Hastings, Wanganui, Nelson and Invercargill, all other centres in the main urban category have some degree of religious diversity worth noting: Rotorua with 222 Hindus, Napier with 102 Buddhists, New Plymouth with 120 Hindus, Dunedin with 570 Buddhists etc.

TABLE 7: DISTRIBUTION OF ETHNIC GROUPS BY MAJOR URBAN AREAS (1991)

	North Auckland	West Auckland	Central Auckland	South Auckland	Hamilton	Upper Hutt	Lower Hutt	Porirua	Wellington City	Christ-church	Dunedin	Total in Major Urban
Chinese	2,724	1,923	9,576	6,039	966	216	1,593	195	4,587	2,835	1,053	31,707
Indian	978	1,632	8,709	3,786	1,137	216	1,344	300	3,552	756	240	22,650
Kampuchean	165	141	405	750	312	54	225	180	579	210	470	3,491
Filipino	270	273	975	303	75	57	135	36	597	273	57	3,051
Vietnamese	93	57	345	789	48	42	111	6	384	210	93	2,178
Sri Lankan	66	117	486	141	105	21	234	36	477	105	54	1,842
Japanese	207	60	738	81	36	9	39	15	210	393	48	1,836
Laotian	45	207	189	210	75	12	105	213	18	3	0	1,077
Iranian	78	78	303	72	33	12	72	12	237	39	57	993
Korean	171	51	279	33	6	3	36	3	90	96	12	780
Malaysian	69	39	234	60	27	18	39	12	129	87	3	717
Thai	63	63	258	42	24	6	15	6	93	99	15	684
Balinese	87	51	186	36	9	0	27	6	123	24	9	558
Lebanese	9	39	69	102	6	0	21	0	111	33	66	456
Chilean	24	6	54	48	24	6	18	24	69	66	3	342
Israeli	21	24	120	9	9	3	24	3	63	18	9	303
Pakistani	3	9	147	18	15	3	3	0	12	15	9	234
Sub-Total	5,073	4,770	23,073	12,519	2,907	678	4,041	1,047	11,331	5,262	2,198	72,899
Other Ethnic	285	222	972	552	255	30	189	21	405	402	154	3,487
Total Ethnic	5,358	4,992	24,045	13,071	3,162	708	4230	1,068	11,736	5,664	2,352	76,386
TOTAL POPN	173,160	138,978	299,266	257,811	121,972	35,289	93,114	46,113	146,955	301,455	107,979	1,722,092
Ratio of Ethnic to Population	0.0639	0.0611	0.0500	0.0556	0.0688	0.0764	0.0569	0.0715	0.0507	0.0785	0.0736	0.0576

Source: Unpublished 1991 census data, Dept of Statistics.

TABLE 8 :

DISTRIBUTION OF SELECTED RELIGIOUS GROUPS BY MAIN URBAN AREAS (1991)

MAIN URBAN	Hindu	Buddhist	Muslim	Sikh	Taoist	Sufi
Whangarei	69	78	12	3	9	6
Auckland	9,678	6,438	3,561	885	117	207
North Auckland	*675*	*906*	*213*	*30*	*33*	*135*
West Auckland	*1,068*	*675*	*396*	*51*	*27*	*30*
Central Auckland	*5,493*	*2,874*	*2,295*	*378*	*54*	*39*
South Auckland	*2,445*	*1,983*	*660*	*423*	*6*	*0*
Hamilton	546	462	231	279	9	3
Hamilton Zone	*528*	*450*	*210*	*270*	*6*	*3*
Cambridge Zone	*9*	*3*	*6*	*3*	*0*	*0*
Te Awamutu Zone	*12*	*6*	*15*	*6*	*0*	*0*
Tauranga	36	51	21	9	0	3
Rotorua	222	69	33	9	3	0
Gisborne	21	30	6	27	0	0
Napier-Hastings	102	153	72	123	3	3
Napier	*24*	*102*	*21*	*27*	*3*	*3*
Hastings	*75*	*51*	*48*	*96*	*3*	*3*
New Plymouth	120	87	18	3	3	3
Wanganui	63	45	15	30	3	0
Palmerston North	282	339	168	15	9	3
Wellington	4,296	2,418	858	123	75	27
Upper Hutt	*156*	*117*	*30*	*27*	*0*	*0*
Lower Hutt	*1,089*	*582*	*144*	*24*	*15*	*0*
Porirua	*174*	*351*	*99*	*12*	*12*	*12*
Wellington City	*2,877*	*1,368*	*588*	*60*	*48*	*15*
Nelson	27	153	12	3	3	6
Christchurch	564	846	273	27	39	3
Dunedin	144	570	72	6	6	0
Invercargill	81	27	9	0	3	0
Sub-Total	16,251	11,763	5,358	1,545	282	270
TOTAL NZ	17,661	12,765	5,772	2,061	324	327

The Challenge to the Church

In terms of size, these population groups are relatively small. To this extent the risk is that they will be marginalized in our efforts to see New Zealand evangelized. To some for example, they may not be seen to be 'proper Kiwis'. This is a very short-sighted and inappropriate viewpoint that can only serve to perpetuate the 'hidden' status of many of these groups. Even if their relative size does not seem to merit our attention, their strategic significance certainly does.

Some of these groups are from nations that are closed to the gospel. Out of their normal cultural contexts they are receptive to friendship and the gospel. That needs to be built on. Some of these individuals have moved permanently to New Zealand, but numbers of them (especially those who are here as students) will return home, some of them to positions of influence within their nations. The strategic significance of this for the gospel should not be overlooked. Beyond this, the cross-cultural vision and calling of many Kiwi Christians can be enlarged and sharpened through involvement with these ethnic minorities. There is scope here for relatively inexpensive pre-field missions exposure and training. In addition however, we must be sensitive to biblical admonitions in relation to how we treat "the strangers in our midst." Without being patronizing about this, we need to realise that these people must be included as we "call the whole Church to take the whole gospel to the whole nation".

What should be done from here? At the very least, the statistical information presented earlier needs to be fleshed out with further 'on-the-ground' research. We need to know more about the composition of these ethnic groups (age structures, internal differentiation, occupational and neighbourhood concentrations, language patterns, community networks and living patterns). We also need to know the extent to which they have already been evangelized and the degree of their openness to the gospel. We need to know what evangelistic and church planting strategies are already being used among them and what relative degree of success there has been. Where no strategizing has been done to date we need to give thought to this. We need to know which mission agencies are targeting these groups overseas and what reciprocal benefits can be obtained from mission agencies and local churches working together in closer cooperation. Above all we need to be convinced that these people are loved by God and warrant the evangelistic efforts of the Church in New Zealand.

Some Christians have already been convinced. Scattered throughout the country are specific outreaches, churches and fellowship groups, involving Chinese (Dunedin, Christchurch, Wellington,

Palmerston North, Hamilton and Auckland), Japanese (Auckland, Christchurch, Queenstown), Koreans (Auckland, Wellington, Christchurch) and Laotians (Auckland, Dunedin) to name but a few. A few local churches (such as City Elim in Auckland) have developed effective outreach programmes specifically geared towards internationals. Under the auspices of Operation Friendship, other local churches are beginning to get involved in outreach to non-Christian internationals (students and others) in Christchurch, Wellington, Palmerston North and Hamilton. All of these efforts need to be looked at, learned from and applied wherever appropriate and necessary.

God is bringing the world to our doorstep. We need to be more sensitive to the challenge and the opportunities.

FOOTNOTES

[1] Lawson Lau, *World at Your Doorstep - A Handbook for International Student Ministry* (Illinois: Intervarsity Press, 1984).

[2] Census reports for these years also provide information on place of birth of the resident population. It was felt, however, that the ethnic identification information gave a better foundation for looking at ethnic diversity. Because of the rounding conventions used by the Department of Statistics, some of these totals may not exactly match totals in other tables.

[3] Changes in ethnic identification and classification make true comparisons across these periods difficult. Nevertheless, it can be asserted that the Maori component of the population is increasing and will continue to increase significantly.

[4] For ease of reference, Tables 2, 3 and 4 do not include the Combination and Not Specified categories from Table 1. The Chinese, Indian and Other information in these tables has been drawn from unpublished material supplied by the Department of Statistics.

[5] The information on minority ethnic groups in the rest of the tables in this chapter are drawn from unpublished information supplied by the Department of Statistics. Similar information was not obtained for Pacific Island populations because of the costs involved in obtaining it, and also because it was felt that relatively more was known about the distribution of these Island population segments.

[6] This matches the Single Ethnic Group categories in Table 1.

[7] The only other figure that seems to merit attention here is the 108 Other Ethnic in Timaru. However these were not overly concentrated in any one group (ie. they comprised 39 Filipinos, 15 Japanese, 15 Vietnamese, 12 Sri Lankan etc.).

[8] Chinese and Indians have been have been excluded from consideration in Table

6.

[9] For example: 642 Balinese, 162 Burmese, 3 Shan, 108 Afghani, 129 Bangladeshi, 45 Nepalese, 252 Pakistani, 12 Tibetan, 6 Algerian, 96 Arabs, 60 Egyptian, 138 Iraqi, 18 Moroccan, 96 Turks, 3 Kurds, 78 Argentinian, 18 Bolivian, 90 Brazilian, 432 Chilean, 42 Colombian, 6 Costa Rican, 6 Ecuadorian, 6 Guatemalan, 57 Mexican, 99 Peruvian, 9 Uruguayan, and 24 Venezuelan. It is expected that some of these would have been overseas students. Unpublished figures supplied by the Department of Statistics show that in 1991, of the overseas students who were studying here, 1,315 were from Asia, 35 from South America and 75 from Africa.

18

Reaching All the People Groups

by Bruce Patrick

"A four million dollar lesson in multiculturalism" was how one journalist described the opening night of the 1990 Commonwealth Games at Mt Smart Stadium, Auckland. Most New Zealanders are very aware of the multicultural nature of our society. Given the language, ethnic, and cultural mosaic that now exists, the Church needs far greater flexibility and a wide range of models if it is to reach these various people groups with the gospel of the grace of God in Jesus Christ.

In this chapter, terms such as ethnic, culture, and language are used often interchangeably, always recognizing that every person (with no exception) has ethnicity, a distinct cultural heritage, and a heart language. The writer has his own ethnicity, culture and language, and though he writes from his viewpoint as part of the majority (European) culture in New Zealand, no value judgments are implied at any point.

The Great Commission of our Lord recorded in Matthew 28:19 in fact says: "Make disciples of all the people groups" (Greek: panta ta ethne = all the ethnic groups). Though once referred to as a melting pot society, New Zealand is in reality a pluralistic society composed of numerous ethnic groups, each with distinct language and cultural characteristics. Over 20% of New Zealand's population belongs to one of the minority ethnic groups. Some of these groups are increasing at a much faster rate than the European population through immigration and higher birthrates (see chapter 16).

Over recent years numerous secondary schools, especially in Auckland, have accepted thousands of Chinese teenagers, most of whom do not speak English. Many wealthy Chinese business people are immigrating from Hong Kong and Taiwan, and elsewhere. These are Taoist or Confucian Chinese, speaking Taiwanese or Mandarin. They are a visible minority, not least as they drive rather hesitantly on the roads of suburban Auckland in their Mercedes, BMWs, and large and late model Toyotas. There are many less obvious people groups. We have Buddhist Cambodians, Laotians, Viet Namese, and Sinhalese; Moslem Indonesians, Shintoist Japanese; Jewish Eastern Europeans; Roman Catholic Poles, Italians, Yugoslavs, Czechs; Hindu Indians speaking Hindi, Tamil, Telegu or Urdu; Sihks; Fijian Indians; materialistic Western Europeans from USA, Canada, England, Scotland, Wales and Ireland; both committed and nominally Christian Pacific Islanders from Samoa, Tonga, Vanuatu, Cook Islands; Dutch; Greeks; and so on. All of these and more dwell here with our longer-term Maori and European New Zealanders. The primary evangelistic objective of the Church in New Zealand must be to give every person in New Zealand an opportunity to become a follower of Jesus Christ through hearing and accepting the gospel, then to be nurtured by and to worship with fellow believers.

People Groups and Socio-cultural Groups

People groups are defined as ethno-linguistic groups. Their identity is determined by ethnicity and/or language, eg. Samoans, Turks, Tamils. People groups generally need a congregation or church. There are also socio-cultural groups, defined as groups whose identity is determined by factors other than ethnicity or language. Some examples: Occupational factors: students, nurses, truckies, bikies. Residential class: housing type. Religion: Moslem, Mormon, Hindu. Educational level. Variant: alcoholics, prostitutes. Medical: deaf, blind, paraplegic. Nationality: Irish, Dutch, American. Recreational: rugby players, bowlers. Stage of life: young mothers, teenagers, retirees. When a socio-cultural group is identified as the target group for a ministry thrust, sensible strategies for bridge-building suggest themselves. It may be possible to assimilate them into the church or congregation of their people group.

The Four Forms of Growth

Ralph Winter has pointed out that there are only four basic forms of numerical growth.[1] New Zealand churches have generally concentrated on Internal and Expansion growth. Extension and Bridging growth are now needed if we are to reach the people groups.

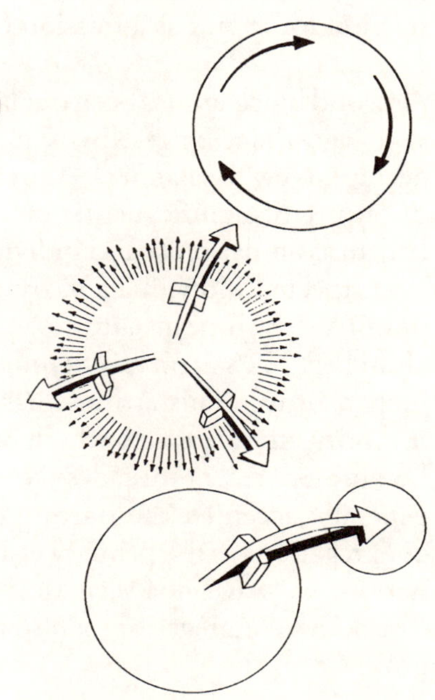

Internal growth (E_0 evangelism)
Christians becoming better disciples,
(quality growth), and the evangelizing
of church members who are not yet
born again.

Expansion growth (E_1 evangelism)
Evangelizing the unchurched
and nurturing them in the context
of a commitment to the local church.
Must cross one cultural barrier:
the 'stained glass barrier'.

Extension growth
(E_1 evangelism by church planting)
Evangelizing the unchurched
and forming them into new churches.
Must cross one cultural barrier:
the 'stained glass barrier'.

Bridging growth
(E$_2$ and E$_3$ evangelism by
cross-cultural church planting)
E$_2$ refers to one degree of cultural
difference, eg. Kiwis reaching Dutch
immigrants. E$_3$ refers to evangelizing
a very different culture, eg. Kiwis
reaching Laotians.

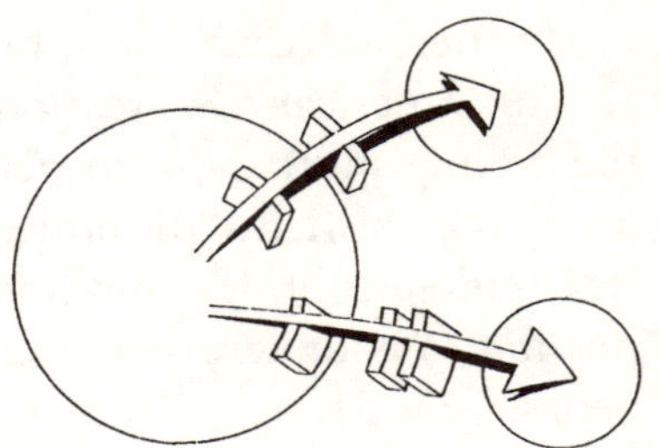

Blockages to the Gospel

It is not uncommon for churches to include among their number people from various ethnic origins. But many of New Zealand's ethnic people have never heard the gospel. There have been three main blockages. One has been lack of vision for cross-cultural mission, or mission generally, in New Zealand. We have regarded New Zealand as a Christian country and the source of the overseas mission force, not as a mission field.

A second blockage has been our lack of cultural awareness. Twenty years ago the average Kiwi Christian was as ethnocentric as the average New Zealander. Our British heritage disposed us to disregard the significance if not the existence of other cultures. We had an assimilationist and individualistic approach to evangelism. We expected individuals of other cultures to assimilate into the dominant European culture and language of our monocultural churches. We said in effect: unless you become like us you cannot be part of us. This attitude has oppressed even Christians from minority ethnic groups who have come as immigrants. Further, because in recent decades New Zealand Christians have not generally accepted the starting of more and more effective new congregations as the primary evangelistic strategy for reaching the nation, we have not seen that the multiplication of culturally distinctive congregations is also the simple key to reaching people groups.

The third blockage is more subtle, coming in the guise of a theological ideal. We have not wanted to develop distinctive culture or language congregations lest it be thought we are undermining unity. We have assumed that "all one in Christ Jesus"[2] must refer to organic multicultural unity. In fact, worldwide, truly multicultural churches are in a very small minority. The vast majority are more or less monocultural, and certainly monolingual, and they enjoy the blessing of God. In practice we may have held unity as a higher value than the value we place on the salvation of other-culture people who cannot be reached by our white middle-class cultural expression of Christianity. There is a false dichotemy here which wrongly pits ethics against ethnics. In fact it is possible to maintain cultural integrity in distinct congregations and at the same time to build fellowship bridges among language or ethnic congregations. Several proven models are described at the end of this chapter.

Culture and language matter. However noble the intention, it is not sufficient for us to proclaim simplistically that the church is open to everybody regardless of cultural and language differences. Church attendance is voluntary. Most people choose a church where they feel comfortable. In multicultural societies, cultures are the context of mission, and congregations are the key.

Lessons from Howick and Henderson

When Christian and Missionary Alliance church planter Richard Applegate settled with his family into Howick in 1987, he envisaged planting a typical Kiwi church. A year later, with a small nucleus of people, he considered reaching out to the Chinese immigrants who were moving into the area in large numbers. Various contact strategies were useful. Numerous practical services were offered, always with a desire to share the gospel of God's love. But people came and went. There was a back door problem. The turning point came when an Asian couple joined the church and began a Cantonese-speaking youth programme. The fellowship grew from a dozen to over 60 in 6 months, the majority of these being unsaved Chinese. "By this time we began to realise our limitations to reach these ones for Christ," Richard said. "Many of the youth spoke Cantonese and English, but some of the parents who were coming regularly knew no English, and I could not speak Cantonese." Richard prayed actively for couples from Alliance churches in Hong Kong to move into the area, who would be willing to take up the challenge of reaching their own people. Within five months this prayer was answered through the arrival of three more leadership couples. Cantonese language services started. By mid 1992 the first Alliance Chinese Church in New Zealand was released as an autonomous church, with its attendance growing towards 100.

Out of curiosity, Daniel Fuemana attended a course on church planting during his third year as a Bible College of New Zealand student. He wrote an assignment on how he might start a new congregation to reach fellow Pacific Islanders and Europeans. He discussed it with his wife Sharon, and God began to grow a conviction in their hearts that this was no mere academic exercise. He took the plan to Ian Wood, minister of their Presbyterian church in Te Atatu South, then to the outreach committee, then the session. It was approved. Two families and three singles met under Daniel's leadership for ten weeks to study evangelism through church planting. The second stage of the plan began when they hired the marae at Henderson High School for Sunday worship services. Their approach is cultivating Pacific Islander contacts and Europeans. They encourage cultural expression and interaction, and after worship have a shared lunch every week followed by informal sports. The sponsoring church is supportive with resources but is unable to provide financial help. Both Daniel Fuemana and his wife work to support themselves. The new congregation reaches people different from those whose culture predominates in the sponsoring church.

First Step: Study the Total Community

Here are some steps to take to reach people of distinct language or cultural groups and establish congregations. People are diverse. These suggestions are therefore very generalized. People of ethnic minority groups are everywhere but they are often 'hidden people'. What are these groups in your community? The national census supplies comprehensive facts about ethnicity.[3] Your church could bring a special task group together to collect information.

Some people groups are quickly identified by physical appearances. Simply looking for different people wherever you go, at schools, shopping centres, recreational areas, and public meetings, will usually reveal their presence. Some people groups are not easily identified. Note non-European or non-English restaurants and gift shops, churches, clubs and organizations, theatres that show non-English language movies, newspapers and periodicals in other languages, non-European sounding names in the local telephone directory.

Make a community survey of possible other-culture areas. It would help to get the following information from ethnic minority families: language spoken in the home, national background, religious preference, and whether or not they have attended a live church. Some will consider themselves Christians by their own definitions. People generally appreciate sincere interest but are cautious about questions concerning their family and background. Avoid a paternalistic attitude. Ask questions sensitively. It is better to do so than to make false assumptions. Seek to learn about the people group. Excellent books are available from public libraries. When the research is ready, maps of the area, locations of ethnic people and organizations, population data, and language and cultural distinctives should be presented to your church leaders.

Second Step: Identify Target Group, Strategy

Your findings will reveal the need for witness and ministry to ethnic and language groups, and may also disclose which of two basic approaches to take:

Expansion growth may result from the ministry of a church to ethnic people. Usually this will involve bringing them into the majority culture congregation with the goal of integrating them into the full programme of the church. This approach may be appropriate with bicultural people or assimilated ethnics, but is unlikely to be effective with nuclear ethnics (see below).

Bridging growth is the establishment of a separate language or ethnic congregation which reflects the linguistic and cultural needs of the target group. Nuclear ethnics need a language or culture congregation. A cross-cultural church planter or a church planter from the target ethnic group will be essential to the success of this approach.

Will the expansion growth approach or the bridging growth approach be more effective for the target group? That will be determined by the language spoken in the home, whether the people are first generation or not, whether they normally follow the habits and customs of their native land, the size of the group, and their religious background. Plans should begin and remain flexible. Often a group that begins in the church through expansion growth will later desire to have a separate meeting place, and may choose to become an independent congregation. What starts as expansion growth may lead to bridging growth. These two approaches are discussed more fully under Step four. Before you make a decision on strategy you must identify your target group carefully. Abandon all stereotypes, and understand the complications caused by ethnic subgroups.

Every Ethnic Group has Major Subgroups

A common error is to view all people of one ethnic group as the same (ie. fitting a stereotype), and then adopt only one approach to their evangelization. They are not all the same. Because they are different, different strategies are required.

Nuclear ethnics are people who are culturally and ethno-linguistically segregated into their own expression of community life, by at least one of the barriers: language, culture, or socioeconomic factors. The majority are usually overseas-born, first-generation immigrants who are in this category unavoidably, though some will be there by choice. These people are the most difficult to minister to through a majority-culture church. They are best reached through a separate language congregation or church. They need, may want, and can attend such a church. Some will remain in this category for life. Some, especially from the second generation, may eventually assimilate into the majority culture. The rate at which they do will depend on factors such as age, education, and experience when they arrived in New Zealand.

Bicultural ethnics are those who remain bicultural by choice. They are usually bi- or multi-lingual, and choose to function in more than one cultural lifestyle. Family units made up by intermarriage of two persons from different cultural backgrounds are often in this category. Grandparents are often caught here while their children and certainly grandchildren are moving rapidly toward assimilation into the majority culture. This group can accommodate to a majority-culture church, but may require a special type of ministry in order to be reached with the gospel: possibly bi-lingual Bible studies, literature, and preaching services. Some may prefer the culture of their roots, especially where they belong to an indigenous people group which is seeking to regain its original identity. Some Maori are in this category.

Marginal ethnics are those who are moving towards assimilation into the majority culture. Many are highly transitional toward assimilation. But some will remain as marginal ethnics till death, and some will even return to the culture and language of their roots, becoming nuclear ethnics once more. These people are best reached by a multicultural, preferably multi-congregational, church which provides cultural and language options.

Assimilated ethnics are those who have moved out of their own culture and have been effectively assimilated into the majority culture. They may or may not have been born in New Zealand.

They speak English and have adopted a Kiwi lifestyle, more or less. These people do not need, and often do not want, separate facilities or churches. They can be evangelized by a caring majority-culture church. Many white Kiwi churches include assimilated ethnics. Because they are people of other races, this may give the superficial impression that the church is multicultural when in fact it is multi-racial. Predictably, most if not all of the cultural factors expressed in the public life of the church will be English/European. Multi-racial is not multicultural.

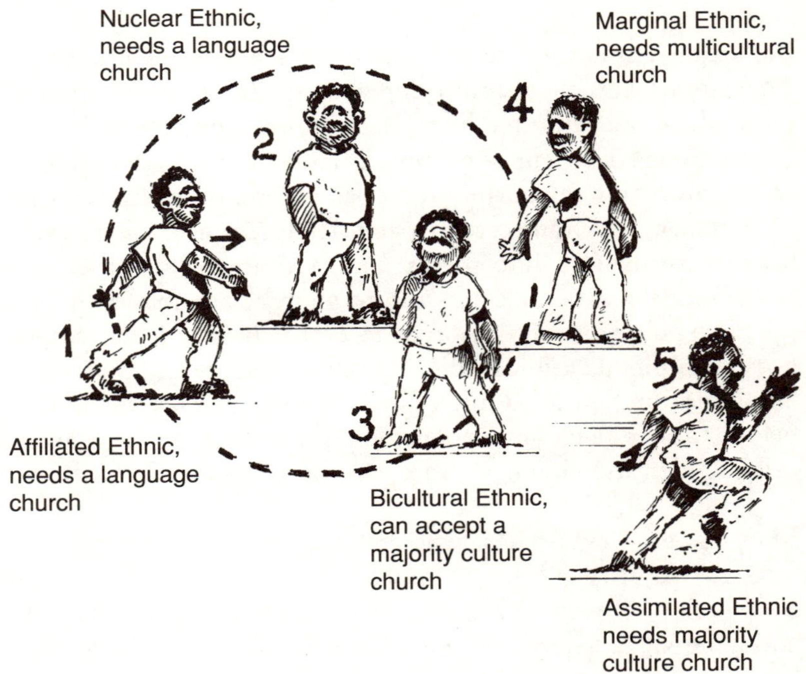

Third Step: Identify Workers, Cultivate Field

The effectiveness of any ministry depends to a great degree on the maturity and experience, the gifting, and the training, of primary leaders. This is absolutely true here. No church can begin an evangelistic cross-cultural ministry without workers who are harvesters. This is a call to prayer.[4] The way God answers your prayer could be the all-important factor in your guidance.

Returned missionaries may be located through overseas missions networks. There are literally hundreds of experienced cross-cultural workers in New Zealand who have returned from overseas. A doctor and his wife living in South Auckland have 15 years experience in medical mission work in Thailand with the Overseas Missionary Fellowship. They have gathered a congregation of Laotian settlers, one of whom is now studying at the Bible College of New Zealand in preparation for a pastoral leadership role.

When establishing a witness and ministry among other-culture people it is important to overcome the tendency to think in stereotypes. Accept the other person as an individual; be friends, be yourself, begin on common ground. If language is such a barrier that you cannot communicate, find help. Where possible meet whole families and seek to win whole families to Christ, even extended families. Take time. Invite the family head to take the initiative, eg. to bring the whole family to attend fellowship and worship activites.

Fourth Step: Begin the Ministry

The ministry may begin centred on a home. It may then develop either within the church, using one of the cross-cultural approaches suggested in the following paragraphs, or by the establishment of a new congregation in the church buildings, or a daughter congregation sponsored by the church. One approach might well lead into another. The ability and desire of the target people group to relate to your church's cultural and language distinctives will largely determine your approach. Many Maori people are bicultural and may relate. Some are not or do not desire to be. Many immigrant Taiwanese do not speak English so will require a language ministry.

Expansion Growth

Adopt a language person or family. Members of the church might wish to adopt an other-culture person or family, inviting them to meals and social events. On occasions all of those adopted could meet at the church building or elsewhere for fellowship meals. This type of ministry is especially effective among internationals, people temporarily in New Zealand for study, training or business.

Bible Study. Many other-culture people are interested to study God's word. The Bible study could be in the church, or a home, or any other suitable place. Scriptures can be obtained from the Bible Society[5] in probably every language spoken in New Zealand. The group may prefer to study in English.

Home fellowship. Home meetings might include singing, teaching, sharing, Bible study and social times. Many who will not come to a church will come to the home of a neighbour or friend. Other-culture people are generally hungry for fellowship with people of their own ethnic background.

Literacy class. Many language or culture people want to learn English. Using well-developed techniques available through ESL[6] courses, people can learn the English language. In some cases, the language groups will want their own language taught to their children. The church might enlist a Christian adult from among their language group to do so, making the facilities of the church available for the class.

Class in Sunday school. A language class may meet at the same time as other classes, with their lesson being taught in their language. Some members of bilingual families might wish to attend an English class while others attend the language class.

A congregation within the church. As the other-culture group grows large enough its own ministry leaders may form a congregation which could meet at the same time as the regular church congregation and the Sunday school, or at another time, or both. Its leaders may be chosen in the same manner as other church leaders, but note that it is essential the congregation members themselves have a voice in determining their own leaders and programmes.

Bridging growth

A congregation may be planted out by the church. Often the cross-cultural outreach of a church will lead to the need for an ethnic, language or culture congregation with a separate identity from the sponsoring church. It may or may not meet in a separate building. The programme of the ethnic congregation should include Bible study, worship, a strong mission emphasis, and training to equip them to reach their own ethnic group. It is important that the sponsoring church not take a paternalistic approach, but allow the group's leaders freedom to assume responsibilities and to experience growth and maturity. The relationship with the sponsoring church should be carefully defined in regard to finances, receiving members, the calling of pastors, Bible study materials, and equipment.

If starting a new congregation, the following notes may be helpful:

1   Keep foremost the primary need of the people-group to find salvation through friendship, and to have an opportunity for ongoing worship experiences appropriate to their culture and language.
2   See the congregation as a New Testament fellowship of believers even though it may be using a different language, a different cultural style of worship, and have other cultural differences.
3   No programme, facility or building should be begunwhich is beyond the ability of the other-culture congregation to maintain.
4   Financial assistance from sources outside the congregation should be considered temporary and understood as such by the other-culture congregation.
5   The responsibility for calling a pastor or other workers should be the daughter congregation's, in cooperation with the sponsoring church.

6　The congregation should function in agreed ways as a church, recognizing, while in the establishment phase, the need to have approval of the sponsoring church for actions in the areas of policy and finances.

7　The sponsoring church should provide periodic opportunities for review of the progress of the culture or language congregation.

Fifth Step: Provide Growth Assistance

Like a newborn child the newly established language or culture congregation will need some help as it grows toward becoming a self-sustaining church. The congregation should build its potential for growth and make definite plans toward self-support. If a separate building is needed, it is usually preferable to defer building plans until the congregation has developed sufficient strength and stability to shoulder such efforts themselves. Priority should be given to enlistment and training of leaders from the people group. The pastor may be part-time, bivocational, or full-time depending on the local situation and the potential for growth. The pastor should be able to communicate in the language of the people served and understand their culture. The most successful pastors of such congregations are those who are from the language or ethnic group being served.

Bibles and Bible study materials in many languages are available from the Bible Society and foreign language printing houses. It may be necessary to adapt English language materials to fit the needs of the group. Assistance from the sponsoring church should decrease as increasing responsibility is assumed by the other-culture congregation and its leaders.

Living Models

An autonomous ethnic or language church. Every Sunday on the seventh floor of Christchurch's Vacation Inn a Japanese congregation meets for worship in Japanese, followed by a shared meal. Why a separate congregation? Ken Roundhill, a young over-70 year old, who with his wife Betty served the Lord as a missionary in Japan for 40 years, says, "The Japanese are very different culturally, and very few of our contacts speak English. But even fluent English speakers find the cultural gap immense. In one marriage between a Japanese woman and a New Zealander the cultural gap was so serious she eventually committed suicide." Asked about Ephesians 2:14-16 which speaks of Christ removing all barriers between races, Ken Roundhill responds, "But which barriers? Japanese thinking processes are peculiar to Japanese people. And language barriers are not removed by conversion." This congregation is effectively evangelizing a mobile and fairly short-term population of Japanese who are in Christchurch to learn English.

A daughter ethnic congregation. The Northcote Baptist Church commenced an English language class for Chinese immigrants in mid 1989. Three months later a second class was requested, to explain the Christian faith. Why? They were puzzled that their teachers were working as volunteers. Now about 65 Mandarin-speaking adults and children attend the normal Sunday morning service, then exit before the sermon for their own Mandarin worship service and sermon which, if in English, is translated into Mandarin. Interlinear Mandarin/English hymnbooks are used. Many attend who are Buddhists and ancestor worshippers, noticeably more open to the gospel away from the patterns of their homelands. With increasing spiritual maturity the Chinese are taking more responsibility for leadership, including midweek Bible studies and contact visitation. A Chinese pastor is being sought. Though older Chinese will always need Mandarin, their heart language, for worship and counselling, the congregation prefers to remain integrated, especially for the sake of children who are quickly assimilating into Kiwi culture.

A multi-ethnic, multi-congregational church. Eden Chapel in Mt Eden is affiliated to the Brethren Assembly movement. The congregation is led by elders with the help of full-time pastoral worker Rob McArthur. Several years ago a Japanese evangelistic home group grew into a congregation with separate Sunday services, under the leadership of returned Brethren missionaries Hayden and Diane Harvey. A Korean congregation led by Korean pastor Park moved into the area to be close to where many Koreans live, and began meeting in the Eden Chapel facilities. These three congregations now have strong relational links, each regarding itself as one expression of the life of Eden Chapel. There are opportunities for combined worship services (the Japanese meet apart only three Sundays per month), and leaders relate together though in an unstructured and informal fashion.

An effective ethnic movement. Having started here in 1975, there are now Tongan Methodist congregations in 14 cities around New Zealand. One of them, the Tongan Parish in Auckland, is unique in many ways. It consists of 15 fellowships, staffed by only one full-time superintendent with two office staff. There are six self-supporting presbyters ordained or in training. There are 15 lay pastors each with a deputy, plus 430 accredited lay preachers, ministering to over 4,200 people, now a sizeable proportion of the Methodist Church in New Zealand. A highly planned weekly programme preserves the methodical approach to discipling and evangelism that was part of the genius of John Wesley. Monday focuses on the family. Tuesday is for lay leadership training, and Wednesday for mid-week worship and Bible study. Thursday is for Wesley class meetings, Friday for youth meetings, Saturday for evangelistic outreach, and Sunday for prison ministry, worship services, and a highly developed Christian education programme.

Extensive printed materials are written and produced in Tongan by Dr Alifaleti Mone, the full-time superintendent of the parish. His Bible readings programme covers the Bible in four years, and provides the basis for the whole life of the church. Another booklet he produces twice each year supplies timetables and themes for each group and activity. Building on the foundation of Tongan

Christianity in the islands, the church here is largely evangelical, traditional, biblical, and central to close-knit family and community life. However the forces of Kiwi culture are affecting Tongans: secularism, materialism, family disintegration, and individualism. In the view of Methodist minister Tavake Tupou these factors necessitate a back-to-basics approach for the evangelization of his people. This Methodist movement is setting a standard for other partners in the task of discipling the people groups of our nation.

Conclusion

Paul stated the basic principle of cross-cultural mission: "To the Jews I became as a Jew to win the Jews. To those under the law I became like one under the law (though I myself am not under the law) so as to win those under the law. To those not having the law I became like one not having the law (though I am not free from God's law but am under Christ's law), so as to win those not having the law. To the weak I became weak to win the weak. I have become all things to all men so that by all possible means I might save some."[7] There are many returned missionaries whose cross-cultural gifts, language and experience could be deployed at home in New Zealand to reach their specific target people here.

Paul's strategy was to equip and release those who could then work within their own culture. In this way the degree of difficulty in Bridging growth is overcome as people reach their own kind in Extension growth. Another world leader in mission, Donald McGavran has made an observation that has become a classic statement for students of the growth of the church: People "like to become Christians without crossing racial, linguistic, or class barriers."[8] People are best reached in their own cultural settings. Mission movements must be established among all the people groups in New Zealand so that congregations are multiplied to reach them.

BIBLIOGRAPHY

Lloyd Martin, *One Faith, Two Peoples*, (Paraparaumu Beach, NZ: Salt Company, 1991).

Donald A. McGavran, *Understanding Church Growth*, (Grand Rapids, MI: Eerdmans, revised 1980).

Donald A. McGavran, *Ethnic Realities and The Church, Lessons from India* (Pasadena, CA: William Carey Library, 1979).

C. Peter Wagner, *Our Kind of People*, (Atlanta, GA: John Knox, 1979).

Explaining The Gospel In Today's World, Church Planting, Gospel and Culture, Lausanne Occasional Papers, LCWE, (Wheaton, Il: 1978).

FOOTNOTES

[1] Outline and diagrams adapted from Roy Pointer, *How Do Churches Grow?* (Basingstoke, UK: Marshalls, 1984), pages 150 - 154, used with permission. This book is highly recommended as a foundational church growth text. Having a British origin it relates well to New Zealand churches and culture.

[2] Galatians 3:28.

[3] Contact the Department of Statistics.

[4] See Luke 10:2.

5 Bible Society, Private Bag, Upper Willis St, Wellington.

6 English as a Second Language.

7 1 Corinthians 9:20-22.

[8] Donald A. McGavran, *Understanding Church Growth*, (Grand Rapids, MI: Eerdmans, revised 1980), page 223.

Chapter

19

AD 2000 and Beyond

by Bruce Patrick

"I am amazed afresh at the unbelievable daring of the Creator Spirit who seems to gamble all the past gains on a new initiative, inviting His creatures to such crazy adventure and risk. The Holy Spirit is not a baby's comforter... It is this incalculable and sometimes violent aspect of the Holy Spirit which the Hebrew word 'ruach' conveys in its primary meaning... Mission is often described as if it were the planned extension of an old building. But in fact it has usually been more like an unexpected explosion... When the ruach of God sweeps into a situation, change cannot be smooth."[1]

Faced with a drop in religious affiliation of bungy proportions, and in the light of the Great Commission, the New Zealand Church must respond in many ways at many levels, as indicated in all previous chapters. The assumption has been made throughout that the New Zealand Church seriously desires to follow in the footsteps of Jesus, who came "to seek and save the lost." This closing chapter is not so much a synthesis of earlier chapters as a specific challenge. It is a challenge to every part of the body of Christ to adopt a ten or twenty year growth strategy. It is a call for multiplication. It will necessitate radical change: nationally, at denominational level, at district level, and at local level. The whole Church must urgently unite around common goals and crucial strategies that will lead most directly to making disciples of the people groups of our nation.

"The key to revival is prayer," is a quotable, challenging statement. Urgent, desperate prayer seems to have preceded every revival in history. The Bible records other important principles which must also be applied in every generation and culture. God is a strategist. This is clear from Old and New Testaments. "Contrary to the belief of some, when a local church carefully plans and develops its strategy, it is reflecting God's character rather than denying his power. It seems strange then that on a national level this vital local lesson is often forgotten or ignored. All too easily we can find ourselves almost wanting to be seduced by the loud but shallow enthusiasm of those who tell us that revival hides just around the corner and that all we've got to do is sit tight, keep singing, and pray a little harder!"[2] A sovereign God can send revival. In fact he may do so as the Church applies nationally these lessons learnt locally. To get to grips with the missionary challenge in New Zealand the Church will have to pray urgently, see a new vision, recover apostolic confidence, think hard and work hard, understand and develop God's strategy, and set growth goals for the 1990s and beyond. We must think at many levels about how to be effective, and then we must act effectively. "Thinkers think, and doers do... but until the doers think and the thinkers do, progress will be just another word in the already overburdened vocabulary of the talkers who talk!"[3]

New Vision

In his book *To Dream Again* Robert Dale offers some most helpful insights to becalmed churches and denominations.[4] Dale points out that every human organization goes through a cycle of birth, growth, maturity, decline and death. Local churches, and denominations, follow this pattern. Healthy new churches are born out of a dream. A group of pioneers dream of a redemptive ministry in a community. As they own that vision they follow God's leading by faith. They join together, clarify their beliefs in their worship life, and set goals and priorities. They formulate policies, approve budgets, and launch ministries. The dream is realized. Over time, if the congregation fails to open itself to revitalization, a plateau occurs. Decline begins. First people doubt the structures. "It isn't working as well as it used to, is it?" they ask nostalgically. Next they doubt the goals. "Is this the best way to do it?" Finally they doubt the basic beliefs of the organization, and some drop out in disillusionment.

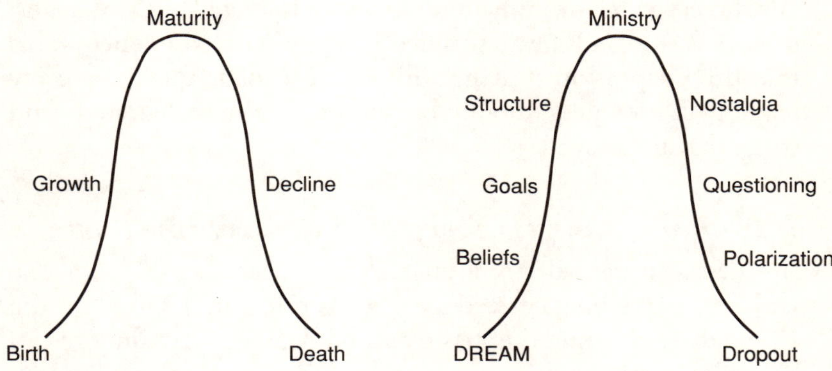

Where is the whole Church of New Zealand, on this cycle? Where is your denomination, and your congregation? Dale goes on to underline the importance of the dream, the vision. When a Christian organization is in decline, the crucial response is not to restructure, nor to set new goals, nor even to reformulate beliefs. It is to discover God's new dream for the organization. It may mean returning to the founding vision; more likely it will mean seeking a new vision that is appropriate for new circumstances, new needs, new opportunities. Churches must dream again! Leaders must continually help their people understand "who we are" (identity, vision), "what we are to do" (destiny, goals), and "how we work together best" (harmony, organization). Out of the new vision valid goals can be set, and suitable structures adopted to release people into vital ministries.

Another very pertinent insight from Dale bears mention. The body of Christ is rich in diversity. Visionaries dream. Theologians operate in the intellectual realm of beliefs. Directors set goals. Organizers design and build structures. Activists perform ministries. Dale goes further. On a less positive note he points out that traditionalists suffer nostalgia, detectives question, fighters polarize, and the apathetic dropout. (In fact where an organization is led by a non-visionary it is often the visionaries who drop out.) Visionaries and directors are not always understood or tolerated by theologians; nor are theologians always valued by activists. Experience warns that this chapter on strategy will not be valued equally by every reader! Differences should be accepted, gifts celebrated, and strengths encouraged.[5]

If Nothing Changes, Everything Remains the Same

Business as usual will not evangelize New Zealand. As someone said, "We have now perfected evangelism for the 1950s!" In the 1990s there is something basic and biblical we are failing to do. What basic strategies must be applied if New Zealand is to be evangelized? VISION New Zealand research confirms what has been discovered world-wide, that while we must strengthen all existing churches, the evangelistic planting of new and diverse congregations grows and conserves the kingdom of God more effectively than any other means.

In August 1992 more than 12,000 pastors, denominational leaders and Christian workers from 2,145 denominations and 45 African nations converged on Lagos, Nigeria. A week-long congress was hosted there by the 85,000 member Deeper Life Bible Church and its pastor William Kumuyi. In his welcoming statement Kumuyi said, "We meet here in recognition of our historical background of civil wars and tribal strife, but we join today as one body in Christ, standing on the promises that Africa will be saved to the glory of the risen Lord. While poverty and starvation threaten many across the land, we know the Church is the pathway to peace and prosperity, and is the salt of the earth." The modern missionary movement began to impact the African continent less than 180 years ago. Huge gains have been made; enormous challenges remain. Church planting is recognized as the key strategy. They have adopted the AD2000 Movement's slogan: "A church for every people and the gospel for every person by the year 2000."

Peter Brierley's massive survey *Christian England* was the research base for the Challenge 2000 Dawn Congress held in Birmingham in February 1992.[6] Over 700 church leaders came from 32 denominations, including mainline except Roman Catholic, the new streams, ethnic churches, and many pentecostals. A visionary challenge was presented to the congress: to believe, pray, and plan towards having 20% of the nation attending churches by the year 2000. It was accepted that church attendance of that level begins to affect a nation's life. The congress experienced an unprecedented degree of cooperation and unity. On the last day, organizations and churches represented were invited to set and share their own goals for church planting by the year 2000. The total came to 20,000 churches!

Pastor Steve Ibbotson[7] later wrote: "Over lunch, feeling quite relaxed and biting through a tuna sandwich, I casually asked the leader of the Anglican stream how they were getting on, and what kind of figure they were looking at. I nearly choked on the tuna! It was phenomenal! Impossible! How could they entertain a figure of that magnitude?" He went on to answer his own question, pondering "the idea of 'planting stock', ie. churches that have the ethos of church planting, either because they've planted a church or because they've been planted. Add the concept of an ongoing church planting policy rather than a one-off approach, and challenge people to set a goal of planting by different points in the decade. I floated these concepts past my own experience in Peterborough. There from one very ordinary, rather traditional and moderately-sized Baptist church, we had managed to plant in 1982, again in 1987, 1989, and 1991. Now in Peterborough we have four churches and congregations with a church planting ethos and commitment, with another church on the way. So then, calculate from your planting stock the number of churches you could plant from that stock, not just once but at intervals throughout the decade. Then add a figure for the number of churches that are growing significantly and are over 100 or 120 members. Get them to plant once or twice in the decade. It adds up. My mind was reeling! Maybe the Anglican figures were based on optimistic assumptions, but the fundamental principles were proved in my experience. They were valid. I was excited."

Ibbotson and the Baptist delegation's final goal amounted to a very challenging 2,000 churches! That same evening a prophetic word affirmed this vision. Steve Ibbotson wrote, "We saw that Christ was inviting us, beckoning us, goading us to thinking that broke the mould of caution, realism, unbelief; and the mere projection forward of a trend on the basis of present experience. We were being asked to dream dreams, see visions, and enter into possibility thinking. God was standing before us and showing what could be if we can rouse sufficient leaders to capture the vision and go forward in faithful, costly, and dependent obedience. Even 500 to 600 churches would mean that it was an issue for other churches. 1,500 to 2,000 means that it's an issue for my church."

In Ibbotson's view, "The Congress demonstrated such energy and vision. I have never previously experienced this with regard to a national strategic perspective. A number of us felt we were at a gathering where history of the English church could well have been in the making."

A National Perspective

The impact of the Church on the nation will be the sum of the effects of individual believers in the full round of their daily lives, the effects of local churches on their communities, the effects of other Christian agencies with specialist roles, and the effects of denominations or families of churches as they pray, think, act, and speak individually and corporately. A three dimensional network must be knitted together, and the mesh made increasingly fine, across the nation. A network consists of many knots joined by strands. The knots are leaders, agencies, or congregations; the strands are relationships.

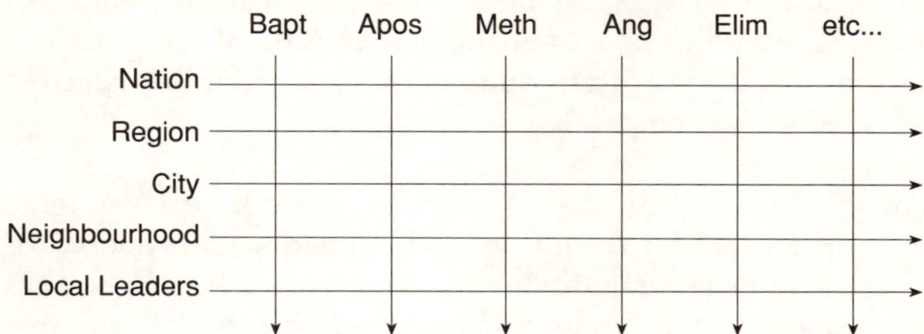

A national strategy requires the involvement of as many denominational strands as possible. Each requires the right information, on the basis of which the most fruitful goals may be adopted and plans developed at a national level. For the plans to work and the goals to be reached they must be owned and expressed by leaders at all levels through to the local level. Some have vision for the nation, others for a region, others for a city, and others for a community.

Denominations Hold the Key

Local churches are the key to evangelizing whole nations. Denominations (or growth movements) hold that key. Our current New Zealand experience, and the history of the expansion of Christianity, show that growth movements occur within relational frameworks. When a family of churches combines to effect missionary strategies, the power released is much greater than if churches worked at mission separately. They are stewards of, and are prepared to share, greater resources of prayer, personnel, and finance. In a new day of mission, local churches should strengthen their commitments to the mission vision of their own movement.

In the churched culture of past decades, denominational structures could survive despite being institutional, conservative, protective of past traditions, and oriented towards maintenance. Often they were led by administrators rather than apostles. Visionaries at lower levels in the structure may have been tolerated but they were not always valued; they often escaped to broader pastures, often into specialist agencies, to find a vision and a challenge worthy of their consecration. Denominations were certainly criticized for fostering the kind of loyalty and narrow perspective that issued in an unbecoming competitive spirit.

Though this image still dogs the Church, a new day is dawning. A growing concern for the mission field under our feet transcends lesser concerns about traditions or secondary beliefs. Renewal has affected many churches, bringing what may best be called simply a convergence of style. Barriers have been reduced, in many cases to the dimensions of lines on a playing field; they are often crossed today.[8] Differences remain, providing a diversity that mirrors the diversity of our nation. This diversity is something to value. It enables different churches to reach different segments of society. In the 1990s denominations are embracing a common vision for the evangelization of New Zealand. Expertize is being shared as each sets its own goals, as each purposes to engage more in mission and in multiplying congregations. Growth specialists cross the lines to assist other denominations develop vision and strategies. Church planters are being trained by one denomination to serve another. Written resources are shared widely. The experience of one benefits others.

If a denomination is to be mobilized for mission, the first essential is a national vision.[9] Some years ago, one denominational leader in an overseas country said, "We are the largest denomination already. We don't have to grow." The result was their very slow growth at a time when others grew rapidly. Another leader had a burning desire to see his whole region filled with live churches reaching people for Christ. The result was hundreds of churches planted, and thousands of people discipled. The Holy Spirit releases great power in the denomination with a vision for effective mission and an understanding of movement principles. This usually occurs where top leaders are recognized and accepted in the churches as having apostolic gifts of vision, faith, communication, and leadership with spiritual authority. In a context of pioneering growth, the neglected leadership gifts of apostle, prophet, and evangelist come into prominence alongside the more familiar gifts of pastor-teacher[10] and administrator.[11]

The Church in New Zealand is still developing home-grown denominational consultants. Current studies will contribute to knowledge of how the Church here grows best.[12] Meanwhile we may quote Lyle Schaller, one of the world's foremost consultants at this level. He writes of twelve assumptions for denominational growth, and then lists eight priorities.[13] His first assumption: a denomination concerned to grow will place high priority on reaching people who are not active in the life of any congregation. His first priority: in any denominational strategy for growth, the first priority must be to organize new congregations, "the most effective single method of reaching people without any active church affiliation."

An overseas study, presented in New Zealand under the name *Rigor Mortis*, identified four major factors that have led to the decline or death of denominations. These four factors were: the failure to find responsive frontiers for growth through the starting of new units; the failure to disciple new believers immediately and systematically; the failure to provide materials for ministries, especially for new church leaders and new believers; and the failure to provide functional training for actual leaders and potential leaders.[14]

Training

World-wide, there has been very little debate over the proposition that the health and growth or non-growth of a church is dependent to a very large degree on the competence, maturity, and style of leadership exercised by the pastor. God is calling the Church in New Zealand to a new chapter in its history, the like of which has never been seen before. Many changes are needed, none more than in the way leaders are prepared for the missionary task. The apostolic challenge to plant and/or grow effective congregations need not lower the quality of theological training, but a new degree of pragmatism is required. This challenge brings denominational training programmes into prominence. They are (or should be) geared to unique denominational and congregational needs in ways that other schools cannot be, training both pastors and church planters. If they are deficient, initiatives can be taken to bring about change. Crucial questions might be asked. What is the mission and what are the goals of the organization being served by the school? What kind of training school would best serve the mission of the organization? What qualities and skills are needed by graduates to lead growth ministries in the 1990s? Who can best model leadership for, disciple, and equip trainees? What models of training are best suited to the objectives? Different agencies will answer these questions in different ways. At the risk of being controversial, some pointers are suggested here.

The adult education boom has focused attention on learning preferences of adults. Adults most desire occupational training and come into such courses highly motivated. They want knowledge that can be applied immediately, which is taught interactively, by proven practitioners. They want some control over how, when, and where they learn. Lectures or classes are highest in appeal, followed by or accompanied by on-the-job training. Short term conferences, workshops, or block courses are also popular, because attendance is less disruptive to family life. Training, rather than classic education, is seen as more desirable by adults: it is learner-centred; affects the mind but also influences behaviour/skills; addresses specific measurable objectives; includes classroom-based, but also activity- and experience-based learning; emphasizes how things are taught as well as what is taught; includes hearing, seeing and doing; the trainer is a player-coach rather than a professor.

Training programmes for growth in the 1990s must recognize contemporary growth factors such as the renewal movement which began in New Zealand in the mid 1960s. Studies in New Zealand confirm that growing churches in Kiwi culture(s) generally describe themselves as conservative or evangelical (in regard to the authority of Scripture) and as charismatic or pentecostal (in regard to dependence on the Holy Spirit). Other studies elsewhere (eg. in the UK) have found the same to be true.[15] Leaders of growing churches encourage the release of spiritual gifts in their people for various ministries. Different streams of the Church may number, define or understand spiritual gifts in different ways, yet most would accept that biblically, gifts of the Holy Spirit are the basis for true God-given ministry. Apart from ministry that is sensitive to and dependent upon the Holy Spirit, his gifted people will never accomplish his mission.[16] In the light of world-wide evidence it would be difficult to overstate the effects of these factors for growth. If growth is a priority, they will be taken seriously in the training context and in church life.

Many graduate from training institutions to "Go and make disciples," but have themselves never been adequately or systematically discipled. They lack personal experience in discipling to pass on in their churches. This is all too evident when one visits churches which lack a decentralized discipling dimension. Pastors and church planters require training with exposure to the humbling and refining effects of the Spirit and the authority of Scripture, through a person who gets close enough to lovingly assist the maturing process as immaturities surface. Part of discipling is modeling. Where necessary, academic staff could be supplemented by part-time trainers who are leaders of growing churches.

Some schools are perceived to lack a mission orientation. They do not adequately teach (in any systematic or committed way, in the classroom or in the field): evangelism (theology along with contemporary practice), church planting, indigenous church growth principles, church management principles and practice, leadership, training (ie. how to train others, and how to train trainers of others), basic discipleship (and how to disciple others, and how to train people to disciple others), prayer and power ministries. These areas of knowledge are essential for mission. Practical, growth-related skills are also needed, especially training skills, church growth skills, witnessing skills, management skills, leadership skills, prayer ministry skills, etc. An enthusiastic atmosphere will be a feature of mission-oriented training, where people are encouraged to be full of vision, faith and the Holy Spirit, enthusiastic and zealous for God, for the gospel, and for the growth of the kingdom through the Church.

At one traditional college in an overseas city known to the writer, a change of heart and mind to mission theology was needed to initiate radical changes for re-orientation towards mission (especially evangelism and church planting). This involved introducing several new staff and new courses. Now focused on their city's multi-cultural millions, this college has quickly become the springboard of denominational growth, after 50 years of decline.

District strategies[17]

A gathering of pastors in the Bay of Plenty heard Alan Withy of VISION New Zealand describe the VISION process. One asked, "How can we pick this up in Tauranga?" The answer to this crucial question is being modeled in St Helens, an English industrial town of about 170,000 people to the east of Liverpool. Over 22,000 (13% of the population) attend churches weekly, including 14,500 Roman Catholics. After the large evangelistic missions of the mid 1980s, several Anglican leaders continued to meet for prayer and encouragement. In December 1990 they were introduced to the idea of developing a strategy to evangelize St Helens. Bob Hopkins, Anglican church planting leader, and migrant Phil Pawley from Youth With A Mission in Hamilton New Zealand, shared the Dawn strategy and how it might be used at a district level. A steering committee was appointed to investigate the strategy further and to research the state of the churches in St Helens. A consultation was held in March 1991, when 47 church leaders representing 40 churches from all denominations in St Helens considered this information. The facts were interpreted to reveal the challenge facing St Helens churches for the 1990s and beyond. They accepted the vision of the body of Christ working together, united in their common purpose of obeying the Great Commission, and established SHINE, St Helens Inter-church Neighbourhood Evangelization. Coupled with prayer, SHINE is creating an environment for church growth and multiplication that will allow churches to multiply after their own kind in a climate of mutual trust, respect and sensitivity.

Having adopted a Dawn-type approach, they decided to proceed immediately with a cooperative research project, known as the Mission Assessment Programme (MAP), which was used to mobilize the churches. It exposed church people to the thoughts, feelings and opinions of the general public. It also enabled churches to take a serious look at their own strengths and weaknesses. The community data was presented publicly in the town square. The church data was presented at a town-wide church congress in June 1992. This historic SHINE Congress brought together over 100 leaders from 30 churches. In a climate of prayer, the data was pooled and analysed as a basis for realistic goal setting and planning. A blue-print for coordinated mission and outreach was developed. During the day denominational and inter-denominational groups consulted. Communication between churches is being enhanced and co-operation is being encouraged where feasible.

There are six distinct phases to SHINE, plus a related prayer strategy that runs throughout the process. The phases are: catalyse the vision; draw leaders together for consultation; conduct in-depth research of the area and the churches; provide a goal-setting congress; plan and implement goals; evaluate and review goals. The prayer strategy has three thrusts: bi-monthly prayer concerts at the Town Hall; prayer triplets encouraging people to pray for friends, neighbours and family; and intercession for society, aimed at the seven major arenas of influence: arts and entertainment, business and commerce, church life, the media, education, family, and government.

A national strategy for the evangelization of New Zealand must lead to regional and city strategies such as that initiated and facilitated by New Zealander Phil Pawley in St Helens. Each step in the process described above is essential. Further study is advised before action is taken. A mis-fire at this level can prejudice future efforts.

Local Churches: the Key to Evangelizing Nations

A national strategy requires the involvement of as many denominational structures as possible. Information is gathered, plans are developed and goals are set at national level. These must have regional or district expression, and local expression. It is through the ongoing ministries of local churches that nations are evangelized. These churches must be of a certain quality, and of sufficient numbers, targeting every small community of people, throughout New Zealand. "We will encourage Christian leaders to strengthen the quality and multiply the number of growing, caring, Christ-centred churches until there are sufficient to affect the spiritual and social climate of New Zealand. The task of evangelizing New Zealand will be attainable when there is at least one such congregation sharing Christ within easy access geographically, culturally, and linguistically of every person, ie. approximately one for every 500 people. We will encourage every denomination in their commitment to growth, and every specialist ministry to assist denominations and churches in mission. Together we can do it!"[18] This is the vision of VISION New Zealand. The contents of this publication are intended to serve the vision at every level. Kingdom mission can only be effective as disciples are multiplied, and as leaders are multiplied to multiply churches that multiply disciples and leaders, who then do all that mission for the kingdom of God entails.

The Whole Church

There is a cry on the lips of laypeople of all ages desperate for meaningful Christian service that is facilitated and appreciated by their pastors. Unemployment is not working, in the church. The mission field is outside the church building, where only the lifestyle evangelism and market place ministries of laypeople will penetrate society. All research confirms that the majority of people are drawn to Christ as a process over years, through relationships with credible Christians. The message is clear: increase the workforce out in the community. Pastor-teachers have a primary role "to prepare (equip, disciple, encourage, work with, enable) God's people for works of service, so that the body of Christ may be built up."[19] Denominations also face a new challenge, to re-theologize and reorganize where traditional dogma and institutionalism blocks lay participation in church leadership. This is of particular importance in regard to releasing church planters, many of whom may be less trained and unordained.

There is another cry on the lips of many people in New Zealand. Journalist Beulah Wood speaks for them when she writes: "The problem starts a long way back in youth groups where eager young women are often overlooked by youth leaders for opportunities to speak or exhort in front of the group. Church leaders seldom look them out to encourage them to train for up-front leadership or seminary training. It may even still be true that a woman has to be twice as good as a man to be considered half as good." Beulah Wood goes on to quote K.M. Haubert: "Male superiority is given acceptable social garb; lack of mutual submission is sealed with the stamp of church approval; female inferiority is embedded into the fibre of womanhood; gifts of the Holy Spirit lie dormant; and many churches suffer unnecessary constraints."[20]

"When I visited the largest church in the world in Seoul in 1978," wrote well-known Australian Roland Croucher, "I was not surprised to learn that 80% of their small group leaders were women. I attended one of these, led by a woman. The Church is immeasurably impoverished when more than half its members are debarred from exercising leadership ministries not on the basis of the presence or absence of giftedness or competence, but simply because of gender. The time has now come to practise the principle that in Christ social, racial, and sexual barriers have been removed."[21]

Beulah Wood: "The failure to accept all the gifts given to women has wasted resources God gave for his work on earth. The church is stunted as a result. Women have demonstrated their zeal and loyalty during the 15 decades of the Church in Aotearoa. Let's now give them equal authority with their brothers in Christ, to grow the kingdom of God."[22]

The Whole Gospel

The gospel of God's love demands expression, in word, sign and deed.[23] There are open doors in every community. Following a thorough community survey in Balmoral the report stated, "Sadly, the vast majority have no idea of any activity offered by any church. However when presented with possibilities, youth clubs, elderly home help and child-care are the activities they most want. Among the courses, aerobics was the favourite by far, followed by car repairs and managing finances."[24]

Dangers in the trend towards social work are frequently pointed out. Christians must beware on the one hand of using community ministry as mere bait on a gospel hook, and so failing to treat people with true compassion and dignity. They must beware on the other hand of failing to share Christ by word as well as by deed. C.B. Samuel, Director of the Evangelical Fellowship of India Commission on Relief (Eficor) wrote of the results of a survey conducted by the Social Concern elective track at the Lausanne II Congress in Manila 1989, a survey of 68 social concern projects on all five continents. He said, "The most important finding was that evangelism takes place best when the target community is treated not as a project but as people who have dignity and deserve respect. The way people are treated rather than the benefits they receive contributes most to evangelism in social action. Thus the process attracts people to Christ more than the product. This process should reflect the compassion and the justice of God and involve Christians in sharing the struggles of the poor. A second finding is that evangelism takes place most effectively when the team includes someone with the special gift of evangelism. A local community of Christians should be channels of the work with an evangelist as part of the team.

"The effect of a combination of evangelism and social action brought clear changes in the values and attitudes in communities; marriages were strengthened; people accepted themselves as created by God and thus as of great value; deep respect grew for the word of God... Almost all groups mentioned an increase in church attendance and the growth of new churches through their work."[25]

The Whole Nation

Mrs Joy Gill was a member of the Te Awamutu Baptist Church, 78 years of age. As she relates it, in early 1990 the Holy Spirit told her to go and live on the West Coast at Kawhia, where she was to intercede for that small community of several hundreds. Growing out of this prayer ministry arose a vision for a new congregation of Christians which is now meeting regularly and reaching out to the people of the area. Where God gifts certain people for intercession, leaders do well to listen. As we listen to the Lord he reveals his plans. "Surely the sovereign Lord does nothing without revealing his plan to his servants the prophets."[26] His vision for New Zealand is totally inclusive; God will thrust out labourers into the whole nation, into every rural and urban village, to every small pocket of people.[27]

If a vision is to be shared, it must be communicated. It must be subject to the wisdom of the community of Christians who receive it. They may affirm it, and they may modify it according to their collective insights. This is an essential part of the process of guidance. The best way for this to be accomplished is to commit it to paper. "Write down the vision... make it plain... so that he who reads may run with it!"[28] In this way the vision may be translated into faith goals, or objectives, which then become the steps the church takes to advance. Every goal is a statement of faith. And, "Without faith it is impossible to please God."[29] Goal setting demands clear definition, releases faith, focuses effort and expenditure, awakens objectivity, and brings accountability. Good goals are shared goals, and they are SMART goals: Specific, Measurable, Achievable, Realistic, and Time-based. Peter Wagner says, "For some reason I do not fully understand, some power is released through setting positive goals that otherwise remains dormant." Growing denominations, and growing churches, almost invariably have prayed through and worked through their options, and come to clarity in regard to where they are going, how they will get there, and by when.

Now is The Time

For many years New Zealand's top missionary expertize has been exported. It is time to develop a New Zealand theology of mission, and a New Zealand movement for mission at home. In the 1980s and 1990s a new generation of leaders has emerged with competence in many fields: missiology, theology, community ministries, evangelism, overseas mission, aid and development, healing ministries, music and worship, children's ministries, youth ministries, prayer, cross-cultural mission, communication, media, etc. God is speaking through New Zealanders today, about New Zealand. It is time for the Church to stand on its feet and take responsibility under God, to launch out with a fresh vision, to make disciples of the people groups of New Zealand. It is time for the whole Church to take the whole gospel to the whole nation.

FOOTNOTES

[1]John V. Taylor, *The Go-Between God,* (London, UK: SCM, 1972), pages 33 - 54.

[2]Steve Chalke, Foreword in Martin Robinson and Stuart Christine, *Planting Tomorrow's Churches Today,* (Tunbridge Wells, UK: Monarch, 1992).

[3]E. Jacob Taylor.

[4]Robert D. Dale, *To Dream Again,* (Nashville,TN: Broadman, 1981).

[5]1 Corinthians 12

[6]Peter Brierley, *Christian England*, (London, UK: MARC Europe, 1991).

[7]Stephen Ibbotson, *2,000 by 2,000*, a personal diary-style summary of the Congress sent to the writer.

[8]Numerous overseas observers have stated that in their opinion the body of Christ in New Zealand enjoys a unique degree of unity. VISION New Zealand grows out of and contributes to that unity.

[9]Denominational leaders and those wishing to promote a denominational vision and process for growth through church planting are recommended to read Jim Montgomery, *DAWN 2000, 7 Million Churches to Go,* (Pasadena, CA: William Carey Library, 1989). See especially Appendix 1: "13 Steps to a Successful Growth Programme", page 211.

[10]Ephesians 4:11,12.

[11]1 Corinthians 12:28.

[12]A brief study of the recent growth of the Apostolic Movement can be found in Bruce Patrick, *A Clear Call to Mission in New Zealand*, (Auckland, NZ: MISSIO**NZ**, 1990).

[13]   **Twelve Assumptions**

1 A denomination concerned to grow will place high priority on reaching people who are not active in the life of any congregation.

2 The effective implementation of a denominational growth strategy requires that a full-time staff person be charged with that responsibility (nationally and/or regionally).

3 Long established middle-sized and small churches tend to remain on a plateau in size.

4 The smaller the congregation the greater the changes to be managed in successful growth (and by implication, the greater the growth skills needed to manage the changes).

5 Every denomination has only limited resources to allocate for growth.

6 Therefore cost effectiveness must be assessed, favouring strategies that give greater results for lower costs.

7 Diverse types of pastors (with respect to educational level, ethnicity, socio-economic background, gender, etc) will be required to reach diverse groups in society.

8 Administrative rules and traditions will be adapted to attain objectives. For example to reach new ethnic groups new approaches will be acceptable.

9 Every denomination will want to include several programmes in its total strategy and therefore must determine an order of priority. It is impossible

to have three number one priorities.

10 Inevitably there will be trade-offs. You cannot have growth without change. You cannot have change and keep everyone happy.

11 An effective growth strategy will link evangelism with the incorporation of different categories of people: new converts, longer term Christians, church re-entrants, and membership transferees.

12 Outsiders, third party observers and consultants, will be enlisted and trained to help churches.

Having listed these assumptions, Schaller asks, "What are the assumptions on which the church growth strategy for your denomination is based? How do they compare with the assumptions listed above?" He then goes on to suggest eight priorities in order of importance:

Eight Priorities

1 The first priority in any denominational strategy for growth must be to organize new congregations, "the most effective single method of reaching people without any active church affiliation."

2 Encourage the numerical growth of larger churches, the second most effective means of reaching more people.

3 Develop programmes designed to help congregations assimilate new members, closing the 'back door'. This must be a very high priority for all denominations.

4 Train pastors and new pastors in principles of church growth, especially how to grow a church beyond the single cell to a multi-cell church.

5 Encourage and equip pastors for longer pastorates. A long pastorate will not automatically result in numerical growth, but sustained growth usually requires it.

6 Provide third party consultants to help generate new growth for plateaued middle-sized churches.

7 Change the reporting system (the annual statistical returns) to encourage churches to set goals for new member growth, and to hold themselves accountable to these goals. The denomination could then assist with evangelistic support. Goals influence priorities. Evangelism and growth should be the highest priorities.

8 Encourage all auxilliary organizations of local churches (youth, women's, social services, etc.) to see themselves as agents of growth.

[14] Bruce Patrick, *Rigor Mortis,* 1988.

[15] Tong Ng, *A Focus on the 20 Fastest Growing and Declining Baptist Churches in New Zealand,* (Tauranga, 1984); Dick Holland, *Break Through for Growth,* (a study of the 20 fastest growing Presbyterian churches in New Zealand, Te Puke, 1991); and Paul Beasley-Murray and Alan Wilkinson, *Turning the Tide, An Assessment of Baptist Church Growth in England,* (a study of a broad spectrum of 330 Baptist churches. London, UK: Bible Society, 1981).

[16] 2 Timothy 1:6. Cf. David Watson, *One in the Spirit,* (London, UK: Hodder and

Stoughton, 1973), page 18: "Dorothy Sayers once expressed it pithily like this: 'There are those who would worship the Father, the Son and the Virgin Mary; those who believe in the Father, the Son and the Holy Scriptures; those who found their faith on the Father, the Son and the Church; and there are even those who seem to derive their spiritual power from the Father, the Son and the minister!' The pentecostal explosion has largely been a reaction to this, with a fresh recognition of the Third Person of the Trinity, and a deep longing for the same wind of the Spirit that energized believers both in the first century and in all the revivals of the Church down the years."

[17] The material for this section is derived from several sources: *Challenge 2000, Discipling A Whole Nation,* (Sunbury-on-Thames, UK: Challenge 2000, 1992), the handbook for the English congress described earlier; C. Phillip Pawley, *District Strategy, Creating an Environment for Church Growth and Multiplication,* (St Helens, UK: 1991); correspondence between Bob Hopkins, Phil Pawley and the writer; and visits to St Helens.

[18] From the Mission Statement of VISION New Zealand.

[19] Ephesians 4:12 (NIV).

[20] K.M. Haubert, *Woman in the Bible, and the Implications for Leadership,* (Los Angeles, CA: Women's Commission of World Vision International, 1992).

[21] Roland Croucher, *Christian Leadership Letter,* (Australia: World Vision, Autumn 1992).

[22] From an article by Beulah Wood, written at the request of the writer for this chapter.

[23] Refer also to chapter 4, where other levels of the mission of the gospel ar enjoined

[24] *Balmoral Community Survey,* (Balmoral Baptist Church: 1992)

[25] From a newsletter of Servants to Asia's Urban Poor, 1990

[26] Amos 3:7 (NIV)

[27] Matthew 9:38 commands us to pray a prayer God is bound to answer: "Ask th Lord of the harvest, therefore, to send out workers into his harvest field" (NIV)

[28] Habakkuk 2:2 (slightly adapted)

[29] Hebrews 11:6 (NIV)

Postscript

by John Evans

Over 25 years ago Joseph Bayly parodied evangelistic methods in his book *The Gospel Blimp*. He told of a group who sought to reach their friends and neighbours with the gospel. They hired a blimp, a balloon, and from the safety of its cradle high above the neighbourhood dropped gospel texts like bullets onto the heads of people below. We would like to think we had learned more sense, but have we? We cannot reach our hurting society or touch our community or win our nation for Christ from the distance of clinical isolation. It can only be achieved by God-given means, by incarnating the gospel. That was his means when in love God sent His Son into the world. Biblical evangelism identifies with humankind. It is involved in the human situation of suffering and brokenness. It therefore requires costly self-giving. For Jesus it meant the cross. All true evangelism since has some dimension of the cross etched deeply into it.

Our contributors have shown that as this century has advanced, what was just a drift from public profession of Christian faith and from the societal norm of church affiliation, even in the loosest sense, has become a torrent. Various chapters explore some of the factors and some of the contemporary social phenomena: the pressure of secularism, the tide of modernity, the increase in alternative spiritualities, the lure of materialism, the tensions which produce alienation, fragmentation and polarization within society, as well as the 'long black cloud', the pervading sense of hopelessness, hanging over Aotearoa.

If our commitment in Aotearoa New Zealand to the sense of God's call to a new day in gospel advance is to mean anything, it will include deeper dimensions of **discipleship**. Too often we give the impression of playing at church or of going through the motions. Discipleship requires that we recognize the demand of Christ's Lordship over our lives. Jesus' words at Caesarea Philippi cross the centuries and the cultures with compelling power and urgency. "If any want to become my followers, let them deny themselves and take up their cross and follow me" (Mark 8:34 NRSV). We prefer to pamper ourselves, to pander to our self-indulgence. Jesus calls us to self-denial. We want to follow, but at the least cost and the least personal inconvenience. Despite our protests, we do believe in cheap grace. True discipleship is costly; a cross is at its heart. We are summoned to follow: faithfully, painstakingly, joyfully and obediently. "Why do you call me 'Lord, Lord', and do not do what I say?" (Luke 6:46). Still he is sending his people. Still he commands, "Go!" Why will we not do as He says?

If our commitment in Aotearoa New Zealand to the Decade of Evangelism is to mean anything it will include a new commitment to and a new experience of the **unity of the body of Christ** across the churches. This will be a unity manifesting the spirit of John 17 and our Lord's prayer for his own. It will be a belongingness to one another which eschews any iota of rivalry or competition. It will be a unity which has eyes only for the harvest and the glory of God. It will be a unity of lasting relationships and ongoing cooperation rather than sporadic, or some short-term phase. It will be a unity modelled by leaders for members, and demonstrated to be a priority.

If our commitment in Aotearoa New Zealand to sharing the good news of Jesus with our nation is to mean anything, it will include a new commitment to **prayerfulness**. For so long we have paid lip service to the concept. Biblically and historically prayerfulness and renewal are linked together. So often we appear to have schemes and programmes aplenty. In recent years we have learned something of the dimension of intercession as spiritual warfare. With renewed earnestness we need to encourage Christian groups, congregations, and organizations to tap into these spiritual resources as a fundamental strategy.

If our commitment in Aotearoa New Zealand to ministering the gospel to our people is to mean anything then we need, in our time, to become pioneers again and be engaged on the **new frontiers of mission**. This will mean coming to grips with the challenge of diverse cultures around us, of ethnicity, of religions, of worldview. It will mean employing basic evangelistic and mission strategies to multiply the church here at home. It will mean engaging with the pain and sickness of our society at its deepest levels. It will require a new commitment to the cause of truth and justice (cf. Amos 5:21-24). We will need to stand for righteousness against all unrighteousness, including institutionalized unrighteousness, as well as standing with the oppressed, the powerless, the hungry, the destitute and the hurting.

If our commitment to a new era of evangelization in Aotearoa New Zealand is to mean anything then it will require a new **integrity** in authentic gospel proclamation. It will doubtless require the very best we can bring in terms of technique, or style, or strategy. More importantly, it will require the very best we can be in authentic gospel living. This will be so in our personal Christian discipleship and in our corporate, congregational life. Increasingly, society, the world, will need to see something authentic of the kingdom of God in us. In the account in Acts 4:13-14 where Peter and John are defending themselves before the Jewish Council for their act of kindness to the lame man, it says, "They took note that these men had been with Jesus. But since they could see the man who had been healed standing there with them, there was nothing they could say." Their words and their ministry matched up! Their profession and practice were as one. There was the evidence both of their words and actions which attested to the truth. That is integrity in ministry. Our lives, and our lifestyle, must match our proclamation!

The Exodus generation of Israelites are not remembered for their boldness. In Exodus 14 we read of their pursuit by the Egyptians. In their fear, with the oncoming foe behind them and the Red Sea before them, they clamoured to go back. Moses, confident in God, urged them to "Stand still, and see the salvation of the Lord." But when God speaks it is to command them, "Go forward!" The Church in Aotearoa New Zealand cannot go back to some idealized past situation, rose-hued only in our faulty memories. Standing firm and looking to the Lord can sound spiritual but may absolve us from responsible action in obedience to Christ. Our present position demands that we go forward to the year 2000 and beyond, facing a new challenge with new resolve, with new boldness and faith expressed in costly action, and with new vision for Aotearoa New Zealand.

Appendix :
What New Zealanders
Think of the Church

by Barry Tetley and Max Scott

The sample survey

Students of the Bible College of New Zealand under the direction of Barry Tetley surveyed 540 people of 15 years of age and over. This took place during the first half of May 1992, in the inner city, suburban and rural areas of Greater Auckland with some additional input from Hamilton, Cambridge and Tauranga. While a random sample was attempted, some surveyors reported that only one person in three approached was willing to participate. Nevertheless, the demographic profile of the group surveyed compared favourably with that of New Zealand as a whole. The following chart compares religious affiliation of the group with that of the 1991 census. Apart from the high number of Baptists, chart 1 indicates that religious affiliation of the people surveyed resembles the religious affiliation of New Zealand as a whole.

Chart 1 : A Comparison of Survey Religious Affiliation with the 1991 Census

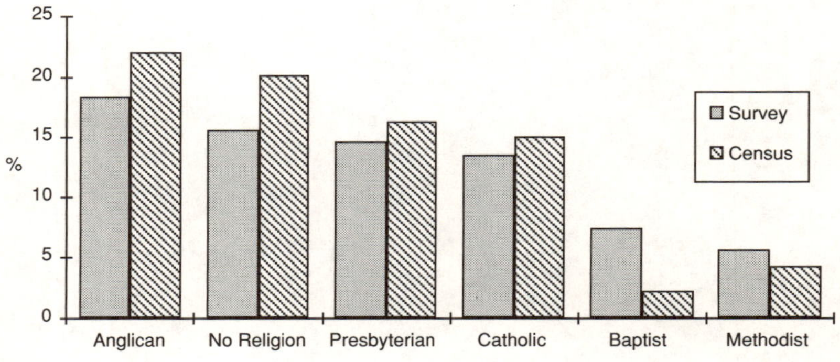

Attendance and belief

The survey asked which of the following categories described the person's attendance at a church service over the past 12 months (excluding funerals, weddings, etc.): Not at all; 1-3 times; 4-10 times; 10-25 times; Over 26 times; Radio only. For the purpose of the analysis, a churchgoer was defined as a person who had attended a church service 10 or more times over the last 12 months (208 people), or who said "I don't attend church but I do listen to religious broadcasts" (5 people). 39% of those surveyed fitted this definition. When compared with national statistics for church attendance, this indicates a much higher level of attendance than would be expected. It tends to confirm the impression that people over-estimate their level of attendance.

People were also asked questions about their belief. The purpose of the survey was not to make judgements about a person's faith. The answers to some questions were evidently 'orthodoxly Christian,' while others were not. 'Orthodox' included all who: Believe Christianity has a true view of the ultimate realities; Said "spiritual realities are important to me"; Said "acceptance by God is important to me"; Believe God is a personal being"; Expect "there is something more after death"; Believe "human beings are frail and need the help of God." Orthodox people answered all these questions affirmatively. There were 178 (33%) surveyed who fitted this definition.

For the purpose of this summary, the religious affiliations chosen were: No religion (NoR); Anglican (Ang); Assemblies of God (A/G); Baptist (Bapt); Brethren (Breth); Catholic (Cath); Methodist (Meth); Presbyterian (Pres). These religious affiliation groups are those which contain at least 2% of those surveyed. Chart 2 shows the percentage of people from each religious affiliation group who fitted these definitions of churchgoer and orthodox.

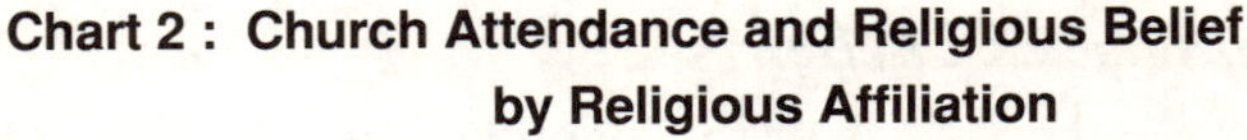

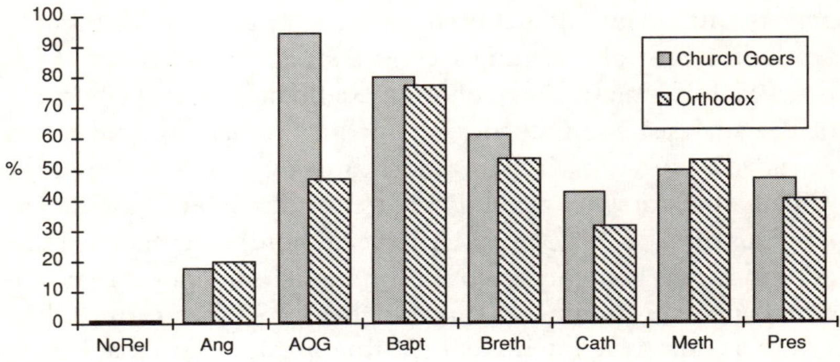

As expected, the mainline churches have a large number of people who associate themselves with their denomination but who do not attend regularly.   The pattern of belief follows the pattern of attendance except for those who associate with the Assemblies of God. This group of people had the highest attendance ratio, but were significantly down in the ratio of people with orthodox belief. This could be unduly affected by the smallness of the sample.

From the two variables relating to church attendance and belief, four categories can be constructed. These are churchgoing and orthodox (CO), churchgoing and unorthodox (CU), non-churchgoing and orthodox (NO) and non-churchgoing and unorthodox (NU). Chart 3 shows the relative numbers in each category.

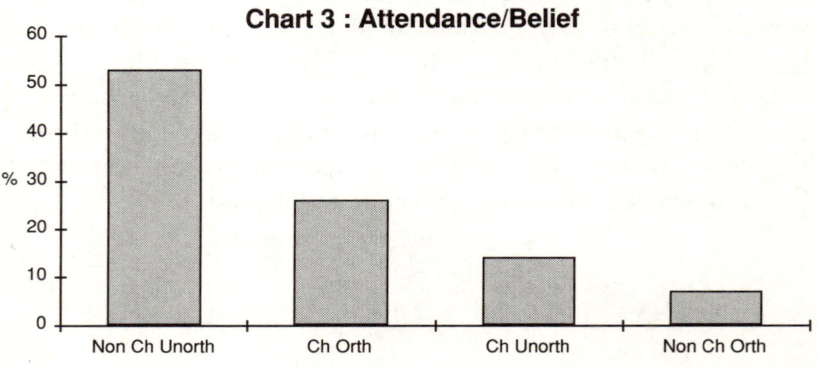

How is the church represented in the media?

The statements made were "In the newspapers the church is usually represented fairly," and, "On the television the church is usually represented fairly." A number was obtained by subtracting the percentage in each category who disagreed with the statement from the percentage in each category who agreed. This provided a number which ranged between -100 and +100. A negative number indicated the level of disagreement with the statement, and a positive number indicated the level of agreement.

Chart 4 shows that almost all groups regarded the newspapers as giving a fairer representation of the church than television. Those affiliated to the Assemblies of God believed that the newspapers and television were equally unfair in their representation of the church. People who have no religious affiliation, and those who were not church attenders but may have an orthodox Christian belief, tend to regard the media as presenting a reasonably fair view of the church.

Chart 4 : The Representation of the Church by the Media

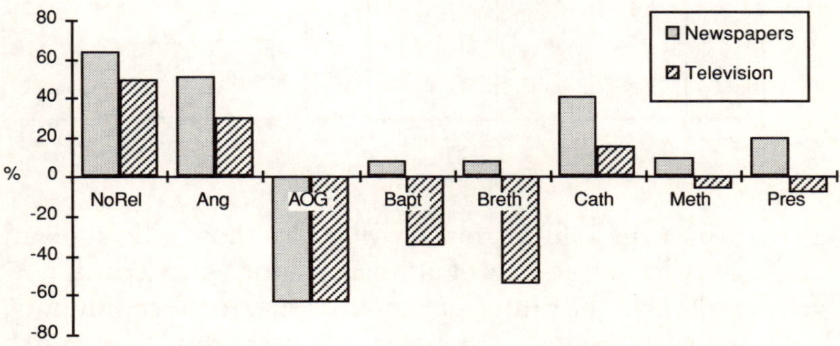

How well does the church present its views of ultimate realities to the community?

The first question determined whether the person surveyed believed that Christianity had a true view of reality. Chart 5 indicates the level of agreement with this statement for each category using the same statistics as that used for the previous chart. As expected, those who had no religious affiliation did not view Christianity as having a true view of ultimate realities. Baptists agreed most strongly with this statement.   Because of the definition of orthodox belief, there was total agreement with this view by those so classified.   Unorthodox churchgoers recorded a positive agreement with this view and unorthodox non-churchgoers recorded a small level of disagreement with this view, this being low because many people in this group did not know or preferred not to answer.

Chart 5 : Christianity has a true view of ultimate realities

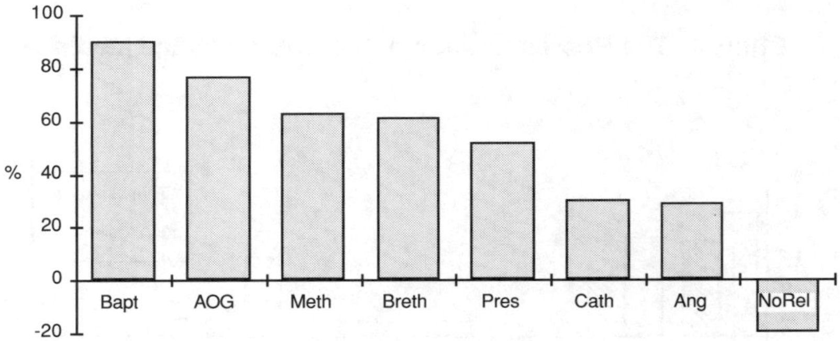

Chart 6 uses the information provided by those who thought Christianity has a true view of ultimate realities, and records how well they thought the church presented its view to the community. It shows that orthodox Catholics and Baptists think the church presents its views well, while those affiliated to the Assemblies of God and Methodists do not. Orthodox churchgoers tend to think the church presents its views poorly, while unorthodox churchgoers tend to think it presents them well.

Chart 6 : Christianity has a true view of ultimate realities which the church usually presents well to the community

A : Agreement by Religious Affiliation

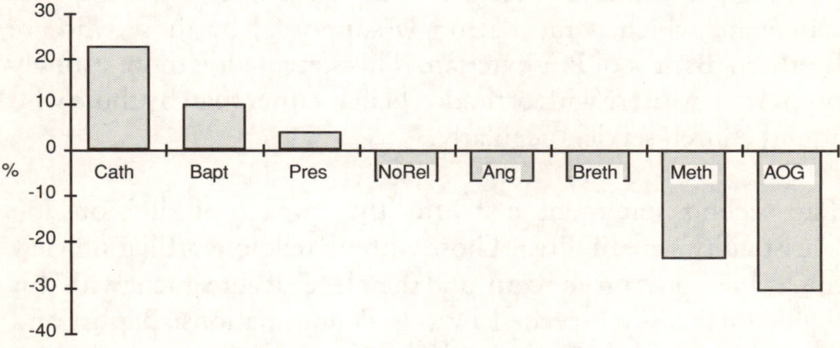

B : Agreement by Attendance/Belief

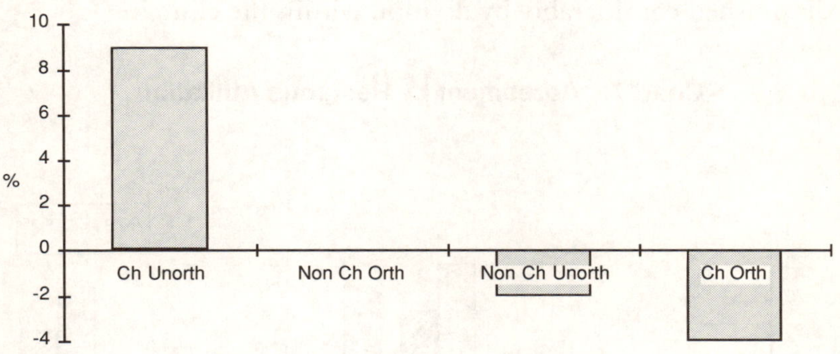

Attitudes towards Christianity and the Church

The credibility of Christianity
Two statements in the questionnaire related to the credibility of Christianity. The results are presented in charts 7a and 7b.

Statement 1: Christianity is the more credible because it is accepted by people of many cultures and ethnic backgrounds. **Statement 2** :The credibility of Christianity suffers from divisions within the church.

All groups of respondents agree with both statements. Those with no religious affiliation record weak agreement with the first statement, which is most strongly supported by those who are Brethren, Baptist or Presbyterian. This statement is more strongly supported by those with orthodox belief, rather than by those who attend church services regularly.

The second statement concerns the impact of divisions on Christianity's credibility. Those with no religious affiliation view this as an important concern, and their level of agreement with this statement is only exceeded by two denominations: Baptist and Presbyterian. Chart 7b shows that the level of agreement with this statement is highest among churchgoers. However, both churchgoers and non-churchgoers see the credibility of Christianity diminished considerably by division within the church.

Chart 7a Agreement by Religious Affiliation

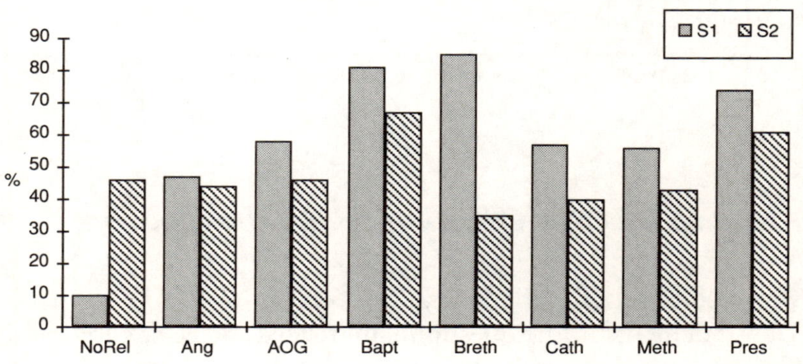

Chart 7b Agreement by Attendance/belief

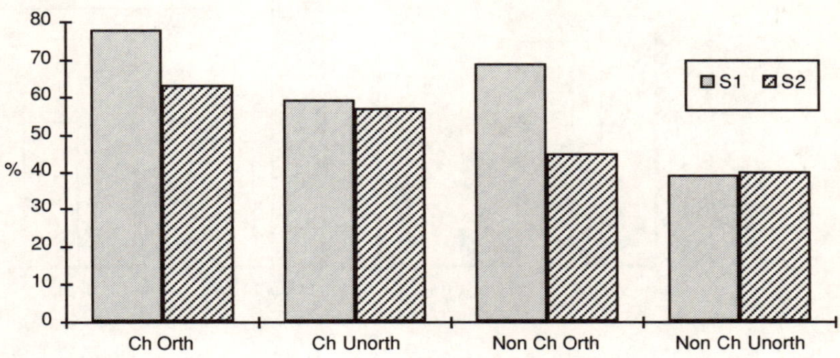

Positive attitudes towards the church

Three statements in the questionnaire made positive affirmations about the church:

Statement 1: Generally speaking, I think the church is changing to adjust to the times.

Statement 2: Generally speaking, I hold church leaders in New Zealand in high regard.

Statement 3: The church seems open and welcoming to people of exploring minds who want to investigate the Christian viewpoint.

Chart 8A : Agreement by Religious Affiliation

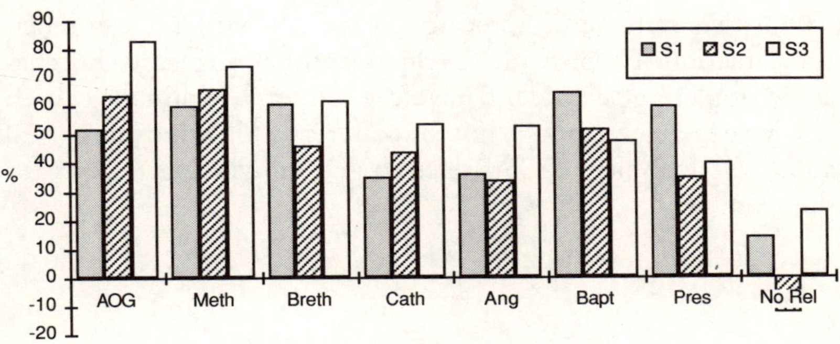

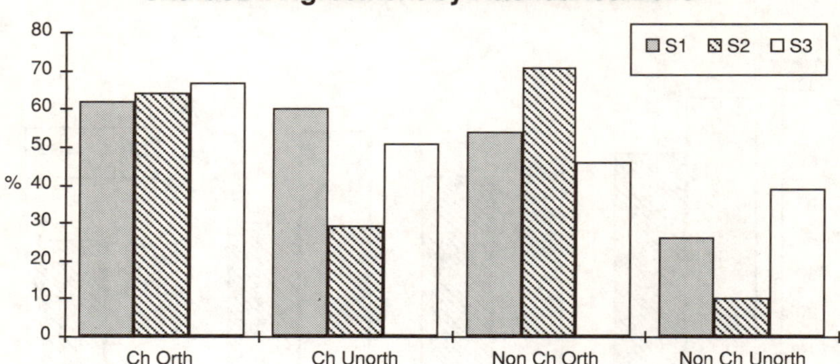

Charts 8a and 8b show that in general the church is regarded positively. This regard is least amongst those with no religious affiliation. Church leaders are not held in high regard by this group. Interestingly, the orthodox non-churchgoers have the highest regard for church leaders.

Negative Attitudes Towards the Church

Two negative statements were also made in the questionnaire about the Church and Christians.

Statement 1: In my opinion the church manipulates people.

Statement 2: Christians often seem to be very strongly convinced about their faith but unable to give convincing reasons to others for the hopes they hold.

These two statements indicate a problem with the churches' proclamation. People with no religious affiliation regard churches as manipulating people, and it is clear that some within the church also have this view (though not the majority). All groups are agreed about the inability of Christians to give convincing reasons for their beliefs.

Chart 9a Agreement by Religious Affiliation

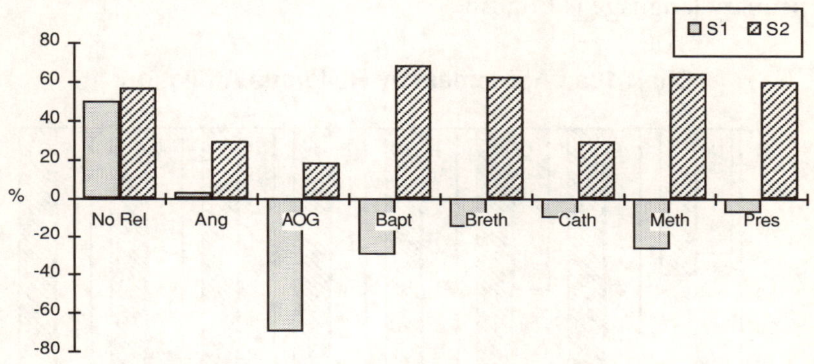

Chart 9b Agreement by Attendance/belief

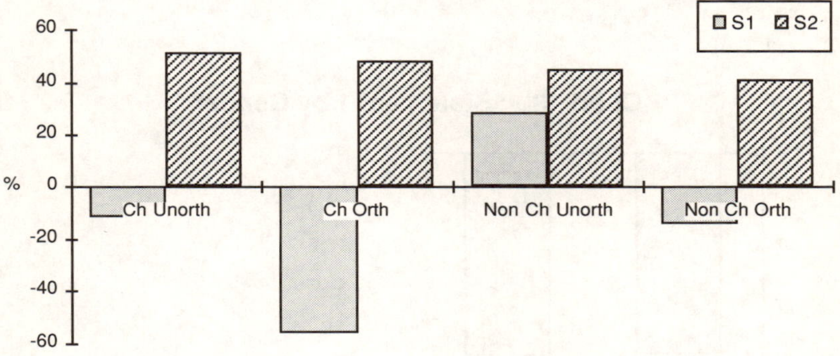

Alienation from the church

Two statements were concerned with alienation: one by gender and the other by cultural background.

Statement 1:   I have felt alienated by the church because of my gender.

Statement 2:   I have felt alienated by the church because of my cultural background.

As shown in charts 10a, 10b and 10c, most people do not feel alienated from the church by reason of gender or cultural background except a small minority whose spoken language is not English.

This is significantly different from the feelings of those whose primary language is English.

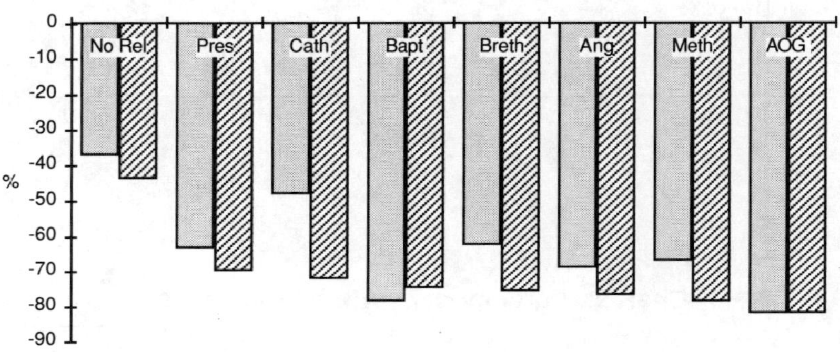

Chart 10a : Agreement by Religious Affiliation

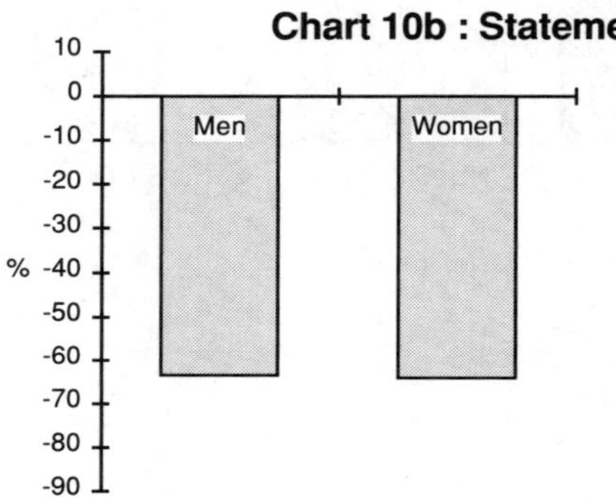

Chart 10b : Statement 1 by Gender

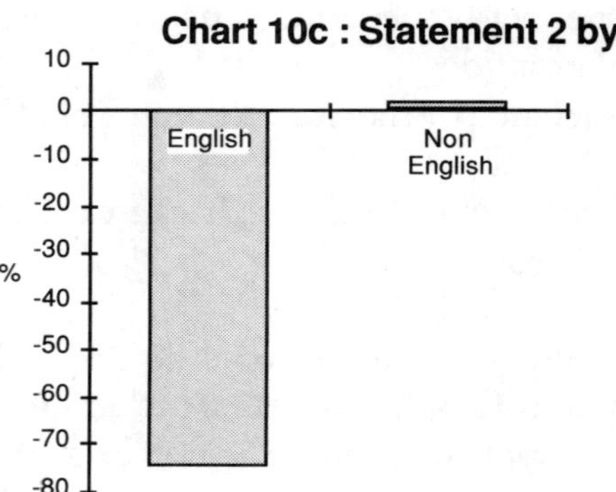

Chart 10c : Statement 2 by Spoken Language

The nature of mission

A further statement concerned the nature of mission. It was:
The Christian church as a whole could better serve the needs of the
many cultural, ethnic and social groups in New Zealand if there
were more Christian congregations. As shown in charts 11a and
11b, those with no religious affiliation see no need for more
Christian congregations. Baptists, together with orthodox
churchgoers, see the most need of more congregations. Orthodox
non-churchgoers see least need for more congregations.

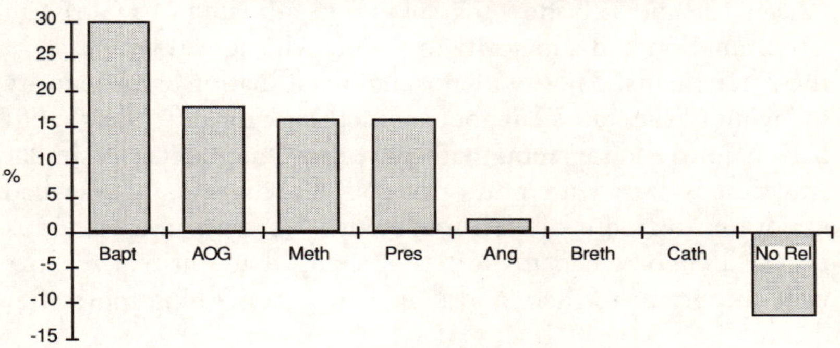

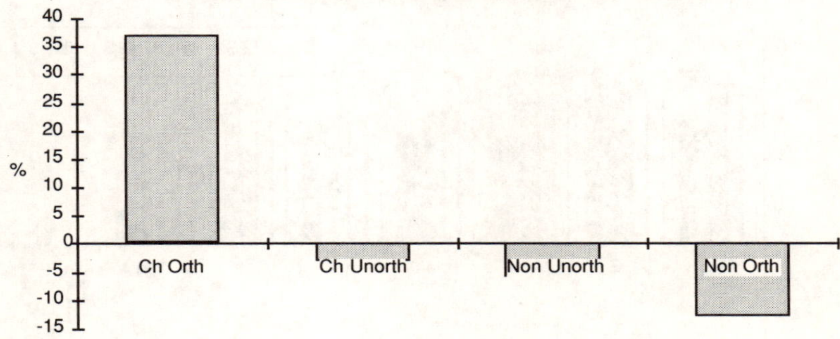

Beliefs

Five statements from this section were used to determine orthodoxy. The following charts relate these to religious affiliation and church attendance (non-orthodox).

Statement 1: Spiritual realities are important to me.

Statement 2: Acceptance by God is important to me.

Statement 3: I believe God is a personal being.

Statement 4: I expect there is something more after death.

Statement 5: I believe human beings are frail and need the help of God.

Charts 12a and 12b show that all groups affiliated to a Christian denomination had a majority of people who agreed with each of these statements. Those with no religious affiliation had a majority in favour of the statement about something more after death, but had majorities disagreeing with the other statements. A similar situation is seen with non-orthodox churchgoers. These had majorities in favour of each statement. However non-orthodox non-churchgoers had majorities agreeing that spiritual realities were important to them and that there is something more after death.

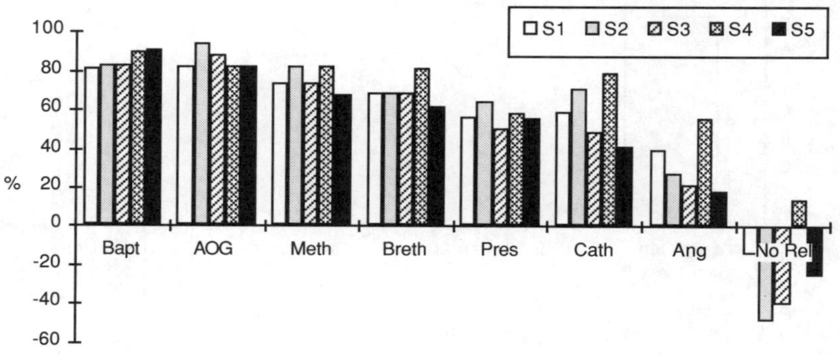

Chart 12a Agreement by Religious Affiliation

Chart 12b Agreement by Attendance/belief

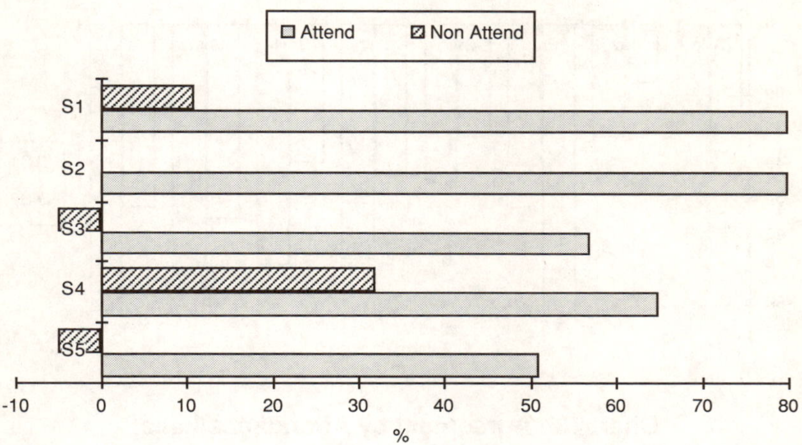

Belief in non-Christian practices

Two statements concerned belief about non-Christian practices:

Statement 1: I believe we can make contact with the dead

Statement 2: I believe our lives are affected by the stars as astrology says.

Charts 13a and 13b show that the majority of people in each group disagree with each of these statements. They also show that those with no religious affiliation are more likely to be sympathetic towards these beliefs than are those who associate with a church. The exceptions to this are Anglicans and orthodox non-churchgoers, who are more likely to believe in astrology.

Chart 13a Agreement by Religious Affiliation

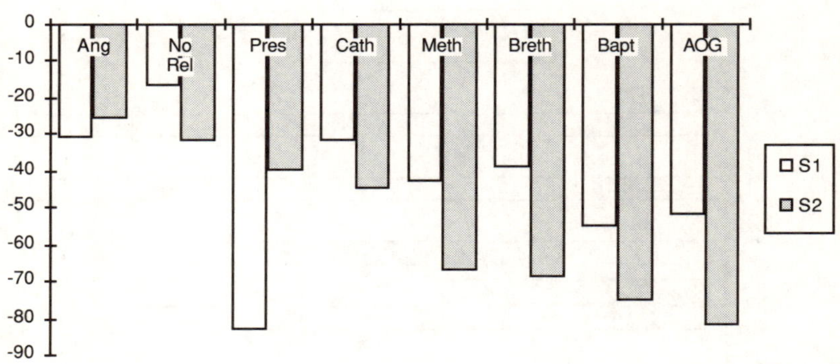

Chart 13b Agreement by Attendance/belief

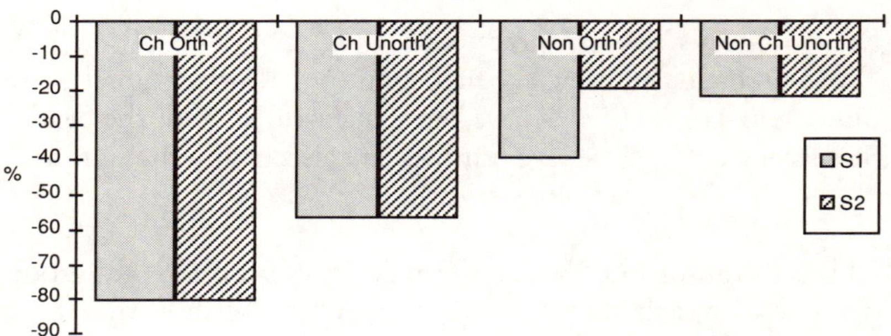

Would Use the Church for Ceremonial Occasions

A question was asked concerning making use of the services of the church: If I needed to, I would call on the church for services like weddings and funerals. As shown in charts 14a and 14b, most people would call on the church for services they require. Those with no religious affiliation are least likely to do so. Orthodox non-churchgoers are more likely to use the services of the church than are non-orthodox churchgoers.

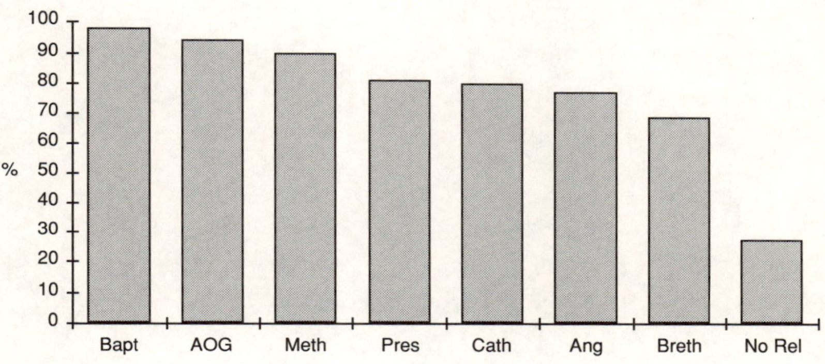

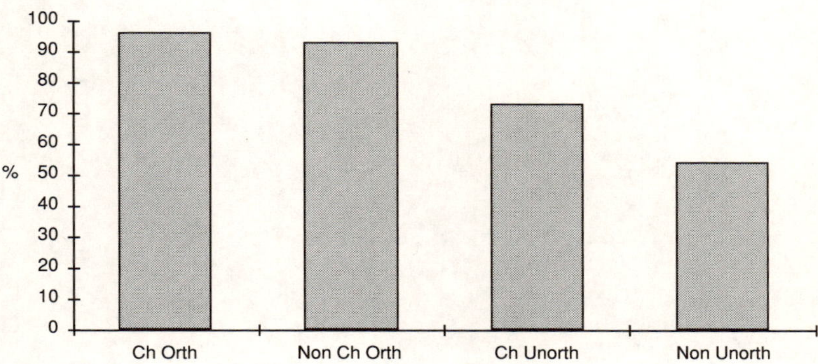

More information regarding this survey can be obtained from the writers.